HAVING RESEARCHED AND WRITTEN about Irish men serving in the Hong Kong Police Force and their families, Patricia O'Sullivan became curious about the lives of those around them – both the Chinese who were starting to call Hong Kong 'home' and the Westerners. The men had their jobs, their gambling dens or opium haunts, clubs or lodges, and could move about easily. But what of the women? How did they cope? The material available for the pre-1941 period gives few clues – except when things started to go wrong. Through the stories of women's encounters with the forces of law and order we get a little glimpse into how they lived their lives, their cares and anxieties, and the challenges they faced day to day.

O'Sullivan lives in Britain, but since 2009 she has been spending a few months of each year in Hong Kong, researching the lesser-known by-ways of its pre-1941 history. Before embarking on her 'big Hong Kong adventure' she taught for Hertfordshire County Music Service for 25 years.

Her first book, *Policing Hong Kong – an Irish History* is also published by Blacksmith Books. Her website is at *www.socialhistoryhk.com*.

WOMEN, CRIME
AND THE COURTS:
HONG KONG 1841-1941

Patricia O'Sullivan

BLACKSMITH BOOKS

For D. A. C.,
who started me on my Hong Kong journey,
with gratitude, always.

Women, Crime and the Courts: Hong Kong 1841-1941

ISBN 978-988-79639-8-1

Published by Blacksmith Books
Unit 26, 19/F, Block B, Wah Lok Industrial Centre,
37-41 Shan Mei Street, Fo Tan, Hong Kong
Tel: (+852) 2877 7899
www.blacksmithbooks.com

Edited by Paul Christensen

CONTENTS

HONG-KONG, KOWLOON AND ADJACENT TERRITORIES.

HONG KONG, 1912

Courtesy of Wattis Fine Art

To locate individual areas, streets and buildings named in the text, the reader is advised to consult www.gwulo.com/map-hong-kong-streets for a variety of expandable maps from this period.

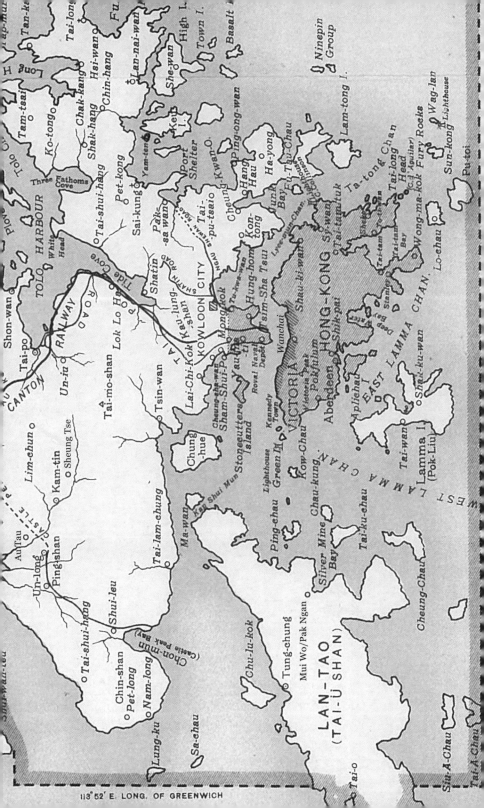

Acknowledgements

Books, I am learning, depend for their coming to fruition almost as much upon the people around the writer as that person herself. At any rate, that is my experience of the process. Throughout the journey to bring this work to print, I have had great support and encouragement - and long after I deserved it, given that I spent an age 'tinkering round the edges' of the subject. Of those to whom I am indebted, foremost is Dr Christopher Munn, whose has given unstintingly of his knowledge and insight. His expert guidance has saved me from many faux pas. Those that remain are all my own work, and have nothing to do with him.

Hong Kong is blessed with generous historians, many of whom have helped me along the way. David Bellis and the Gwulo community have been a constant source of information. May Holdsworth, with her expert knowledge of this field, together with Jonathan and Vicky Wattis, Dr Louis Ha, Annemarie Evans, Roy Delbyck, Greg Robb and Diane O'Hare are just some of those who have contributed to my endeavours. Jenny Fearns, formerly a history teacher in Hong Kong schools, gave me great practical research help, especially at times when I could not be in Hong Kong. She was always ready to listen to and discuss my 'thinking through' of the stories and issues I found. Jenny's sudden and untimely death in September 2020 is keenly felt by many. I am so sad that she did not get to see this book published.

I thank all the friends who have told me of their eager anticipation of this book – even though they must have despaired of my ever finishing. I have been encouraged and spurred on by many in the lovely virtual community of focusmate.com, and have even had useful specialist advice from some. I am indebted to Dr Nicola Ferreira, without whose steady support the book might well have taken another year to complete.

The final stages of the manuscript coincided with the first months of the Covid-19 pandemic, and brought home to me my reliance on the superb facilities we have both in the UK and Hong Kong: The National Archives, Hong Kong Public Records Office, Hong Kong Libraries and Hertfordshire County Library Service.

I sincerely thank my editor, Paul Christensen, who spotted all sorts of mishaps in the manuscript and whose welcome constructive criticism challenged me to improve the text in many places. Finally, I am immensely grateful to my publisher, Pete Spurrier, whose dedication to keeping books appearing in difficult circumstances is magnificent, and whose forbearance and good humour seem inexhaustible, even towards a tardy writer.

Patricia O'Sullivan
October 2020

INTRODUCTION

My interest in this topic was piqued even before I had determined that I would write my first book. Some years ago, I began to unravel the lives of my relatives and their townsfolk who were in Hong Kong from the mid-1860s until just after its reoccupation by the British in 1945. They were ordinary men and women, from farming stock, not poor by the standards of the time, but without any silver spoons to smooth their way. The men came out for good jobs, the chance to send money home to support elderly family and unmarried sisters, and with the prospect of a valuable pension. They returned from home leave with brides, young women from their town who could have had only the haziest notion of what awaited them. I soon became aware how interconnected lives were here – with other westerners and the longer-term residents from Macao, and then with the Chinese community all around them. Necessarily they lived not on the privileged upper reaches of the Peak, but in the very midst of the town itself. I tried to find out how all these other people lived, what their life experiences might be, and in what ways their living in a British Crown colony brought contrasts to the lives of their families in China or Macao. But as with so many aspects of Hong Kong's social history, there were few resources on the subject.

However, because the group I was then studying were mainly policemen, and there turned out to be quite a lot of them, I kept stumbling across crimes they investigated that had been committed (or not) by women. As my reading broadened, I realised that these cases supplied at least a partial answer to my question about the lives of all women in the colony during its first century. True, we're learning about them, both Chinese and western, when things go wrong, and sometimes dreadfully so. But even the reports about trivial little misdemeanours or transgressions give a glimpse of what was happening day to day. And these crimes were reported – although they were a tiny fraction of the total, newspapers regarded 'women criminals' as good copy, so we hear about them, and often with a little more detail than those of their menfolk. So I make no apology for including the brawl for water, the attempt to purchase a few sweets with dodgy five cent coins or the prosecution for illegally hawking a small tray of cakes. They and their ilk have their place in the wider story, just as do the murders and kidnappings which are recounted.

I do not read Chinese, and I freely admit that my knowledge of the wider region is relatively superficial. I may have family roots that go back 150 years and more, but my personal experience even of Hong Kong dates only to 2009. Thus I am wary – very wary – of reading into the lives of people whose culture I do not share. Even the temporal distance between myself and my grandmother's generation, for example, who arrived in Hong Kong over a century ago, feels like a hurdle, although admittedly one easier to surmount. That all said, as I read the varied cases and started making selections from the accounts, I was struck by the common themes that ran through. Looked at with the bird's-eye view of hindsight, these thread their way through the stories, despite differences in backgrounds and race. Not surprisingly, the main themes are of poverty and powerlessness, of taking control when it was possible, of abusing that control, and of the limitations that women's isolation and lack of access to education created in their ability to deal with a moral code built on an (alien) philosophical system. I believe that the reader will observe these here, especially in the longer stories recounted.

The women who appear in this book were part of a rare breed. On average, and until 1930s, less than 5% of the defendants appearing at the magistracy were female. Those who stood trial at the Supreme Court were more exceptional again. This contrasts with the situation in England and Scotland during the first half of the period covered, which saw lines of 'unfortunate females' waiting their turn before the bench and then accounting for between a quarter and a third of the total prison population. In these places overcrowding was a frequent problem in the women's prisons. Hong Kong magistrates could 'rattle through' cases with scant regard for the defendants as well as any in the 19th and early 20th centuries, but in cases which had required more investigation or longer consideration, the reader is often left with a suspicion, at least, that the gender of the defendant has played a part in the treatment meted out to her. As the century progressed, there was a real awareness of the limitations under which these women lived, and how that affected their motives and actions. It is also worth noting that, in the English-language press at any rate, women standing trial for murder were not demonised, as frequently happened in the West. Sensationalist language, even in the most dreadful cases, was remarkably rare in the reporting, and absent in the courts.

Many of these cases are 'stories' in their own right. For that reason, the reader will find that some are treated in a more narrative style than those chapters that recount multiple incidents. When speech has been reported in the newspapers I have tried to use it faithfully. Some has been conjectured, but where this has been done, it is only to express the sentiments conveyed in the reports, or to move the story on. No such additions have 'created' events or motives. When I have suggested the latter, these are in my own voice, and not put into the mouths of those who cannot now dispute them.

I do not claim to have included all the most 'significant' crimes which involved women as protagonists during the century 1841-1941. My sources have primarily been the newspapers, the Colonial Office Records and the specialist histories of this region and time. I have given over two chapters to investigating the small Female Prison that existed throughout the 100 years, since there is an almost entire absence of literature on this. Until the recent and very welcome publication of May Holdsworth and Christopher Munn's book, *Crime, Justice and Punishment in Colonial Hong Kong* (sadly appearing too late for the present work to benefit from), books on the subjects of the Prison and their inmates have been very light on research.

I am hoping that my modest efforts might spur others, perhaps with access to Chinese-language material in addition to that I have used, to conduct more in-depth research on the subject. But from the foregoing, I hope it will be apparent why I have not attempted any grand 'drawing together' in a conclusion at the end of the book. Thus when we get there, we will leave these stories with Molly Cecil sailing off to a new life – heaven help Australia!

Some notes on terminology

The transliteration system used for the names of both places and people from Chinese evolved over the period covered by this book. I have adopted the policy of using the spelling given in the accounts of events being related, but providing the modern usage where this differs significantly to the earlier one. Some newspaper reports of trials include two or even three spelling variations of individuals' names. The 'majority' spelling has then been adopted.

Chinese names are written in the normal form of family name first, followed by given names.

The terms "prison", "gaol" and "jail" have been used in accordance with the period and institution. In the early days, the place of detention was referred to as a prison, but in official records the person in charge of it was the Jailer. The new structure, built in the early 1860s, was named "Victoria Gaol", an appellation which remains until this day. The facilities at Lai Chi Kok and Stanley were always known as prisons. The place where female prisoners were confined was, throughout the whole period, known as the Female or Women's Prison.

All references to dollars are to Hong Kong dollars. Amounts are generally specified in (HK)$ unless the item (salary, payment, etc) was specifically defined in another currency (normally sterling). One pound (£) sterling was (until 1971, when it became 100 pence) divided into 20 shillings (s.), which were in turn divided into 12 pennies (d.). Where conversions between the two are shown they are at the prevailing exchange rate of the time in question. For reference, this varied from about 4s. 4d. (about £0.22) per dollar in the 1850s and 60s, to a low of 1s. 9d. (£0.08) in 1903, gradually increasing thereafter.

Glossary

A short glossary follows of some of the terms used more than once in the text (the definition also generally appearing in the text or as a footnote on first use):

Amah – a female domestic employee, comparable to a maid in western countries. Some amahs had specific roles, e.g. baby amah, wash amah. The term is also used for the female general servants in the hospitals.

Compradore – a Chinese agent employed by foreign businesses as an intermediary between themselves and local firms and labour.

Exclamations – *ai yah* = (roughly) oh dear; *gau meng* = save life.

Foki – a male employee, usually in businesses but occasionally as an outdoor servant to a household.

Mui tsai or 'pocket daughter' – female child transferred to ownership of wealthier woman (the 'pocket mother') by poor parents. In intention a form of charity towards the less fortunate, but in perhaps the majority of cases resulted in bonded female slavery, as the girl was tied to the woman, paid no wage and not free to leave.

San po tsai – the transfer of a female child to another family with the expectation that the girl would marry a son of that family, and was thus a 'daughter-in-law-elect'.

Tael – a common measure of weight in East and South-East Asia; its size has varied between locations and over time, but in Hong Kong it has always been one and one-third ounces, i.e. about 37.8 grams.

Sly brothels – brothels unregistered and thus illegal under the legislation of the colony.

Wives – *kit fat* (tie up hair): the primary or first wife; *tin fong* (fill in room): the principal concubine, taking prime place in the event of the death of the *kit fat*.

CHAPTER I

CONTINUITY AND CHANGE – WOMEN'S LIVES IN EARLY HONG KONG

I n the period covered by this book, the lives of most women in this distant British colony were defined and shaped in relationship to the men in their immediate circle. Those men exercised varying degrees and forms of control over them, some less beneficent than others. The gender balance in all the different sections of the population was weighted towards males, females in Hong Kong only achieving demographic parity during the 1950s.

Three years after the arrival of the first colonists, enumerators reckoned the population of the new colony to be 19,463. Having just been awarded its status as a British colony, Hong Kong had to submit its first annual *Blue Book*.[1] It was the responsibility of the Colonial Secretary's office to collate all the required data for dispatch back to London. Inevitably, the figures that could be produced at relatively short notice, and with only an *ad hoc* mechanism for the count, were an approximation, especially in terms of the numbers of Chinese. While not too much emphasis can be placed on the precise numbers, they do give an indication of the size of the town and the villages, and the rough proportions of males to females. Of the population thus counted, 978 were married Chinese women, although there must also have been many such amongst the 5,368 floating population, which was only given as a total figure. The column headed 'adults and children' amongst the Chinese population is probably so labelled to take account of the brothel residents. The total number of females here was 759 and whilst there were more 'boys' than

---

1 The blank, blue-bound books were issued to all Crown possessions to be filled with the statistical, descriptive and legal information required by their various pre-printed pages. Figures here come from CO133/1, *Blue Book for 1844*.

'girls' in the villages (355:220), in Victoria the reverse applied, males being outnumbered almost threefold (205 to 539). Chinese men in the villages and the town, those present temporarily employed on building projects and those in domestic labour with Europeans totalled 11,904, although that last named group probably included a few women as amahs and baby amahs. Amongst the westerners, there were 355 men and 99 women, which figures probably include a few infants and children. This count excluded the men and women attached to the garrison.

So although Hong Kong was, for many years, a predominantly male place, this scant 13% of the population represents the gender imbalance at its most pronounced.[2] Thereafter, women were still well in the minority, but steadily grew in numbers and occupied a significant place in Hong Kong's story. That this share has largely been ignored by commentators and historians is no surprise. While male hegemony takes a large part of the responsibility, there are also many real difficulties and limitations to be overcome, or rather, circumvented, when an attempt is made to write either a specific or even just a more inclusive account of that story.

Female pop	mid 1850s	mid 1860s	mid 1870s	mid 1880s	mid 1890s	mid 1900s	1911 census	1921 census	1931 census
Chinese	11,596	23,910	27,881	31,995	49,601	75,015	134,945	210,845	321,959
f:m ratio	1:3	3:8	3:8	>1:3	>1:3	1:2.5	>1:2	<2:3	3:4
Floating	6,792	9,330	8,605	11,028	11,700	16,133	20,652	25,847	28,040
f:m ratio	2:5	<1:2	1:2	<2:3	>1:2	3:5	<4:7	2:3	3:4
Foreign	298	659	1,248	1,814	2,391	4,377	4,749	5,617	7,810
f:m ratio	1:4	1:2	2:3	2:3	2:3	2:3	<3:4	>3:4	<4:7
men (all)	50,742	85,500	101,232	115,369	157,585	222,826	289,752	380,915	481,572

Figures taken from Blue Book census returns. 'Foreign', in most cases, includes all non-Chinese, except a very small number with the mercantile marine and although it encompasses other nationalities, including, at varying times, Portuguese, Indians etc., the largest group throughout were British.

---

2 The female (land) population of Hong Kong (1844) as a proportion of the total.

But these are just overall figures and, in multiply divided Hong Kong, a resident of that time might have received a rather different impression, depending on where they lived and how they were occupied. The colony was divided not just on racial grounds, but also by financial and social status, and this not only amongst the class-obsessed British. For those in the upper echelons of power or privilege, shared commercial interests, similar levels of education and a common interest in preserving the status quo allowed for social as well as business interaction, although with well-defined limits. Those in less exalted positions had frequent contact with those of similar status from other races in their day-to-day lives. They could respect the other and appreciate their interdependence, but it rarely went as far as forming friendships outside their own milieu. For those on the lower rungs of the social scale, fear, or at least wariness of the 'other' prevailed. Open hostility was less frequent, but, for example, the labouring westerner would look down on the 'uncivilised' locals around him, unaware that his Chinese neighbours considered him just as uncouth and unpleasant in his habits. And the situation would appear different again to those living, for example, in the New Territories north of Boundary Street. Even in the 1931 census, just 8.5% of Hong Kong's population lived there, and, unlike the rest of the colony, women slightly outnumbered men, showing how little this area had been changed by its accession by Britain in 1898. In this entire region, too, there were just 35 western females in 1931, most of whom were police wives and daughters.

As a constituent part of the British empire, Hong Kong's role differed from that of its counterparts in Africa. It was not taken to be plundered for its mineral or agricultural resources, nor was it part of the 'carving up' of a continent amongst dominant European powers. Its function was always commercial: to be a locus of communication between China and the wider region on the one hand, and Europe and America on the other. Although it was intended to serve British interests, its possibilities were soon realised by the Chinese. Building business concerns alongside and often with the British and other Europeans, they too started to construct the stable social and economic world on this small island that would contrast so starkly with the very unsettled and troubled land to their north. Although lack of mutual understanding was a problem for the colonial administration in the early years, traders and merchants were swift to find effective ways of communication. Hong Kong was a place of transience: a city to which men – and some women – came for a time to make money before returning home, be they Chinese, British or from other parts of the globe. But despite this, there emerged a nucleus of settled residents who, although with no common purpose other than pursuit of financial success, built the idea of Hong Kong as 'home' very early in its history. These were Cantonese-speaking Chinese, both merchants and compradores, but also family businesses, as well as those from other ethnic and national groups, including a few British.[3] It is perhaps this broad range of traditions and cultures which gave resilience to the early colony. Old Portuguese families from Macao, who saw Hong Kong's star rising, brought commercial, clerical and linguistic skills with them. Enterprising individuals from many parts of India and the wider region arrived and flourished in the new colony. Their families created small but stable communities, often with easy relations with the British, given the long relationship between those countries. Marriages between Europeans and Chinese produced Eurasian families of which many were financially successful and although being 'outsiders' on two counts, often provided another conduit for interaction between races.

Finding women's stories

The stories and information in this study come from several contemporary sources. Foremost of those are the newspapers, with official information coming from the government reports, including the annual *Blue Books*. Accounts and commentary appear in a few books of the period, with secondary studies consulted for the broader picture. Printing presses were producing English-language papers from the start of Britain's engagement with the region and the tiny colony, together with traders and merchants in Canton and around the coast, were served by newspapers in the 1840s. Initially, these appeared either once or twice a week, with the editor/owner assisted by a nominal staff. *The Hong Kong Register, The Friend of China*

---

3 A compradore was a Chinese agent employed by foreign businesses as an intermediary between themselves and local firms and labour.

(which included the official bi-weekly *Hongkong Government Gazette* until 1854) and *The China Mail*, which started in 1845, served a variety of purposes at the time and now provide much of our knowledge of daily life in the new colony. The first two did not survive long but from 1857 the reading public enjoyed a daily paper, the *Hongkong Daily Press*. The *Hongkong Telegraph* followed in 1881 and the *South China Morning Post* in 1903.[4] All these competed for readership amongst what, including the English-speaking Chinese, were perhaps ten or fifteen thousand people. In the 1840s and 50s, circulation could be counted in the hundreds. But they thrived, particularly in a port city where shipping lines took many column-inches every day, and where firms of all descriptions found this a convenient way to advertise their wares or services.

But what of daily life can be gleaned from these early broadsheets? Editorial columns might give an appreciation (or otherwise) of the character of a prominent figure in Hong Kong or British public life. Obituaries and funeral reports were regular features of this most unhealthy place. Initially, the passing only of western residents was noted, but from the 1880s onwards, mentions of prominent non-western men appeared. Marriages (western only until the 20th century) were reported as "A pretty wedding…" with plenty of costume detail, whilst government, military and naval appointments, leaves etc., relevant to Hong Kong were recorded. Detailed accounts of social events, such as the annual balls of the national societies (the St Andrew's Society being particularly prominent), 'smokers', amateur theatricals and concerts give us a little idea of how the comfortably-off westerner might employ his or her leisure. But for anyone who seeks illumination into the daily lives of the residents of the colony – Chinese even more so than western – it is the *Police Intelligence* or *Around the Courts* columns that give at least some hints and, occasionally, well-drawn word-pictures. The sound business base of the papers meant that soon they could employ reporters specifically to attend sittings at the Magistracy and the Supreme Court, journalists who usually had enough understanding of Cantonese to be not wholly reliant on the court interpreter. Of course, their reports are not of usual daily life, but of the exceptional days, when a defendant came into contact

---

4 The *South China Morning Post* is the only survivor.

with the law in the shape of a tall British or, more likely, Indian police constable. Here, at least, we do find out a little of the situation of the ordinary folk of the colony, of what concerned and motivated them, and, just sometimes, we hear their own voices.

Chinese women's lives in Hong Kong

The lives of affluent Chinese men in early Hong Kong are not well documented. Still less can we know about the ordinary working man who had regular employment with the government, a commercial firm or business, or a family. Of the men who hired themselves out by the day or hour, making just enough to ensure sufficient food for when there was no employer, only a few scant descriptions exist. We might, though, hear about these last two classes in particular, through these police reports. Not that these individuals needed to commit any heinous acts to be thus noticed. British law, impartial and even-handed as it was in the minds of the legislators, fell particularly heavily on the Chinese. It was they, and especially the poorer amongst them, who had to negotiate a maze of repressive and intrusive ordinances, designed primarily to protect the interests of a minute proportion of the population, specifically the 'respectable' British residents. However, the Chinese appeared not only as defendants or witnesses at the magistrate's court, but as complainants too. The early colonists had created a legal system for its European population modelled closely on that of England, but then promptly declared that all people living there were subject to it. Thus, almost unwittingly, Hong Kong had made available to the majority Chinese a very different system of law than that to which they traditionally had access.

The English-language papers tell us of the offence and status or occupation of defendants. They only give the names of the Chinese sporadically, although almost always give them for westerners. Sometimes a reporter inserts an unflattering physical description of the man but rarely is interest shown in the reasons that the crime was committed. We do not hear whether a man had a pressing need to be out after dark, for example, to get some medicine for a sick friend, and had not time to get the required police pass. The poor aged man who is brought in for hawking a few paltry wares without a licence does not get to tell the magistrate that he had recently been robbed of his money, and until he sells these bits, cannot afford the necessary permit. The Magistracy was a production line, and there was insufficient time to give attention to the case beyond the bare facts. Near the end of the century, the press described a later magistrate as running his court 'at railway speed'. Not that the defendant, before the mid-1860s, would have much chance of being understood had he launched into an explanation. The paucity of Cantonese speakers amongst the courts and law-enforcers meant reliance on locally engaged interpreters, and a general lack of communication. As the century progressed and more European policemen learnt something of the local language, there is the occasional report of a compassionate officer who fills the magistrate in about the problems of the accused. Equally, as interpretation in the courts improved, and the magistrates were more likely to have substantial language training, there are cases where the man in the dock and the man on the bench speak directly to each other. But overall these men varied in their attitude to the mass of humanity they encountered in their courts, and the levels of compassion they displayed. And even for the most humane of men, and some appear in this study, the pressure of the sheer number of cases militated against much enquiry.

Yet as invisible as these men individually are, and for all the lack of testimony from them, far more so were the women.[5] Early Hong Kong had many detractors, quick to stress any apparent depravity or lawlessness in the new colony. Writers both contemporary and later considered that most women in Hong Kong were prostitutes.[6] A misreading of the 1845 census produced by the first Registrar General, Samuel Fearon, resulted

---

5 For an authoritative and nuanced study of the lives of enslaved women in Hong Kong and China, the reader is referred to the two early books by Maria Jaschok, details of which are in the bibliography.

6 The first such to highlight the level of female slavery and prostitution on the island was Robert Martin, in his report to the British Parliament in 1844 (*British Parliamentary Papers: China 24*, p. 115). In later years, Magistrate Charles May's oft-repeated 1876 statement that five-sixths of the Chinese women were prostitutes was echoed four years later by barrister J. J. Francis, who estimated that there were just 4,000-5,000 'respectable women' compared to 18,000-20,000 prostitutes amongst the Chinese population (*British Parliamentary Papers: China 26*, p. 102-3).

in the myth that the colony had 32 brothels but only 30 families, an error which can still be found in standard histories, whereas the report specifically records that there were 315 Chinese families in the town at the time.[7] The statistics produced for that first *Blue Book* a year earlier, on which the opening of this chapter is based, showed 978 married women for the whole island – and, even if this was an overestimation, the majority of those were just that. They looked after their homes and families, engaged with their spouses in trade or other industry but for the most part, stayed within a small distance of their residence and out of notice. Of the various cases found during the first three decades, many involve those who are not brothel inmates, but are women going about their normal, if sometimes nefarious, business. The schools established in these years, whilst mainly being for boys, include a few for Chinese girls, and although the attendances at any of the schools was never great, this does imply a parental home life for some female children. Women occupied traditional roles, as midwives and wet-nurses amongst others, while many widows became small-time traders or hawkers on their own account. Poverty reduced the less fortunate to living on the margins of other people's lives, begging for their daily rice. Examples from most of these groups can be found within the newspaper columns headed *Police Intelligence*. When they appear as plaintiffs, prosecuting a man for a theft or assault, reporters frequently describe them in terms such as "a very respectable married woman prosecuted…". All this serves to show that there were women living recognisably ordinary, domestic lives in the early years of the colony.

The boat people, or 'floating population', as official documents often describe them, occupied a more anomalous position. Fearon's report indicates that women far outnumbered men in this group – 600 men, 1,800 women and 1,200 children are his estimations. There appeared to be an expectation, a tradition, almost, that many of the women here would engage in prostitution. And yet many plied their various more

---

7 The census, in CO129/12 pp. 308-9, states that there were 30 'family houses', which, from the accompanying report, can be seen to refer to substantial houses owned and occupied by Chinese merchants, compradores and others of means, whilst the many of the Chinese lived in the 436 brick houses in within the city of Victoria.

Young boat-women, from the collection of Roy Delbyck, with kind permission.

legitimate trades, providing the *ad hoc* ferrying services to and from the larger craft in the harbour and the floating shops that brought provisions to those same ships.

Brothel inmates

All that said of the women on Hong Kong Island during the first decade, it is certainly true that soon, driven by the great influx of men from neighbouring south China, the majority of women were serving them either directly or indirectly. Mostly living in brothels, they were held in financial bondage to their owners and were physically as captive as any slave on a sugar plantation or in the cotton-fields. While in this work the term *prostitute* is occasionally used, since it generally implies a woman working with at least some autonomy, *brothel slave* might better capture the situation of many. However, since these houses also contained women and girls who worked in other capacities and yet were similarly owned by the brothel-mistress, the term *brothel inmate* has been generally employed.

So, whilst the 'respectable' Chinese women of Hong Kong had little presence in the public forum, even less did many of the brothel inmates.

Their appearance on the streets in an attempt to escape would attract immediate attention and be recognised for what it was. This invisibility translates into an absence of the majority of Hong Kong's female population in the records and accounts of the day.

Anti-slavery legislation had at first been proposed, but the Colonial Office advised that, since protection both from slavery and serfdom was enshrined in British law, there was no need for a separate ordinance here. And yet Captain Elliot's declaration that Britain would leave Chinese customs alone in its administration of the colony was sufficiently fresh in the mind. The law-makers engaged in a very dubious sleight of mind to allow for the tradition of established brothels and daughter transfers to be considered beneficial in the light of contemporary Chinese practice. As in England, prostitution itself was not illegal. Soliciting by individual women was an offence, but, due to the prevalence of brothels, was almost unknown in 19th century Hong Kong. Through the operation of the *Venereal Disease Ordinance* of 1857 and its successor in 1867, brothels were considered legal if they and the women therein were registered with the Registrar General. The Ordinances required that those brothels serving European men sent their inmates for a weekly examination at the Lock Hospital. Any found to be infected were confined to the Hospital for treatment until cured. Such measures were not put in place for the benefit of those who had to submit to the inspection, but to ensure a supply of 'clean' women for their clients, who were predominantly members of the British Army, the Navy and the Hong Kong Police Force. Failure on the part of the brothel mistress to comply with the requirements could cause the establishment to lose its licence and be closed down.

In general, through this period, in registered brothels the women themselves were not prosecuted. However, by the mid-1870s the campaign against 'sly' (unregistered) brothels had escalated and the police attached to the Registrar General's department became increasingly determined to obtain convictions. The operation became more ugly with the use of paid informers to trap the women (and the brothel owners), such as were used by Inspector Lee in his time as Inspector of Brothels. Only when the inquest on two women who had fallen to their deaths while trying to escape the inspector brought the methods used to public attention were these subjected to scrutiny and then abandoned.[8] Insp. Lee had sent three Chinese men to a sly brothel in No. 42 Peel Street to have a meal and then stay with women there.[9] At 1 a.m. Insp. Lee raided the house and two women, Fung Asee and Ho Tai-yow, scrambled out onto the roof to evade him. There followed a chase across the rooftops, which, according to the policeman, was quite a usual feature of such 'investigations'. However he did not manage to arrest the women on this occasion, as, in their panic, they both tumbled down an unguarded smoke shaft, falling about 40 feet (10 metres) to their deaths. At the conclusion of the inquest, the Coroner, Mr Russell, gave it as his opinion that the women had died as a result of misadventure, since neither they nor the policeman had known of the smoke shaft. Insp. Lee had, perhaps narrowly, avoided prosecution for manslaughter, but he was reprimanded for exceeding his authority.

Yet, however assiduous were the police and the Registrar General's department in closing down the illegal establishments, there was a continuous demand for women, and not just for the brothels in the colony. Traffickers brought in girls from Guangdong or other parts of southern China. Sometimes they came individually, sold to the go-between by parents or other relatives, but often they were kidnapped from their villages and sold through a succession of traders until they arrived at a brothel in the colony. Some were themselves the daughters of prostitutes there or of the brothel mistresses, whilst the latter would often buy young girls to act first as servants and then train them to their profession. Another source, particularly in the earlier years, was from the boat-people. Rather despised by the land population, these prejudices would force these women into the lowest class of brothel, or into those serving western men.

Perhaps least unfortunate amongst all these women were those in a fashionable and 'high' or 'first-class' establishment. These catered for the merchants and compradores, who would come to relax and be entertained by beautiful singing and music performed by the inmates, or

---

8 The case was covered by *China Mail* from 17th October 1877, with the adjourned conclusion in the edition for 29th October 1877.

9 This was within the area – the eastern stretch of Hollywood Road – which was reserved for brothels for European clients.

CHOW-CHOW (CHINESE SUPPER) AT HONG-KONG.

Chow-chow in a high-class brothel, Charles Wirgmann, 1857.

hold business meetings over sumptuous feasts, waited on by the women. The sexual encounter was secondary and the women who lived and worked there were skilled in music, singing, mahjong and conversation. But for the vast majority of women, life was much less cushioned and often brutal. Officially, the establishments were in one of four categories: those that catered for westerners (and could not admit Chinese or other non-Europeans), and first, second and third class Chinese brothels. The 'European' houses were markedly less agreeable places than the 'first-class' houses described. The men they catered for were the ordinary working men of the colony, the police and gaol warders, the clerks and store-men, the soldiers and seamen as well as all the riff-raff of a port with international connections. European men with sufficient means preferred to 'keep' a woman in a small apartment in the town than to frequent the brothels. The second class Chinese brothels catered for the craftsmen and salaried men, offering meals and some degree of comfort. The worst, for the 'coolie-class', as day or hour labourers were termed, made no pretence about offering anything other than sexual services. These were in squalid, foetid tenements or even shacks, where the women quickly lost their youth and health. Sickness ran rife through all brothels – not just the obvious venereal disease, but all the many infectious diseases which abounded in the early colony. Typhoid, dysentery, smallpox and cholera all made inroads into the population, unchecked until the advent of vaccines and then penicillin. In the worst of these places, the fortunate women were those who succumbed to an early death.

Mui tsai and child slavery

In her illuminating study of the Tung Wah Hospital and its development in the 19th century, Sinn points out that in Chinese law the adult was not, *per se*, the free agent that he or she was in British law.[10] Rather, for many adults – and thus children – there were levels and types of bondage that restricted their autonomy and tied them, in many cases for life, to their financial or social superior. This was the case for apprentices, sons, nephews, etc., as it was for wives, concubines and *mui tsai*. It goes some way to showing how difficult it is to identify the relationship between all the young children in the colony and the adults in charge of them. The smallest children, male and female, became servants, and the masters or mistresses to whom they were attached often had scant resources themselves. The child then became a tradable commodity, with a seven-year-old sold to another master for perhaps $20. Writing in 1939, Geoffrey Sayer, who had been in the Hong Kong civil service since 1910, blamed the arrival of 'respectable' Chinese women for the appearance of *mui tsai* in the colony, but perhaps they had been in Hong Kong long before the British.

The practice of daughter-transfer, known as *mui tsai*, which defenders were keen to present as having a long and venerable history in China, was a way for lower-income families to deal with their surplus of girls. Apparently tracing its roots back to the Confucian writings on domestic rites, at its best it was a charitable act reaching across social class. Parents with more daughters than they could provide dowries might present a young child, usually less than eight and sometimes as young as three years old, to a better-placed woman, who would then bring her up as a 'little sister'. All daughters, whether natural or *mui tsai*, were expected to undertake many household chores, be docile and show respect to

10 Elizabeth Sinn, *Power and Charity*, p. 97.

their mistress/mother and to apply themselves to learning the arts of housekeeping. In the best situations, the girl would receive some education and, when of marriageable age, a husband of suitable means and status (often higher than that of her birth parents) would be found, and a dowry supplied. The mistress would then look round for another *mui tsai* – thus ensuring that she had a 'daughter' to look after her as she grew older. The mistress, sometimes called the 'pocket mother', gave the birth parents some money in compensation for that which they had spent rearing the child until she left their home. Known as 'rice, ginger and vinegar money', this was a nominal amount, and was not understood as payment for the child.

That was the system both in intention and at its best. Examples of such did exist, and, amongst the better educated or more affluent families, it was the experience of such adopted girls. But the system was wide open to abuse, and for the majority of girls who were transferred to a mistress, life became one of bonded slavery, from which escape, even in adulthood, could be very difficult. Usually the problem was that the mistress had insufficient funds to keep enough domestic help, so the child was a useful source of unpaid labour, and over whom the money paid (no such niceties as compensatory monies here) became an overt bond. The *mui tsai* received no wages, not even when she was adult, and was less free to leave than a paid servant and was thus, in reality, a slave. As if this were not enough, the distinction between *mui tsai* and brothel slave was frequently blurred. Girls were bought by brothel mistresses, often having been sold on through a series of intermediary owners. Alternatively, a married woman who did not like the child she had acquired or found her disobedient might easily sell her to a brothel, and realise a profit on the transaction. Many, perhaps the majority, of cases of brothel slavery involved women who were (still) *mui tsai*. Not all the children sold stayed in the town – the demand for women for the brothels in Singapore and other parts of south-east Asia saw the regular trafficking of girls out of the colony, while others were kidnapped often from Guangdong and dispatched through Hong Kong.

Alongside these traps for girls and young women, the emergent emigration trade was another great threat to their safety (not that the majority of Chinese men affected fared much better). The Abolition of Slavery Act of 1833 might have had the effect of outlawing overt slavery in the British Empire, and focussed attention on the transportation of peoples from Africa and the Caribbean, but the demand for cheap labour had not diminished. The opening of the treaty ports and the establishment of a foreign base in Hong Kong allowed for the recruitment of labour on a huge scale from much of eastern and southern China. Boat loads of men were ferried down the China coast to Hong Kong, which was used as a giant clearing house. Often these men had been kidnapped or decoyed, so the Legislative Council rapidly passed ordinances to place some control on the process, in part to counteract suspicion that this was slave trading by another name. These laws gave some minimal protection for those boarding the coolie ships, but also ensured that disease was neither brought unchecked into Hong Kong nor exported to British interests elsewhere. Alongside the warehouses and godowns on the Praya, and later in British Kowloon, emigrant sheds held hundreds of men bonded to serve as labourers, usually for ten years. The Harbour Master (as Emigration Officer), Registrar General and Colonial Surgeon were responsible for ensuring the 'legality' and health of these men.

But as the trade established itself, so too did the unspoken but evident call for young women to follow them and serve in brothels. Most were, like the men, decoyed or kidnapped from their villages. Dealers could make large profits selling the girls in the USA, Latin America or nearer to home. Harbour Office officials questioned the potential exports, intending to ensure all were travelling of their own free will. However, their temporary owners had trained them to give the right answers and so they had to be allowed to leave, and go outside the reach of any colonial power. This dreadful situation, however, could be prevented or at least remedied to some extent in Hong Kong, and it was concerned members of the Chinese community, rather than the British administration, that took the lead.

Chinese community solutions – the Tung Wah and Po Leung Kuk

With an ancient tradition of remedies and medical practices developed long before and without reference to western ideas, there was a general suspicion of and antipathy towards European medicine and hospitals. The movement for a Chinese hospital was started by some ordinary tradespeople in the town and then promoted by more prominent men. The Tung Wah Hospital opened in 1870 and gave people access to their own medicine and medical procedures, but provided much more than its name would suggest to European ears. Here poor Chinese could receive help to get themselves back to their home villages if need be, or help with burying their dead. The Man Mo Temple in Hollywood Road was where townspeople brought many disputes to elders for their decisions, but the Tung Wah also served this purpose. In short, it was a source of support and assistance, provided through the charitable efforts of the wealthy in the community towards the wider Chinese population, both in and out of health. From its earliest days the Tung Wah was regularly removing girls and women thought to be at risk of being kidnapped into prostitution, and returning them to their home villages. But some on the Tung Wah committee, and prominent merchants from Dongguan, were anxious to extend the work. They also deemed it advisable to separate, to some extent, the medical and social aspects of the Tung Wah's work, since there had been much criticism in the press that the hospital was overreaching its legal authority. If they formed a discrete organisation that was granted legal status specifically with this aim, they hoped that this would silence the critics. They envisaged that this society would take over the Tung Wah's role, even to the extent of employing detectives. In 1878, they petitioned the Governor, Sir John Pope Hennessy, for permission to start the Po Leung Kuk – Protect the Innocent Society, to investigate and adjudicate on suspected kidnaps and repatriate those affected. The idea received the Governor's enthusiastic support, but the Colonial Office and members of the Hong Kong judiciary were less happy, and refused him permission to establish it by ordinance. It was realised that the Tung Wah were attempting to make a distinction between what customary Chinese practice considered legal and illegal monetary transactions for people. English law prohibited all such commerce – slavery – since this was (now) anathema to the British. The Tung Wah had pressed for legislation to protect females from trafficking, which all parties considered unacceptable. However, the resulting ordinance, the

Protection of Chinese Women and Female Children Ordinance, of 1873 and its amendment two years later, had gone much further than they intended and outlawed customary practices of concubinage, *mui tsai* and *san po tsai* (future daughter-in-law) as well as the purchase for adoption of male children.[11] The promoters of the Po Leung Kuk were attempting to uphold customary Chinese values in a manner outside of government control and yet with the sanction of that government. The Colonial Office perceived the threat to its authority if such an organisation, especially one that had quasi-police and -judicial functions, was so legitimised.

The Protect the Innocent Society was duly formed, with its lesser powers, but worked closely with the Tung Wah. For over fifteen years it had no base of its own, and operated much as before, since all its activities came from and led back to the Hospital premises. The Society had to hold the women and girls rescued within the Tung Wah, where their accommodation was so basic that it gave the impression that they were being punished, which was far from the intention. But it had a separate constitution and directorate and continued its work of tracking women and children in brothels or being trafficked, while also providing assistance to destitute adults in the colony. But it was its work with the rescued young women that continued to alarm the European population. For those not 'restored' to parents or husbands, the Society found marriage partners, although this would often mean that the girl became a first or second concubine. This, of course, in western eyes, pushed them into bigamous relations. In 1892 the Governor called a commission to investigate its activities. This very thorough-going enquiry, led by the Registrar General, James Stewart Lockhart, met over ten months and eventually produced a 170-page report. They had interviewed a wide range of people with experience of the Society and of the stories of women and girls helped.[12] Under Lockhart's leadership it was no real surprise that the Po Leung Kuk emerged stronger from the investigation and the report recommended that the Society be given the same legal status as the Tung

11 *Hongkong Government Gazette,* 10th May 1873, Ordinance No. 6 of 1873, *For the better protection of Chinese Women and female children and suppression of certain abuses in relation to Chinese emigration* and, of the same title, Ordinance No. 2 of 1875, *Hongkong Government Gazette,* 20th March 1875.

12 *Report of the Special Committee on the Po Leung Kuk,* Sessional Papers 1893.

Wah.[13] The administration had already addressed the need for separate premises, but its solution had been to build a series of houses, with the top floors of each reserved as a Home. This was quickly seen to be quite unsatisfactory, and a piece of land, on the eastern corner of Taipingshan Street and Po Yan Street, opposite the Tung Wah Hospital, was designated as a site for the new home. The Governor, Sir William Robinson, laid the foundation stone on 18th January 1896 and it was completed ten months later.[14] Designed by local architect, Albert Denison and built by Wing On contractors, it stood some 16 feet (about 5 metres) above street level, its stone walls faced with mandarin-green brick and topped with white tiles. It incorporated rooms for Tung Wah outpatients, but had spacious rooms for 100 inmates and staff, meeting rooms, gardens and courtyards. It was lit with gas throughout, and special attention had been paid to installation of the most modern cooking and sanitary facilities on every floor. Amidst great pomp and ceremony, both Chinese and British, the Governor was again there on 13th November to open it. He presented the Society with a plaque, with a quotation from the Chinese Book of Odes, which he believed would be most appropriate. The inscription read, "I regard them as my own children".

Colonial solutions – the Registrar General's Department

From the outset, the Government's intention had been that the Registrar General would control the Chinese. Ordinance 8 of 1858, an *Ordinance for the Regulation of the Chinese People,* bestowed on the office a range of wide reaching powers, affecting the majority population.[15] Registration and licensing of all kinds, with accompanying powers of search and forfeiture, meant official interference in many aspects of life. Tickets were required for market stalls, rickshaws, meetings, boats and much else besides. Officers from the department could inspect boarding houses, and the department regulated fares for all forms of transport and set labour rates. A prominent early office holder, Daniel Caldwell, who was a rarity

---

13 *The Po Leung Kuk Incorporation Ordinance,* No. 10 of 1893.

14 *Hongkong Weekly Press,* 22nd January 1896, *Hongkong Telegraph,* 13th November 1896.

15 *Hongkong Government Gazette,* 15th May 1858.

in the 1840s and 50s Hong Kong in that he was fluent in Cantonese, had the title 'Protector of the Chinese' added to the post. Throughout the entire period it remained the most outward facing, and often the busiest, of government departments. Besides all its prescriptive functions, it was the office to which ordinary people could take their problems, whether with other government officials or in their neighbourhood. When normal Chinese routes or the District Watchmen were not appropriate, or when there was a need for the stronger hand of British law, it was to the Registrar General's office, with its Cantonese speaking staff, that residents could turn. In the years after Caldwell's removal (of which we shall hear a little more later), it looked set to become merely a form-stamping office, until the charge of it went to the very young Cecil Clementi Smith in 1864. One of the first three Civil Service cadet officers in the colony, he had used his two years' immersion in Cantonese to good effect and gave the department structure and expanded purpose. But it was James Stewart Lockhart, a later cadet officer, who occupied the post from 1887 to 1901, and who transformed it into a deeply Chinese-oriented office of the Colonial Government. Lockhart, too, had steeped himself in Chinese literature, customs and culture, and, feeling that Hong Kong's eventual future would be back with China, supported the development of local organisation as far as he could. Chinese community leaders appreciated his support and sought his endorsement of local interests. Lockhart's promotion of the Po Leung Kuk was just one example of this.

Meanwhile, the office continued to oversee the functioning of what would become known as the '*Women and Girls Ordinance*'. Since its first enactment in 1873, it had sought to control the emigration abuses and thereafter, in various re-draftings, gave increased rights to women in brothels, through to the 1941 Japanese occupation.[16] The Inspector of Brothels, a policeman (since the power to arrest was imperative) reporting to the superintendent of the Lock Hospital from the time of the *Venereal Disease Ordinance* of 1857, worked closely with the Registrar General's

---

16 The last full enactment of this was Ordinance No. 5 of 1938, *Hongkong Government Gazette,* 13th May 1938.

office.[17] After the rescinding of this ordinance and its successor, these inspectors also came under its direct control. In 1915 the name of the department was changed to the Secretariat for Chinese Affairs (S.C.A.). From the 1920s it coordinated the measures to prohibit the *mui tsai* system under the *Female Domestic Service Ordinance*.[18] This established the rights of any girl to leave their employer, forbade further contracts and required the registration of all *mui tsai*. The Secretariat used seconded police as inspectors, but from the mid-1930s also appointed women to this post. Most notable was Phyllis Harrop, who became Assistant Secretary to the Secretary for Chinese Affairs in 1938. She was a fearless champion and protector of many girls, not only household *mui tsai,* but captive brothel slaves, and earned great esteem from many of the police with whom she worked.[19]

Families between two worlds

There were a few women whose lives crossed cultural divides. Mary Ayow Caldwell, the Chinese wife of adventurer and government official, Daniel Caldwell, brought her children up within both cultures. For all her husband's rather chequered career, she was known for her charity and virtue, although she remained something of an outsider in the narrow-minded world of the self-styled elite. She is, though, rather an anomaly in this 'sub-set' of the women of Hong Kong. Many well-placed European men kept mistresses in the town, providing for them a comfortable home while they were 'out east', but rarely acknowledging paternity or providing for any children of the liaison, much less marrying the woman. Among those working-class men whose lives were set to continue in Hong Kong, some preferred to settle down with a Chinese woman in a semi-permanent relationship. Others, with a steady job but insufficient funds to think about returning home, would apply to one of the convent

---

17 Lock Hospitals were established in Britain and its colonies from the late 18th Century to specialise in the treatment of sexually transmitted diseases.

18 Ordinance No. 1 of 1923, *Hongkong Government Gazette,* 15th February 1923.

19 Phyllis Harrop made a daring escape from Hong Kong just a month after the occupation, and was one of the first to give information about the battles and Japanese atrocities during those weeks to the British Government.

orphanages for a suitable young woman, whom they would decently marry in a Catholic church. The story of sailor Thomas Legg's family is one particularly tragic example. He lived with his Chinese wife, Amni, and their three adopted (Chinese) daughters in Wanchai, and they came to public attention when their five-year-old daughter was mysteriously murdered. The events of the evening in 1887 and the subsequent investigation, trial and acquittal of the eldest daughter aroused much interest in all sectors of the community.[20]

Italian Convent Orphanage.

Foreign women's lives in Hong Kong

Who were the foreign women in Hong Kong? Whether the question is about the 100 or so in the first decade or the 4,000 at the turn of the century or at any other point, we know for certain they were as cosmopolitan a group as the men at those times. It must be admitted that, while the intention here is to include in the term 'foreign' all non-Chinese, the earlier census forms defined people by skin colour. Thus, the figures until the 20th century somewhat understate the number of

---

20 The story is recounted in *Policing Hong Kong – an Irish History,* pp. 108-10.

women in Hong Kong counted by the more inclusive criteria. In the first decades, alongside the majority British, there were Americans, Japanese, women from many parts of India and parts of south-east Asia, a few from the West Indies, Germany, Italy and France, not forgetting the Portuguese and Macanese from neighbouring Macao. And as Hong Kong's importance as a world trading centre grew, people came from central and south America, Sweden, Denmark and Russia and settled for a shorter or longer time. Harking back to the opening of this chapter, most women in the colony were wives, and were there because of that. But that broad description hides a great variety of situations, according to their nationality and financial position, and their (perceived) social class.

It is probable that the first western women to step ashore were the wives of ordinary soldiers, relieved to be getting off the troopships that had been their homes for too long. Even life under canvas, sharing a tent with three or four other couples, and on a rather marshy piece of flat land in the east of the island would be preferable to the cramped, unhealthy sailing ships. Until about the 1870s women regularly arrived in the colony thus, since the army permitted wives to travel with their husbands as service was frequently for five or six years, and there was no means of support for women left back at home. These women would find how disease ridden were their camps: early mortality amongst them and their children was high. They may well have urged spouses to purchase their discharge from the army and take a chance on a post with the emerging firms or the colonial powers on the island. Many a woman became a policeman's wife overnight in this new world. The navy did not permit the families of ordinary ratings to travel, but those of senior officers were some of the earliest women in Hong Kong at the other end of the social spectrum. With better quarters on board, they could wait a time for a house of some sort to be erected, and then could soon move from that mat-shed type home to a proper granite built house along the shoreline. Soon the wives of merchants, ambassadors, doctors and lawyers joined them, and they became the first 'elite' of the place.

As years went by and Victoria began to bear less resemblance to a gold-rush place, the social hierarchy of Britons removed from their usual world emerged. At the top of the tree – the salaried upper middle class, in the absence of any aristocracy or landed gentry – family life might be remarkably similar to that which they could expect were they at home. Men who had acquired senior roles in the banks and trading firms or in the civil service might expect to marry whilst still in their mid-twenties, perhaps only five or six years into their career, bringing the young woman out with them at the end of their first long leave. The exigencies of life in Hong Kong would be mitigated by the presence of servants, usually in a far greater number than they had in Britain. In earlier times these women brought their lady's maid with them, but as the century progressed the responsibility for a young unattached female in the household, plus the difficulty of finding young women willing to work in such a difficult and alien situation soon persuaded most to employ a Chinese amah, and train her into the role. Within a few years of marriage, the man's salary was sufficient to pay for a first-class passage home for his wife, if the climate and place proved too deleterious to her health.

But most of the women who arrived as new brides had husbands some ten or more years their senior. These were the women who had married the engineers, supervisors, police sergeants, insurance brokers, or one of the many men listed as Assistant in the Jury Lists to the banking, merchant and shipping lines. Either regulations or their pay had not permitted them to marry until they had worked for ten years or so, and now, perhaps seeing that their longer career might be in this far-flung part of the empire, had decided to settle down. They, often with the active involvement of mothers and sisters at home, had selected a young woman, who would now need to adjust to this very different life. Not all of these women were from the British Isles – European and American firms had soon set up offices in the town, and their employees also brought their womenfolk. But many of these men would still have financial responsibilities to families at home. In the days before state pensions, the bread-winning son would expect to look after parents in their old age, and any unmarried sisters also had to be supported. Men sent considerable portions of their salaries back to Britain for this purpose. Most of the new families in Hong Kong would know that their sojourn 'out east' was temporary. Forty-five was considered a suitable retirement age for a man, such as a police officer, whose work took him amongst the people, whilst fifty-five was a good age for an office-bound worker to achieve, given the many virulent diseases that stalked the town. For these couples there would be periodic leaves, perhaps every three or five years, and sometimes enough money for the wife to return home before her husband, if need be.

Not so for many of those discharged soldiers' wives. Unless they had secured a good post, their husband's low pay meant a continual struggle to preserve some sort of European way of life, living in the grimmer parts of town, with many poor Chinese as neighbours, and no chance to put anything by for the future. They had to reconcile themselves to the likelihood that they might never see their homeland again, although, in the constant battle against disease, any long-term view was an unaffordable luxury. These were the women, like some early matrons of Victoria Gaol, who would find themselves widowed and marry a friend or colleague of the late husband, only to be widowed once more. Epidemics of typhoid, smallpox, malarial fever and common old dysentery took many, especially those who had not the funds to ensure they bought their food from the better, cleaner, class of shop. Women in this stratum of society might find themselves abruptly abandoned in the colony. It was not unknown for a man, tiring of a tedious, ill-paid job and with a marriage fractured by the strains it had been under, to go straight from the paymaster's office to the shipping line and purchase a passage, just for himself, perhaps to Australia or California. It was after such an experience that some women had to make their keep how they could and became the western prostitutes that were always present. But further up the financial scale, widowhood, if not comfortable, received some attention. Firms and government repatriated their employees' widows. Now without incomes, or with the much-reduced means of a pension from a widows' and orphans' fund, they would be an inconvenience if they stayed in the colony. Much better that they were returned home where their families could support them.

There were also, and from early days, women arriving and living independently here. Some of the most vivid pictures we have of 19th-century Hong Kong are from female travellers, whilst missionaries travelled both as part of married couples and as single women, intent on saving souls and alleviating distress. Female religious congregations sent sisters out, with the French Daughters of Charity of St Paul de Chartres arriving in 1848. Bishop Forcade had sent for them to set up a school for Irish and Portuguese girls and an orphanage to rescue the abandoned Chinese infants. The Italian Canossian teaching sisters arrived in 1860 and were immediately joined by the daughter of the Governor, Emily Bowring, against the wishes of her staunch Protestant father.

With its long history of trade in the region, Macao was a rich source of literate men, used to working in more than one language and quick to acquire a working knowledge of English. As the hub of the Catholic church's missionary work in south China, it had boasted the first western-style university in Asia, Colégio de São Paulo in the 16th century.[21] Even now, it had many good schools, where the curriculum was delivered in two and sometimes three languages. With this education, young men found ample employment in the trading firms, insurance brokers, banks and shipping lines that were being established in the neighbouring colony. Macao's climate was more benign than that of Hong Kong, so until the new place was firmly established, there was no need for wives and families from the Portuguese colony to immediately uproot themselves. But within a few years the Portuguese/Macanese community in Hong Kong was flourishing, although, for at least a century, families kept close ties with their homes in Macao. Of other nationalities, initially there were few wives accompanying the many Indian regiments that served in the region. But when these men, too, moved into jobs in the town, and could afford separate accommodation, they sent back home for their families. Japanese trader and finance firms soon established themselves, but whilst this resulted in a few settled families, many Japanese women were prostitutes, with brothels set up in the Ship Street area of Wanchai.

But this brief overview cannot do justice to the rich contribution foreign women made to Hong Kong's first century. The best introduction to this, at least the western women's part of the story, is to be found in Susanna Hoe's 1991 study, *The Private Life of Old Hong Kong*. Out of print at the time of writing, second-hand copies can still be found of this

---

21 Founded by the Jesuits in 1594 to prepare their missionaries, St Paul's College functioned until 1762.

fascinating book. With meticulous research and access to many private papers, diaries and letters, alongside official records and contemporary material, Hoe gives us an open window into lives of women from all walks of life, from the early milliners to governors' wives, the pampered wives and daughters of early merchants to Hong Kong's first female doctor. Anyone who seeks respite from the distinctly irregular life events of many of the women portrayed in this present book will be richly rewarded should they find a copy of Hoe's book.

Hong Kong before the British

Before moving on to the first encounters that women in Hong Kong had with the law, it is perhaps worth remembering how different and remote this place was when that interaction first began. Long before the British arrived in Hong Kong it had a small but apparently continuous population, linked by family and clan to the people of the villages on the mainland, across the water. The little island off the Kowloon peninsula was a long way from the centre of the empire, and its few inhabitants had a settled, unchanging way of life. It was self-sufficient, with some agriculture in the wide paddy-fields of Wong Nei Chung, but most of the 3,000-4,000 population were fisherfolk. The scattered villages and hamlets around the southern side of the island were home to many. The majority, though, lived on sampans and other fishing vessels, moored in the island's many creeks, inlets and natural bays. Fish and granite from the small quarries were the only products traded with the mainland. Contact with Canton, the principal city of the Guangdong region, was limited, although the communication routes were well established. Occasional visits from the assistant magistrate, who came to collect taxes and register the island's fishing boats, were among the few times villages might expect to see outsiders.[22]

The high Qing dynasties of late 17th and 18th centuries had been succeeded by emperors whose hold on power was less secure. The many uprisings in distant parts of the now-huge China cost these administrations dear in influence, manpower and money. But another threat to the coherence of the empire was on its way, and by the 1830s

---

22 John Carroll, *Edge of Empires*, p.19.

Canton was already feeling the effects of that as it became the first city to have significant contact with foreign merchants.

British domestic markets had an insatiable desire for goods that China produced, principally tea, silks and porcelain, but had nothing to offer which that country wanted – except silver. To create an alternative currency to its finite reserves of silver, the East India Company and independent merchants began to ship opium to China. British India was producing an abundance of the drug, and it was already used by some in China. Its beauty, as far as the merchants were concerned, was that it would create its own demand. But the emperor was very alive to the destruction it could wreak on society and forbade its use in trade. The British government, wedded to the supremacy of free-trade, and unused to encountering opposition on this subject, responded by sending its military and naval might. To the goal of trading its opium for Chinese merchandise was added another, long obvious to the merchants. Britain required sovereign territory in the region, a naval and military base, but equally one where western merchants could live, untrammelled by Chinese regulations.

From the late 1830s many shipments of opium were stored in hulks in the deep water between Hong Kong Island and the peninsula. At the outbreak of hostilities in Canton, the British and European community boarded ships and moved to this harbour. The villagers of Hong Kong, even those on the southern side of the island, could not but be aware of these strange, huge ships and even stranger people whose presence disrupted their contact with Kowloon and disturbed their fish-stocks. It was the military and naval need for a shore base that prompted the landing of January 1841 on the island, ahead of the Treaty of Nanking the following year. Intended initially as a negotiating tool, the island soon became a *de facto* possession. Much needed workshops and stores were erected, tented camps of troops sprung up and Chinese labourers in their hundreds crossed the harbour to seek employment.

Hong Kong in the 1840s & 1850s
In the months that followed Captain Belcher's planting of the British flag at Possession Point on 26th January 1841, in the camps were what might

seem a surprising number of women. The campaign on the China coast had begun in earnest two years earlier and for the next twenty years and more steady a stream of servicemen converged on southern China. Troop ships carrying regiments allowed wives to accompany their men folk. There were also many tradesmen that had to accompany such a large body of men on the move: tailors and barbers, carpenters and mechanics, whose families also travelled with them.

The military did not long have sole possession of the narrow strip of land between the hill and the shore. Many of the local Chinese who crossed the harbour for work in those first years were people on the margins, since the Qing authorities had declared that those leaving China or working for foreign powers were traitors to the Emperor. Only those already compromised by their commercial activity in Canton, or those so poor they had little to lose, could risk coming to Hong Kong. As a free port the merchants, who had first decamped back to Canton, quickly saw the advantages of trading on British territory. Soon they were followed by merchants and shopkeepers from Macao, both Portuguese and others, who were swift to see which way the winds of trade and commerce were turning in the region. Three months had been sufficient to produce an outline of a town, with a long road connecting the drained Wong Nei Chung, now, ineptly as it would transpire, renamed 'Happy Valley', where the soldiers had their camps of tents and mat-sheds, to the Navy's dockyard out at West Point. From 1842 Chinese craftsmen and labourers arrived in yet greater numbers, to construct the fabric of a commercial centre, as demanded by the merchants and compradores. Thus, well before the proclamation of the *Charter of Hongkong* in June 1843, which the Queen had signed some two months earlier, or the first meeting of the Legislative Council in January 1844, there were many timber houses, shops and godowns (warehouses) along the length of this road. There were now more substantial granite buildings, often constructed on the incline above the road. The prison and the magistrate's residence were the first such.

The colonial life of the emerging town can be seen through the advertisements in *The Friend of China*. In some of the earliest issues, in 1842, businesses advertise themselves by house number on Queen's Road.

These are emporiums of 'all sorts' – paint, anchors, and sail needles for the ships alongside iron window gratings, lemon syrup, brandy and fine flour for a broader market. A gentleman advertises himself as a commission agent and overseer for the construction of houses, whilst in June one Mr Dutronquoy tells Hong Kong that he is opening the London Hotel on the same model as his successful business of that name in Singapore. What is perhaps Hong Kong's first hostelry, Britain's Boast, needs no advertisement, since it is regularly mentioned in the Police Reports. Two years later shops started to specialise, rather than accept any merchandise they can import. A chemist and druggist is established on Queen's Road, while businesses that previously had ironware and timber amongst the foodstuffs now advertise such delicacies as raspberry vinegar and French olives. Liquor merchants abound, while a watchmaker, based at Lane's Hotel, had just arrived in the colony and seeks commissions. London-based fire insurance firms book space in the paper, whilst many of the names of firms – Gibb Livingston, Dents, Jardine Matheson, John Burd, Holliday Wise, etc., are those that will dominate Hong Kong trade in years to come.

The Chinese labourers and craftsmen who were flocking to the island needed their provision merchants and services, some of which were supplied by itinerant traders, but soon Chinese shops were established side-by-side with western concerns. At first there was little oversight as to the buildings in Queen's Road, and the lanes off that, but in 1844 the government passed an order prohibiting Chinese from owning houses in that area and insisted that they move to Taipingshan, further west and slightly above the harbour. The homeowners banded together and successfully demanded some compensation. Soon the *Blue Books* would provide lists of numbers of Chinese businesses and trades, from rice sellers and tailors to coffin-makers and joss-paper merchants. Not all the Chinese arrivals were from the labouring class. Merchants and commission agents who had successfully traded with the British, and were thus outlaws in Qing China, made Hong Kong their home, and built a powerful elite group, ready to take on the colonial government where necessary, but also able to support their own people. Contractor Tam Achoy and merchant Loo Aqui were two such, building the island's first post-colonisation temple, Man Mo Temple in Hollywood Road in 1847.

The spiritual needs of the western community brought one Father Joset from Macao to establish the first Catholic church early in 1842, on (now) Wellington Street, close to the barracks. The little mat-shed saw its first public service in February and Irish soldiers soon spread the word, not only amongst themselves but through the Portuguese community, so that from the second service the church was too small. Foundations of a larger and more permanent church were dug, and a stone laying ceremony was held four months later. In 1847 building commenced of St John's Cathedral to serve the needs of the colony's Protestant community. The Catholic orders and other missionary groups ran some small schools and hospitals, but most were short-lived. The latter, when intended for Chinese, ran up against the aversion the local people had to many western medical practices and their unfamiliarity with the idea of a hospital as a place of cure (in theory, at any rate) rather than just of aid. The Seamen's Hospital, out in Wanchai, was more successful, patients' fees being paid by the shipping lines or the Navy. In 1843 the Governor directly appointed the first Colonial Surgeon, rather than wait for London to do so. But the rigours of this most hazardous job saw the demise of the first three post-holders within a decade.[23] Private medical men, who could pick and choose their patients, were more fortunate.

Moreover, the roads and lanes of Victoria still bore more resemblance to a poor country village than any self-respecting town. Even Queen's Road, which was built by convict chain-gang labour, broke up into rough pools under Hong Kong's torrential rains, and the paths up the hill became little more than mud-slides. There were some horse-drawn carriages – necessarily light ones, but for the majority, the safest way to negotiate the terrain was in two- or four-man sedan chairs. James Norton-Kyshe, in his great two-volume *The History of the Laws and Courts of Hong Kong*, paraphrases the *Hongkong Gazette* for 1st January 1842. He records that in the first year "The population, then, was stated to be hard-working, industrious, and cheerful, the people too much engaged apparently with

23 More on the early attempts to provide medical services in the colony can be found in Moira M. W. Chan-Yeung, *A Medical History of Hong Kong*.

their own affairs to have time for idleness, crimes having been anything but of frequent occurrences…"[24] However, that was not a situation that prevailed for long. Just a few months later, it seems, gang robberies were a frequent occurrence, and no westerner ventured forth without a pistol to hand, even by day.

In the business of crime women lagged behind men, perhaps remarkably so, given that the challenges and tribulations of life were no less for them than their brothers and husbands. Few of the more prosperous Chinese would bring their households to Hong Kong in the very first years, although there was a small 'society' of wealthier western families, the wives and daughters of whom led privileged and sheltered lives. Most Chinese women were from the strata of society where all had to labour for the daily rice. Soldiers from the camps were purchasing their discharge and moving themselves and their families into the town, picking up jobs with little difficulty, even if most proved to be too ill paid to meet their needs and their wives had to scrape along somehow. For the majority, life in Hong Kong was raw, alien and unhealthy. But, for all that, the court and prison despatches show female rates of offending or imprisonment which are just a few percent of those of men. However, the court reporters would pounce on any such example. Even a small offence, that would not even make a separate entry in the paper if committed by a man, merited a few lines. Perhaps a Chinese boatwoman had inserted a pin into the harbour wall to secure her craft, or a barrow pushed by a woman had created an obstruction in a lane for an hour or two. These were newsworthy just because the perpetrator was female. A hundred or more years later, these are indeed very trivial cases in themselves. Yet they provide some of the few insights we have into what life was like for the ordinary Chinese or European woman: what was important to them, what difficulties they encountered and how they got by day to day. But happily – and, yes, that is the wrong word – women were involved in crimes of a more serious and complex nature in the course of Hong Kong's first hundred years of colonial rule.

---

24 James Norton-Kyshe, *The History of the Laws and Courts of Hong Kong, vol. 1.* p 11.

CHAPTER 2

WOMEN IN CRIME IN THE 19TH CENTURY

Hong Kong's first Europeans had quickly set about countering Lord Palmerston's description of the new British possession with plantations of fast-growing trees at strategic points.[25] Those at Wong Nei Chung, planted to assist drainage of this former paddy-field proved too great a temptation for four Chinese women, who, in the early summer of 1847, saw the possibilities of converting them into lucrative firewood.[26] The *Tepo* (local headman) had warned the women off and told them not to destroy or even cut the trees.[27] Disliking such interference with their plans, the four turned on him and assaulted the man. The *Tepo's* men caught them and Mr Hillier, the magistrate, sent them each to gaol for three days. Another plantation came under attack in June of that year. Described as being above the Naval Stores, these were then at West Point, close to what is now Kennedy Town, and not yet at the recently acquired naval area in Central. The insubstantial nature of these sheds was a continual headache for the police who, with the army, had to share responsibility for the security of their contents.

On Thursday 3rd June a sharp-eyed constable, Thomas Mitton, noticed a lot of fir saplings lying on the ground near the Stores and saw a man in the plantation in the act of chopping down more trees.[28] Realising that the policeman had seen him, the man ran away, but P.C. Mitton

25 The British Foreign Secretary, in 1841, called Hong Kong a 'barren island with hardly a house upon it.'

26 *China Mail,* 27th May 1847.

27 The *Tepo* was part of an older Chinese system of local self-governance resurrected by the early colonists in a pragmatic attempt to marry British hopes for the rule of law with the local reality.

28 *China Mail,* 10th June 1847.

outpaced and soon caught him. The constable then found a hut nearby where an enormous amount of wood, some just tied into bundles, some already chopped for firewood, was being stored. Mitton alerted Inspector Thomas Smithers to his discovery. The inspector had earlier entertained suspicions about the inhabitants of this hut and had, he said, repeatedly warned them against cutting the trees, but they only laughed at him. It was estimated that there was more wood in this stash than twelve coolies could carry away, and the plantation was almost entirely destroyed. Insp. Smithers, with his prior experience of these people, knew that the man found by P.C. Mitton and two others were not the main culprits: it was a woman, the owner of the hut who had directed the business. Mr Hillier gave the men the choice of a $5 fine or a whipping, but the woman must pay $10 or go to gaol for fourteen days. Since $10 was about the amount a servant might expect to earn in two or three months, it is likely that she chose the latter option. The question why he had 'taken his eye off' this hut was not raised, but Insp. Smithers was the sole inspector at that time.[29]

A rather unusual case of fraud came to light later that month when two women were convicted of trying to obtain a licence for their boat (a 'boat register ticket') by falsifying the requisite documents. It was customary for a sampan owner to ask a respectable shop-owner or other businessman to countersign – with their chop – their application for the licence. The agreement was that the man would guarantee the good conduct of the boat owners. Because of this, the guarantors were careful only to endorse the forms of people known to them. It so happened that a particular shop-owner's chop had appeared on several forms in the last few weeks and the police, suspecting a forgery, made enquiries from him. Since he professed to not having endorsed any applications recently, their suspicions were well-founded. It transpired that the women certainly knew that the chop was a forgery, if they had not fabricated it themselves. Such deception of both the government and the businessman must be censured, and the magistrate imposed a penalty of $50 or two months'

---

29 The Police Force comprised, in 1847, one inspector, two deputy inspectors, 25 sergeants and acting sergeants and 124 constables, of the latter rank over half of whom were former soldiers from the British Indian Army.

Chinese amahs and their European charges, Charles Wirgmann, 1857.

imprisonment on each. Once more, it is unlikely that the women could have found such an amount, so they probably became part of that year's tally of gaol inmates.

As in the cases described, Chinese defendants were frequently not named, a situation that continued well into the 20th century. Editors of the newspapers would hardly expect any of their readers to know the offenders, and the transliteration of Chinese names was still a very inexact science. Jobbing journalists were not always the most diligent of people in this respect. Acoustics were poor in the hurriedly constructed Magistracy, and even in its later reincarnation. Unfamiliar names were thus easily lost against a background of noise from outside the court.

In this respect, Mr Rangel's female servant, Wong Akum, was an exception. Her job was to look after his children, but on an autumn morning, with her quarterly wage still in her pocket, she suddenly left. Wong did not return until the evening, when she said that she intended to collect her box. Since it was an offence for servants to leave their employment without giving notice, Mr Rangel held her in the house until the police arrived. At the station she was very insolent to the constable. The magistrate fined her $1 – a large proportion of the wages she had just received since here, as elsewhere in the world, women could command only a fraction of the male wage.

A body of law that would cover most situations had been hurriedly created by the early colonists. Ordinance 14 of 1845, for the *Preservation of Good Order and Cleanliness* was a 'catch all' law. In its vast sweep of prohibitions, it gives the impression of being a list of regulations compiled by the lawyers and administrators after a brainstorming session, with little discernible coherence to the whole thing.[30] The errant servant had been prosecuted under Section 3, Note 3 of this law, whilst the tree cutters' offences came under Section 10, which specified a term of imprisonment not exceeding fourteen days. For the courts administering these laws, language, and not just the names of those involved, was an ongoing problem. The colony had the services of one western-born man with a command of Cantonese, Daniel Caldwell, who had arrived in 1842. However, his extensive knowledge of the region and his language skills saw him performing many functions in the early administration, leaving him little time to act as interpreter for the courts. Thus most of this was undertaken by Chinese clerks, often with only pidgin English. The magistrates and judges had only the most rudimentary grasp of the language. To add further problems, because of the small number of westerners in the colony, men from mainland Europe, with only a basic command of English (let alone Cantonese) often served on juries. Yet trials continued, with, on average, just over two thousand people a year appearing before the magistrate and one hundred before the Supreme and Admiralty Courts between 1849-53. The cases against brothel keepers in 1851, quoted by Norton-Kyshe, in his *History of the Laws and Courts of Hong Kong*, exemplify some of the difficulties.

In the autumn of 1851 two Chinese constables had charged Chow Sam-mooey with the keeping of a bawdy house.[31] Here English law was coming up against Chinese custom and practice. But this allowed considerable latitude to the police to exploit the gulf. The woman was

---

30 This replaced Ordinance No. 5 of 1844, which was, if anything, even more a 'stream of consciousness' list of all possible offences. It was not dissimilar to sections of the Metropolitan Police Acts of 1829 and 1839.

31 James Norton-Kyshe, *The History of the Laws and Courts of Hong Kong vol. 1*, p. 308.

convicted and sentenced to twelve months' hard labour at the Criminal Sessions of 15th October 1851. Yet at the same sitting, the two constables and their sergeant were charged with "laying brothels under contribution for the benefit of the Chinese members of the Police Force", i.e. extorting a sum from each as protection money against being raided or closed down. Upon this being made public, there was a feeling that the court had wronged Chow and the Governor overturned her sentence. Then at the December Sessions, another woman faced a similar charge, through the evidence of the same men, and her case had to be dismissed.

Although there was a strong repugnance felt by the higher-minded of the western population against reading about prostitution and brothels in their drawing rooms and offices, the press of the time were liable to see the Criminal Sessions as grist for their mill when there was little else of local interest, although the level of reporting of the lower court varied according to the interest of the editors, and the availability of space and reporters.

When in July 1852, another woman was charged with the same offence, the jury found her guilty, but, in an unprecedented move, 'instructed' the Acting Chief Justice to release her.[32] She had, the jury contested, already been in prison for three months on remand, following her appearance before the magistrate, and had therefore served the appropriate punishment. The jury also censured the magistrate, Mr C. B. Hillier, for sending such cases to the Sessions, and thus into the public notice. Mr Hillier wanted the woman to receive a longer sentence than he could impose, and thus stand as an example to other brothel keepers, that such houses would not be permitted in British Hong Kong. However, the jury thought he should have dealt with this himself. The Chief Justice declared that it would henceforth be the role of the Public Prosecutor to decide where such cases would be heard.

The Chinese population may have been unaware and unused to English law, but many of those administering it were equally ignorant of Chinese law and customary practice. Cases that sought to employ both were generally fruitless, as in another case recounted by Norton-Kyshe. Twelve-year-old You Tsoi was living with her mother in Macao when the

---

32 Norton-Kyshe, *op. cit.,* vol. 1, p.326.

older woman borrowed $120 from Chun Atee, an elderly female.[33] When Chun demanded payment, in late 1851, six years after the loan had been given, compound interest had increased the amount to $355.50. Whether the mother was still alive is unclear – perhaps she had already died. But Chun had nothing to worry about: the mother had pledged her daughter against the loan. She had gone in search of the (now) eighteen-year-old You Tsoi and demanded the money. The girl protested that she could not pay it, so Chun took her to the Registrar of the Court, where she burnt a piece of joss paper, ratifying her assertion that this girl had taken on her mother's debt. The older woman had brought two others with her, who confirmed that You had agreed to this, yet would not or could not pay.

Thus, by a curious mix of Chinese custom and English law, You was arrested and sent to prison. Section 9 of the Ordinance 14 allowed for anyone, of whatever age, to sue or be sued for debt, so her youth was no protection. On 3rd October 1851, the two parties appeared before the Chief Justice Hulme, but the girl disputed that she had ever agreed to pay the money. However, she agreed that she had "pledged her body". But Hulme was reluctant, or more probably, unable to untangle this. Norton-Kyshe records that he cut the hearing short, telling the women to sort out the matter between them. Given the very limited options You would have to raise the money, probably she had to enter a brothel and work there until she could pay Chun off.

In such a young and distant outpost of the British Empire it might not be surprising that there were failures of justice because of the limitations of some of those administering it, and not just amongst the lower ranks of the Police Force. The colony had to take what it could get to fill all but the most senior posts. Some of these men proved energetic and faithful servants, but the majority contributed to its development while paying careful attention to the furtherance of their own interests. This was understandable, for, as the press of the day would often comment, what man would come almost 10,000 miles and endure conditions injurious to their own health, if not for swift and tangible reward. Daniel Caldwell is a particular example of this – a man of immense use to the fledgling colony, but the integrity of whose outside interests could stand

---

33 Norton-Kyshe, *op. cit.,* vol. 1, p.307.

no very close scrutiny. And then there were others, like Irishman Percy Caulincourt McSwyney, a barrister who had already tried his luck in Australia.[34] He inveigled himself into prominent positions, including that of Registrar of the Supreme Court, where he could line his own pockets through swindling and extortion. With little aptitude or knowledge, he even landed the position of Coroner, such was the dearth of reliable men in the colony.

In 1846, he allowed a brothel mistress who had taken active steps to bring about the death of one of her inmates to escape with merely an admonition. In acting so he missed what was perhaps the first opportunity the legal system had to stamp upon the cruel and inhumane treatment of sick prostitutes. McSwyney was the coroner when, on 15th July 1846, an inquest was held upon the body of a young prostitute. Disease – not just venereal – had visibly ravaged her.[35] She had become weak and of no more use to her mistress, Chui a Kwei, so the latter had ordered her servants to carry the girl, almost naked, out to the hills and leave her to die. Chui a Kwei worried that her house would be defiled should the ill young woman stay there longer. Death had been inevitable, but this woman had doubtless hastened it. The jury, under instruction from McSwyney, brought a verdict that she "died by visitation of God", although adding "that her mistress was highly censurable for inhumanity towards her". The coroner told Chui to warn her fellow brothel keepers not to put their sick inmates out into public view again, otherwise they might be subject to heavier sanctions. After public comment, the Assistant Magistrate, Mr Hillier, subsequently prosecuted Chui for "exposing" the girl. She was fined $20, although Norton-Kyshe notes that it is not obvious under what ordinance the charge was brought. The press lamented the loss of an opportunity to impress on the brothel keepers that such inhumane behaviour – which was evidently not unusual – would not be tolerated in British Hong Kong. McSwyney continued to have a colourful career, including periods in gaol. He was half-tricked into marrying a Chinese widow, under the impression that she was wealthy and he would have

---

34 Christopher Munn, *Anglo-China*, p. 211.
35 Norton-Kyshe, *The History of the Laws and Courts of Hong Kong vol. 1.* pp.101-2.

access to her money. This, though, proved to be an illusion, and he died a pauper in the Seamen's Hospital in 1850.

The Magistracy continued to be the busiest government building in the colony. By 1855, the police magistrate heard cases most days, with about 4,000 defendants appearing before him each year, many individuals making multiple appearances. The population was then around 50,000. However, this does not indicate that, in taking possession of the island, Britain had stumbled on an especially criminal part of the world. The colony had created much of the problem for itself, in the raft of legislation designed to prohibit or control behaviour that the local population saw as normal and reasonable. Many 'offences', e.g. hawking without a licence, being a suspicious person, being in the streets after dark, causing an obstruction, were aimed specifically at the Chinese population, and fell heaviest on the unsuspecting recent arrivals from Canton and southern China. But the Chinese were not alone in occupying the magistrate's time, with the misconduct of the many merchant seamen and soldiers appearing with disproportionate frequency in the courts. Their crimes were more often vicious in nature, as they found themselves at the top of a hierarchy of brute force. The victims of their drunken rowdiness were often unfortunate traders or chair coolies, who did at least see their persecutors sent to gaol.

But the usual tally of crimes against person and property were fully represented in the tables produced by the Police Department and sent back to London in the *Blue Books* each year. It was in some of these types of crimes that women were more likely to participate. Official statistics give us little indication, though, of which these were. The figures for the prison are a little more revealing. For example, in 1858, whilst 3,319 men appeared in front of the magistrate only 205 women had to answer such a summons and of those just 74 were convicted and punished either by a fine or imprisonment. Because sentences were short, the gaol matron had a light load, with never over a dozen in her care at any one time, even when the male prison was groaning at the seams with hundreds incarcerated.

Women and their servants

Western women who appear in the courts in cases involving a Chinese servant or tradesman, often display a presumption that the law will naturally favour them. And at a time when in Britain the physical punishment of servants was regarded as a regrettable necessity, these women in Hong Kong often felt no remorse for beatings they inflicted on their employees. In February 1868 a young servant girl, an orphan who, until a few months earlier had been in the Asile de la Sainte Enfance (an orphanage established by French religious Sisters) in Wanchai, had fled to a police station.[36] She told the sergeant on duty that her mistress, Mrs Guelmina Caldero, had beaten her ten strokes and falsely accused her of having stolen a pair of earrings. This wasn't, she said, the first beating she had had from her employer by any means. She was paid just 50 cents a month and food. Caldero had promised her new clothes, too, but had not given her any. The mistress was summonsed, but somehow prevented her young servant from attending the hearing and police had to go to the house to fetch the girl. At the Magistracy, Caldero's story naturally differed from that the girl had told the police. She did not deny that she had beaten her, and this was clear, anyway, from the marks on the girl's body and face. But, Caldero said, she was a very bad girl and had run away from the Sisters. She paid her 6d. every ten days.[37] She had suspected the (unnamed) girl of stealing the earrings, especially since she had refused to search for them. The magistrate, Mr James Russell, suspected something of a sob story from the girl.[38] Yet he was confronted by the evidence of the older woman's attack and so decreed that the girl

---

36 *China Mail,* 11th February 1868.

37 Until 1878, many Government records were still recorded in sterling (e.g. staff lists). The newspapers frequently referred to values in this currency, rather than in the local silver dollar, and it appears that the western population employed both. At the rate of exchange in 1868, six English pence would equate to about 12 cents every ten days.

38 James Russell b. 1843, d.1893, was a cadet officer who had just completed two years of immersive instruction in Cantonese and was one of the few members of the administration very fluent in the language. He used his leave to study for the bar and spent most of his Hong Kong career in the courts, later becoming Chief Justice. He retired to his native Scotland, his health broken and died shortly afterwards.

should leave her employer and was returned to the Sisters. Meanwhile
he considered that although there had been an assault, it had not been a
very violent one. He would fine Caldero only one dollar, but she must
understand that she had no right to attack any servant and warned her
she could not expect such leniency should she repeat the offence.

Mr Russell was again presiding some four years later when Chun
A-ying, house coolie at the Wyndham Street home of Miss Nellie Moore,
charged his mistress with unlawfully assaulting and beating him.[39] The
servant had been told to sweep the large living room carpet but given
only a small broom with which to undertake the task. He told his mistress
this, but started to sweep nevertheless. She had then come in, grabbed
the broom and started beating him with it. He took hold of the handle
and demanded his wages from her, saying that he would leave. Moore
refused and then took a knife to make him leave go of the broom – Chun
had the cut across his fingers to prove it. Another servant of Moore's,
Tong A-tsun, was called to give evidence, but whether he was speaking
the truth or had an eye on keeping his position, he declared that he
had seen no knife and only knew that Chun had refused to beat the
carpet when told to. Moore admitted that she had beaten the man with
a bamboo stick, as his refusal had made her furious. He was such an
impertinent servant, she wouldn't have him back now. She denied using
a knife. Mr Russell told her to give Chun his wages up to that day, but
thought his claim exaggerated, so fined Moore just one dollar, which she
could pay along with the wages to the shroff's office. The court reporter
then had the advantage of seeing what was happening in the foyer whilst
the magistrate started hearing his next case. Chun abruptly demanded his
pay from Moore, before she had had time to hand it to the shroff. Irate,
Moore turned on him and slapped him round the face. Chun rushed
back into court with his complaint, which the interpreter corroborated,
saying that, without provocation, Moore had hit him. Mr Russell then
ordered the woman back, declaring that he had been mistaken in fining
her only one dollar: obviously she was a very violent woman, deliberately
assaulting the complainant when only just outside the door. He would
amend the fine to ten dollars. Moore, very much standing on her dignity,

---

39 *Hongkong Daily Press*, 21st February 1872.

told him she did not carry such a sum on her; he would have to send in his bill. The magistrate sternly told her that the court did not do its business in that way and if she was not prepared to pay the fine she could go to prison for fourteen days.

Meanwhile, Moore had brought a neighbour to the Magistracy to support her, but this woman, a German, was perhaps equally unfamiliar with court behaviour. Quite a crowd of onlookers had enjoyed the contretemps between mistress and servant, especially when they realised that the arrogant European woman was worsted. They jeered both at her and her companion, the latter of whom took exception to this treatment and complained loudly and persistently in broken English, such that her cries interrupted proceedings in the court. Mr Russell ordered her in before him. This did nothing to silence her, so she soon found herself bodily escorted out of the building and right away from the Magistracy compound, doubtless outraged.

Some crimes, committed by women, that came to the attention of the authorities were truly heinous, and had no place in the culture of China or Europe. The horror of the burning case, which first came to public attention on 14th March 1873, comes through clearly in the report of the *Hongkong Daily Press*.

A Chinese girl of between 12 and 14 years of age laid a complaint before the Hon. C May yesterday, in which was detailed an incident of most revolting brutality.[40] The girl's pocket mother, it appears, a fortnight ago sent her out to make purchases, and on her return, some act of the girl's led her to strip the unfortunate child naked, and impress all over her body red hot irons, in some places allowing the iron to sink deep in the flesh. She then locked the girl up in a room, where she was confined till yesterday morning, without any attempt made to heal up the wounds, or to supply her with proper food. On making her escape yesterday morning, she was directed by some other small girl how to act, and was led by her to the Acting Registrar-

---

40 'Pocket mother', mistress of a *mui tsai*, sometimes known as 'pocket daughter' or 'little sister'.

General, who, on hearing the revolting circumstances, at once sent the girl up with Inspector King to the Hon. C May, and a warrant was immediately procured for the apprehension of the inhuman person whom she calls mother. At last accounts she had not been found, but we trust she will be caught and receive her deserts.

Further short articles, reporting that the woman, Acham, had not been found, appeared in the papers on the 17th and 19th of the month. The last added that she was rumoured already to have murdered another young girl by torturing her in the same way, but it was suspected that, knowing that she was hunted, had now fled to the mainland. It seems strange to the modern mind that the Registrar General's first instinct was to send the child to the magistrate, rather than to the hospital, but perhaps Charles May attended to that.[41]

Cases involving servants would continue to appear on court lists throughout the period. Although there are plenty of examples of magistrates censuring their overbearing western mistresses when it is the servant who has brought a charge against her, more frequent are the complaints of the employers. Mrs Mary Hollowell charged an "impudent old woman", Chun-a-leen, who entered her service one Friday then abruptly left on Monday.[42] She had demanded one dollar off the mistress, claiming that she "had no chow-chow" (food), but had not even given service to cover that. Chun was given the choice of a two-dollar fine or seven days' hard labour. But blame could change sides. In December 1867, Mrs Andrews of Wyndham Street gave her elderly amah, Lew A-kew into police charge, claiming that she had stolen $90.[43] But when the old woman was brought before the magistrate, her mistress did not

---

41 Charles May, b. England, 1817, d. at sea 1879. A London policeman, he was sent out to lead the colony's nascent Police Force in 1845. Although efficient and hard working, he had very limited success with this. He never learnt Cantonese and had to rely on interpreters throughout his many years as 1st Police Magistrate. Clever speculation in property made him a wealthy man, but he did not live to enjoy this.

42 *Hongkong Daily Press,* 9th August 1873.

43 *Hongkong Daily Press,* 6th December 1867.

appear, and Lew told him she thought Andrews had her arrested out of spite, as she, Lew, had demanded the wages she was owed. The case was dismissed.

The Parade, Charles Wirgmann, 1857.

Women and the courts

In the ordinary run of life, women do not make many appearances in the *Police Intelligence* columns of the 19th-century papers. It is not uncommon to search through two months' worth without finding a single female defendant, although women, both Chinese and western, were not afraid to bring an action against men who had cheated or wronged them financially. Unlike cases of cruelty to children, which did attract public and press attention, just a few charges of violence towards women by men come to court. How often, though, such took place out of sight we can only guess. One rare case where a married woman, Choi A-chee, successfully charged a man with indecent assault occurred in 1869. Ching A-sam was a barber who rented the front room of her house as his shop and dwelling. Her husband was in Macao when the Hakka-speaking man set upon her. Being a woman of resource, Choi fought him off, then held on to his queue until he went into his shop.[44] Since this room contained the only light in the house, she then knew the identity of her assailant for sure – as did other occupants she had called in as witnesses. She brought him to the Magistracy and arranged for the other people to confirm her account. The man's defence was that, since her husband had been away, she had entertained him. This time they were caught out, having left a light on, and she was covering herself by inventing this story. He brought as witness the man he said had found them together. Unfortunately for him, this man disclaimed all knowledge – perhaps not speaking Hakka and thus not knowing what was required of him. But Choi's case was convincing and well-presented. Ching went to gaol for six months with hard labour, and would receive, in private, two whippings each of 20 strokes of the rattan.

Until well into the 1900s, few cases of rape or indecent assault against women came to court, although they were, frequently enough, the victims of murders or attempted murders. Given the ubiquitousness of violent attacks of men upon other men, often conducted in very public settings, it seems reasonable to assume that such aggression was turned upon women, especially as much of their lives were lived in the private sphere. They, to be sure, inflicted violence on children, since only the young were more vulnerable than themselves. But this behaviour did not arise in a vacuum. What did they, whether in the family home or the brothel, experience day by day at the hands of men?

We rarely see the brothel occupants out and about. Soliciting was an unknown offence in the early days of Hong Kong and does not appear on the annual crime lists until well into the 20th century. But occasionally a woman would make a complaint against a client of stealing from her, or perhaps breaking up furniture in her cubicle. Sometimes groups of women would come to court when they had been creating a disturbance and annoyed neighbours reported them. One such case was heard by Mr Russell, when P.C. John Lindsay arrested two women for making a great noise in the street and running after seamen.[45] P.C. Lindsay said that he

---

44 A queue was the hairstyle involving a plaited pigtail and a shaved forehead mandated for men under the Qing Dynasty until its fall in 1911.

45 *Hongkong Daily Press,* 26th March 1872.

had told the pair to return to their brothels, but they had answered back with a stream of profanities. Fung Chun-you and Chun A-chai disputed his version, saying that the constable had demanded 'accommodation' on credit in Fung's house, which she refused, and then he had hit the other woman with his stock. But the pair had already been observed by P.C. Matheson, a senior constable, who was in charge of the area. The latter man had told P.C. Lindsay to send the women home, and then, when they would not, to arrest them. However, the magistrate must have been in a forgiving mood, or perhaps had other reasons to question the case, for he discharged the women without either punishment or caution. The following case, resulting in each woman and former client being fined 50 cents for disorderly conduct, is more unusual.[46] Described as a "respectably dressed prostitute named Wong-a-ping", she told the magistrate how the "well-dressed boy", Lee-a-on, had come to see her a little while ago. At the time there was two dollars hidden in her bedding. She left him for a few minutes and went to the 'back house'. On her return, she found both Lee and her money gone. She saw him the next day and extracted a promise from him "he would pay bye-and-bye" – but he did not. Then Wong had met him during the evening of 13th March, and yet again asked him to return her money. Mr Mitchell, the magistrate, told her she should have charged Lee with the theft at the time. She could do so now, if she wanted. Lee's account was that Wong had lent him the money. So far he had been unable to repay it and last night she had started calling him a thief and creating a row, even though he told her she would get her money back.

Women pursuing profit: kidnapping, stealing, trafficking and trading
Tam Tai-yow worked in a brothel in a street close to the Central Police Station.[47] She had a small child, still a baby, but since she could not keep the infant at the brothel, Tam had entrusted it to the care of her sister who lived close by. Tam paid this woman, Ho A-hoo, $2.50 each month, an arrangement that helped both, since Ho was a widow. Tam visited the child frequently and sometimes sent for her, but at the start of April

46 *Hongkong Daily Press,* 15th March 1873.
47 *Hongkong Daily Press,* 6th April 1872.

1872 she was distressed not to find her child with her sister. On making enquiries she found that Ho had sold the girl to a woman in D'Aguilar Street for three dollars. With the police station almost on her doorstep, she reported the situation, and soon Ho was brought up before Mr Charles May, the Police Magistrate. Ho defended herself by telling the court that she owed three dollars to the woman in D'Aguilar Street, who was pressing her for repayment. She had not the money so had given the child as security. May found her guilty of selling her sister's child without permission and sent her to gaol for three months with hard labour.

This case, which raises an array of questions in the mind of the modern reader, would have been a very mundane and familiar tale to anyone who had lived in Hong Kong for even a few months in those days. It neatly illustrates the conflict between established Chinese practice, British judicial and moral values and pragmatic necessity. The child was probably a girl, since a male child, being of greater value to families, might well have been sent back to Tam's home in China and Ho may not have parted with him for just a few dollars. But children were property, with a commercial value, and it is not clear whether May is punishing Ho for selling that which was not hers or for selling a child. Nor do we learn what became of the child, if the court and the police used their powers to restore her to her mother. Did Ho leave her own children behind when she went to gaol and did Tam now somehow have to provide for them too? And did the woman in D'Aguilar Street ever get her money? The couple of column inches of newsprint leave many unanswered questions.

The papers and criminal statistics of the 1870s and 1880s, in particular, give a picture of child-stealing, kidnapping and decoying of girls and women as a normal part of Hong Kong life. Throughout this period there was an average of almost one such case per week – and that reflects just those reported to the police or Registrar General. Many families, employers or friends who realised that a young person was missing applied directly to the Tung Wah Hospital, went through the District Watch Force, or Chinese detectives in Canton. Or else they just gave the person up as lost. But to the English legal mind, the crime was an outrageous assault on liberty of the young person and the right of parents, and was viewed with particular severity. An offence that more often than not involved female perpetrators, these defendants could expect no leniency from the bench. The following accounts are just a selection made from trawling the newspapers of these years and display the extent to which children and girls, and occasionally adult women, were commoditised in the minds of those that saw them as a source of profit. Unlike other crime reports, the focus is more on the victim than the criminal, and for the writer, it is they, and not the mercenarily minded kidnappers, who attract interest.

A case with male and female perpetrators, and with family members and neighbours involved, occurred at the end of May 1876 in the Taipingshan area.[48] Boatwoman Yeung A-ng wanted to pay a visit to her relatives and came onshore to leave her four-year-old girl in the care of her brother. We are not told how long she was absent, but the implication is that she was away a few days, perhaps in Canton or the surrounding villages. On her return, her brother told her he had asked another of their brothers to look after the child. This seems to have given Yeung A-ng concern, for she immediately went out to find this brother. She caught sight of him at the Man Mo Temple on Hollywood Road, but on seeing her, he fled. Alarmed now, Yeung put the matter to the police. She was fortunate in the choice of man put on the case: Chinese Constable No. 249 soon had the run-away brother arrested and the story out of him.[49] Yeung Aman kept the child for a while, but soon tired of his role as nursemaid, and attempted to make a little money by pawning her while his sister was away. He had given her to a woman of his acquaintance and received $13 in return. This woman had then pawned her to another for $16. She in turn had sold her to a respectable married woman, Chan Akwai, for $21.50, without telling her that the child was only pawned, and so not really for sale. The constable meticulously followed the trail, arresting women as he went, until the last took him to Mrs Chan's house. This

---

48 *China Mail*, 29th May, 18th & 24th June 1876.

49 As in other police forces worldwide, men below inspector rank were known by their collar numbers. European police usually have their names recorded alongside this number in press reports but Chinese and Indian men do so a lot less frequently. While reflecting their Euro-centric view, it was also of practical use, since the smaller number of surnames used in southern China would otherwise result in duplication and confusion.

woman was upset to find she had been deceived, but readily returned the little girl to her mother. She had a chit or receipt for the money she had paid, and this, with her identification of the last woman, secured the case. All three admitted involvement when they came before the Police Magistrate, James Russell, and in such a clear case, he had no hesitation in sending them to gaol to await the next sitting of the Criminal Sessions.

Although the defendants had all admitted involvement and confirmed their share in the financial transaction, perhaps they did not see it as anything very wrong, so there was no clear guilty plea. Chief Justice Sir John Smale heard the story on 18th June, and the next day *The China Mail* commented that "the jury had very little difficulty in finding them guilty". Yeung Aman's mother, i.e. the child's grandmother, sent in a petition to ask that, if her son could not be wholly pardoned, he at least be spared a flogging. When passing sentence five days later, the relationship between this woman and the child seems to have dawned on the Chief Justice. His comments to her at the first sitting had seemed to give some hope, but now he called her up and told her she was "a wicked old woman." He continued, "Here is a man who steals his sister's child and you justify him! If anything could add to the severity of the punishment he will receive, the light way in which you treat the matter will do that. He stole and sold your own grandson.[50] He will be flogged!" Sir John Smale told the prisoners that he considered this the most cold-blooded of all the child-stealing cases with which he had dealt. He sentenced the man to three years' imprisonment with three whippings of 25 strokes each. The woman to whom he had pawned the child received a two-year sentence and the third, who had sold the girl, eighteen months. All the terms were with hard labour and the more severe one for the first woman reflects, it appears, her greater complicity and knowledge of the affair. The little girl was back with her mother, but Mrs Chan was still $21.50 out of pocket.

The very different attitude in Chinese culture to the status of the individual produced practices outside of western experience, such as bonded servants, brothel slaves and *mui tsai*. Working to regulate such

---

50 Was it the journalist or the Chief Justice who changed the gender of this child?

customs within an English justice system frequently presented the courts with many challenges. But there was no place in Chinese customary practice for child-stealing or kidnapping. The Canton authorities and police were often willing and able to help the Hong Kong Police, as witnessed by their involvement in the next case.

Two widows, who normally lived in Hong Kong, stole a young child, Wong Afoon, from her home in the eastern suburbs of Canton early in 1876.[51] They brought her back to the colony, where she lived with them in Saiyingpun. The parents evidently heard where she had been taken, for the girl's grandmother came down from Canton to search for her. Opportunely encountering her with one of the widows, she sought police help, and soon both were in custody. The police believed that the woman who had been out walking with the child, on their way to buy a cake, was probably the servant of the second woman. It was this widow, they thought, who had snatched the girl from her home. The pair spent some time in gaol on remand, since the investigators wanted to get corroboration of the story from another relative. The police applied to the British Consul in Canton, who enlisted the help of the Canton Police Force, who located the girl's father. However, in court it emerged that he had not seen the kidnapping, so could only confirm the identity of the child. That was sufficient, though. Mr Russell discharged the servant but sent the widow responsible to gaol for twelve months with hard labour.

Whilst the system of control over brothels had as its primary purpose curbing the depletion of the British Army's and Navy's rank and file through disease, it did serve to afford some protection to the women who worked in them. The rather brief report in the *Hong Kong Daily Press* for 14th August 1875 records a tale of the imprisonment and sale of two young women, Yun Ayee and Lai Tuk-kwai.[52] Against their will, they would be taken to Singapore and again sold as prostitutes. Police Inspector John Lee, attached to the Lock Hospital as Inspector for Brothels, charged a married woman with their harbouring and unlawful detention.

---

51 *China Mail* 18th May 1876.

52 *Hongkong Daily Press,* 14th & 16th August 1875.

Untangling the somewhat confused story and making one or two suppositions, which seem reasonable in the circumstances, it appears that Insp. Lee had been 'tipped off' on 8th August. He had been told that the woman Lai Acheong had returned to the colony – perhaps from Macao or Canton – with two young women, and they were now in her house. Perhaps neighbours also told him that the girls seemed to be making some disturbance. However he came to the knowledge, it was enough for him to investigate. He spoke at length (probably through an interpreter) to both and found Yun Ayee the more forthcoming. She had worked (outside Hong Kong) as a prostitute for four years, although she had previously lived in the colony since she was nine years old. Now she had enough of that life and wanted to be a free woman. She thought she had certainly served her time to her mistress. But then the mistress had sold her to a friend, Lai Acheong, who, with another woman, Mah Achee, had been visiting. These two women had taken her and the other girl, Lai Tuk-kwai, back to Hong Kong with them. Yun didn't know Tuk-kwai before this, but now they slept in the same room and the girl had told her she had never been to the colony before.

When they arrived on they had wanted to go out, but were forbidden. In fact, they were not even allowed to look out of the window, otherwise the police would call and declare that the place was a sly brothel. A few days earlier Mah and Lai Acheong told them they would send them both to Singapore. The women did not say what for, but the girls could guess. Yun repeated to Insp. Lee that she wanted to be free, but how could she, now that this woman had paid her former mistress for her? She had no way of getting hold of money to pay off the bond! She was vastly surprised, therefore, when the inspector told her that in Hong Kong she could be a free woman without any payment being made. He would arrest Lai Acheong and perhaps the other woman, and after that, they would both be free.

After listening to the girls, Insp. Lee acted quickly, before any attempt could be made to smuggle the girls onto a Singapore-bound vessel. He arrested only Lai Acheong, but later that day all four women came into the magistrate's court. The Clerk of the Court, having heard the nature of the case from the police, had asked both magistrates, Messrs May and Russell to hear it. The newspaper records that that after Insp. Lee's statement, there was "a deal of conflicting evidence." The magistrates, not being able to settle it there and then, remanded the case to the next morning, Saturday 15th August. Lai Acheong was held in gaol while the two girls returned to the house with Mah. The following day, Mr May bound the woman over for security of $50, to be of good behaviour for three months.

Yet again, there is no chance of finding out what happened to any of those involved. The two young women were now free, and Lai Acheong could not force them to work for her. But free for what? How now would they make their way in Hong Kong, which offered limited employment opportunities for young, probably uneducated, Chinese women? Would they find any job other than that which they had tried to leave?

There are a few stories in this book where a fortuitous meeting turns the tale in a happier, or at least less tragic, direction. This phenomenon reminds us that, whilst the number of westerners in the colony was tiny, by comparison to Canton or other cities in the region the Chinese population was not large. Hong Kong was really more a town than a city, and such meetings were not so extraordinary as they might seem in today's metropolis. From a decade later comes the tale of the six terrifying weeks that Chan Tung-tsoi endured and the serendipity that resulted in a happy ending for her.[53]

The sixteen-year-old was a servant girl to a gentleman in Canton, who owned Chinese chemist shops. She had been born in the city and was happy in her life. Early in the morning of 3rd March 1885, she went out to buy some *samshu* (fermented rice spirit, also known as *baijiu*) that was needed. She had to pass a large group of men, and when level with them, one suddenly threw something in her face. She described it as stupefying her: perhaps it did, or perhaps it was pepper that incapacitated her for a few minutes. It was enough, however, for the men to bundle her onto a boat that took her out to the harbour. From that, Chan was pushed onto a steamer. They landed in Hong Kong, but her journey was not over. The man – he who had thrown the substance into her face – dragged her onto the Macao steamer, sailing from the same pier. In the Portuguese colony

---

53 *China Mail,* 17th & 21st April 1885.

she was kept for two days, when a Californian Chinese man came to the house and bought her from her kidnapper. How long she was with him was not recorded, but then he sold her to a woman, who passed her on yet again to two women, Kwok Asz and Leong Atsoi. These two married women, in their thirties, took Chan back to Hong Kong and kept her in a house until Wednesday, 15th April. Also imprisoned in this house was another young girl, Fan Kan. The reporter tells us nothing about her, except her name and that she, too, had been decoyed and was to suffer the same fate as Chan. On that Wednesday they were told what that was to be. The women were going to take them to Singapore, where they could get a good price for each at a brothel. But, meanwhile, they would have to visit the Harbour Office. Official men would ask them questions. They must say that they were going to Singapore because they wanted to find their husbands, who they thought were there. Doubtless the girls protested, but the women wore them down until they agreed.

But Chan never got as far as the Harbour Office that day. She had started out with Fan and the older women when her extraordinary piece of luck occurred. Chan's master, the Canton druggist, Yune Akwan, also owned the Kung Sai Tung drug shop at No. 331 Queen's Road Central. On 9th April, five weeks after Chan had been abducted, news of her disappearance reached him in Hong Kong. A decent man, he was very concerned as Chan had been in his family's employ since she was six years old, and was probably almost a daughter to him. He had been making enquiries since then and had visited the Harbour Emigration Office several times. Once more, Yune had gone down there that morning at 10 a.m., but the Harbour Master was absent, so he was on his way back to the shop. Walking along Wing Lok Street, he saw Chan with a group of women around her. He called out to her, and when she saw him, she started crying, overcome with relief. He went over to her, and she told him that some people had kidnapped her. They had to leave Fan Kan with the women, but he took her back to his shop.

After hearing the whole story from her, they went out to find a constable, and he reported the matter. Chan was sure that she would recognise the man who had first "flipped the stuff into her face" in Canton. She had seen quite enough of him, since it was he who had taken her to Hong

Kong the first time, and then onto Macao. However, he would be out of their jurisdiction, since the original kidnap had happened in Canton. But the women were a different matter. The police decided that if Yune, Chan and a constable boarded the next steamer for Singapore, they would probably catch them. The ship was due to leave the harbour the following morning. It was reckoned that the party would not loiter in the colony now, after Chan had been recognised. The trio went aboard and it was not long before the girl pointed out Kwok and Leong. They were duly arrested and marched back to the Central Station. Fan Kan had been on the steamer with them, so the detectives had caught the pair actually taking this girl out of the colony.

The pair were charged with bringing both girls into the colony for improper purposes and for attempting to take them out for the purpose of prostitution. Mr Wodehouse heard the various police accounts and that of Chan, then adjourned the case for four days while further enquiries were made. Kwok Asz and Leong Atsoi went to gaol while Chan and Fan, presumably, stayed with Yune. The next Tuesday the women were in court again. This time they had engaged a solicitor, and although he cross-examined Chan closely, her account remained consistent. Yune Akwan also gave evidence and told of how the prisoners had been spotted by Chan on the ship. Magistrate Wodehouse committed the pair to stand trial at the next Sessions. If they could find bail of $100 each they need not go to gaol for the month before the next sitting. It appears that they had adequate funds – women trafficking others generally had some working capital.

But again the accounts now fail us. The Sessions reports include no mention of the case. It does not necessarily mean that it collapsed before the trial, for maybe newspapers did not have enough space to report it. After all, with an average of a kidnapping case in the courts every week, it was not a unique event. Crime figures for the month provide no certain clue since about half those charged with kidnapping offences were sentenced. The prison statistics, which record six women gaoled that year for terms between three months and one year but none serving longer terms, perhaps suggests that they did escape punishment – maybe by absconding. But, as unsatisfactory as it is not to know that Kwok and

Leong received their just deserts, at least there was a good outcome for one, if not both, of the victims.

The ordinary run: disagreements, disturbances and theft

The Magistracy always saw a helping of the banal and mundane disputes and disagreements of ordinary life, and women took their fair share in these. An imputation on the virtue of one married woman by another in 1872 started with a war of words, then proceeded by slaps to one heaving a charcoal stove onto the head of the other. But when a constable tried to arrest them, he was sharply told to keep out of family quarrels. Nevertheless, the magistrate fined the stove-thrower two dollars. Others called him to arbitrate in disputes about roaming domestic animals, property that was moved by a neighbour or a local battle over use of a communal water hydrant. Of course, the more usual route to settle such disputes was to take them to the Man Mo Temple, where they could be put to the local leaders. But individuals might have reasons for avoiding this, and often the situation had come to the attention of a policeman before they had chance to make other arrangements. At the Magistracy such squabbles rarely brought anything more punitive than rebuke from the bench and an exhortation to sort out their own affairs better in future. These very petty cases were not infrequently brought or defended by women. Sometimes the disagreements turned into a brawl, as when the widow Chun A-lun was charged by an unemployed watchman, Sheck Mezan of throwing dirty water and rubbish opposite his house.[54] The summer was still hot and humid on the last day of August, and Chun had, he said, walked round from her street to his to dispose of the waste, which was probably quite noxious. He told her to stop this, but she continued. Mezan told her he was going to get an officer to sort her out, at which the woman rushed at him. She had torn his coat, he said.

On their way down to the police station, they had been intercepted by P.C. Ng A-fat, who reported that the man had hold of the woman by her hair, and she held him by his jacket. At court Chun told Magistrates May and Russell that she was a respectable charwoman, she did her duty by her employers, even occasionally making offerings at the temples for

---

54 *Hongkong Daily Press,* 1st September 1869.

them. She was just sitting for a moment near Mezan's door when he came out and kicked her. At that she grabbed him by his coat, and he pulled at her hair. They were both cautioned and told to behave themselves better in future, before the case was dismissed.

Dogs could always be relied on to provide the court with a few problems, especially as European women were particularly fond of keeping them, both as pets and as guards. Mrs Spencer's dog, who attacked the servant of her neighbour, Mrs Montgomery, was perhaps being over-officious.[55] The servant had only come in to tell Mrs Montgomery, visiting her neighbour, that her meal was ready, after all. Mrs Spencer offered the old amah medicine and 50 cents, but the woman was not satisfied, and decided to pursue the matter through the courts. However, the magistrate told her that there was no remedy to find there and that she had better accept what Mrs Spencer offered. But he warned this woman to keep better control of her dog, and that she should be more generous in her compensation of the servant. Dogs were also the subject of ownership disputes, as when an unnamed Gun Lascar from the Indian Regiment stationed in Kowloon spotted what he believed was his puppy, missing now for four days, with a woman on the island.[56] He towed both woman and puppy off to the police station and then to Mr May. But it proved to be a case of mistaken identity: the woman brought along a basketful of puppies, siblings of the present one, to prove her case. Mr May was convinced.

An unexpected finding of the search through these 19th-century papers is how infrequent were cases of theft or larceny with women as the defendants. There are many incidents of women charging men with theft from their person, particularly of jewellery, or from their homes or market stalls, and often they found satisfaction at court. But whether it was lack of opportunity or superior skills that enabled them to evade detection, this was not a commonly prosecuted crime in the female population then – although this would change come the new century. There are a few little

55 *Hongkong Daily Press,* 19th May 1875.
56 *Hongkong Daily Press,* 20th February 1872. Gun Lascars were low-ranking Indian troops, retained for manhandling and cleaning field artillery including pioneer work erecting batteries.

cases, such as the woman who cannot account for having 50 pounds of coal in her possession, except that she tells the officer she has bought it from young boys who go round the streets picking it up, but beyond this there are few worth recording, save, perhaps, that from one unwary former sailor.

Christmas 1867 was not a pleasant one for John Powell, who was employed by the Sailor's Home out in West Point as a runner. He lived close by, with his Chinese mistress, in a room in Battery Road.[57] A girlfriend of his mistress inhabited another cubicle in that building. He first missed his wallet on the evening of 26th December. It had contained two $5 notes and his gold ring, together with some smaller notes. The only two people who had been in the room that day, aside from himself, were the two women, so he inclined to suspect the friend. But on New Year's Eve, eschewing the usual celebrations, he went to bed at 8.30 p.m. When he awoke in the morning, he found that he was alone – his paramour had left – and going to the friend's room to see if she was there, found this also empty. But not only were the two women missing, but so too was a $50 note. Later that day the police searched the rooms and discovered the large note hidden in a rice jar and the ring in a coat pocket – both items in the girl-friend's room. At court on the following day, this was almost enough for the magistrate, Charles May. One or both of the women was responsible, all that was required was to determine which. May seems to have believed Powell's evidence implicitly: there was no suggestion that he might have 'planted' the items and no questions about his attitude towards the friend. Mr May granted bail to the two women for the week's adjournment, but since they could not find the amount, they had to go to prison.

The next week, his mistress had managed to find the resources to defend herself. By her good fortune, it was J. J. Francis who appeared before Mr May on her behalf.[58] Undaunted by the imperious Mr May,

---

57 *China Mail,* 2nd & 9th January 1868.

58 Irishman John Joseph Francis, b. 1839, d. 1901, was commissioned in the Royal Artillery, but purchased his discharge in Hong Kong to enter a legal firm there. The year after he defended the woman in this case he would qualify as a solicitor, subsequently spending time back in Britain to train for the bar. By 1886 he had taken silk and J. J. Francis, Q. C., became one of the most able

Mr Francis cross-examined both the investigating constable and John Powell, the complainant. He then submitted to the magistrate that no larceny had been proved because the police had not shown that the items – the ring and the $50 note – had been moved with intent to steal. Mr May countered that the removal of an item even an inch counted as larceny. Mr Francis, the specifics of the law at his fingertips, corrected him. The magistrate was right, in that this applied to larceny from the person, but not in cases of common larceny. What was there to show that they might have placed the note in the jar for another reason, in jest, even? Perhaps catching a look of outrage from the bench, Mr Francis hastened to assure him he was not putting this forward as the reason, merely citing an example of the motive for the things being hidden. Mr May was loath to admit defeat, sure that he had one, if not two, criminals in front of him. But, faced with the lawyer's arguments, he was forced to admit that it was not possible to determine which woman had taken the items and so had to discharge both. John Powell, who must have felt bemused by this sudden turn of events, asked the Bench, "Are you not going against the evidence, Sir?" "So far as I am aware, Powell, I am not. You cannot make evidence, you cannot provide the missing link to tell us which woman removed your belonging, so the evidence stops short."

As with so many of these cases, we never hear what happened next. Powell presumably had his property, at least most of it, restored to him, but did he, for example, continue to live with this mistress, or did he move to other lodgings to get away from both women? Since the women could not provide the money for bail (although the papers do not record how much was required), how did one of them pay for legal representation? Being permitted visits by relatives whilst in gaol, perhaps it was one of these who contacted the firm of solicitors for them.

Revenue offences

Women took their share of what the administration defined as 'revenue crimes', those offences where the 'victim' was the purse of the government in some way. Pre-eminent in the list of these offences was

---

barristers on the China coast, often a firebrand orator not too dissimilar to Sir Edward Marshall Hall and other such luminaries.

possession, smuggling or sale of non-governmental opium (i.e. not from the Government Opium Farm and thus on which tax had not been paid). In many years around three-fifths of the male population of the gaol were serving sentences for offences of this sort. These crimes were not so prevalent amongst women, but they did occur, and not always with the female defendant merely as an adjunct to a man. However, the cases featuring women alone were usually very trivial ones, where the magistrate, to keep the gaol from bursting at the seams, would impose a very small fine, often just 10 or 25 cents.

A slightly more curious case, with pleasing elements of serendipity, occurred at the end of August 1890. A woman tied up her sampan near the Praya wall and came to shore with a basket, in which was hidden 85 taels (about 3 kilograms) of prepared opium. This she would sell for $170, a huge amount, twice the annual wage of a labourer. But her activities were known to the police, and an excise officer was waiting to examine the basket. As he stooped to do so, two men rushed him, knocking him over. By the time he came round, they and the woman, but not the opium, had disappeared. It seemed to the police that the matter had to end there – at least the smuggled opium was now in official hands. But three days later one woman brought a charge of assault against another. She said that her assailant had accused her of telling an excise officer that she (the assailant) was carrying some opium, and now she had lost $170 by this. Unless the complainant repaid her, she was going to kill her. But the excise officer happened to be in court just then, and all this sounded somewhat familiar to him. Recognising the woman he had intended to arrest, he informed the magistrate. The smuggler was fined $15 for assaulting her complainant and $150 for the original offence. If she failed to pay these, she could go to prison for a total of three months and two weeks.

One case which breached the regulations of the Sanitary Board involved the enterprise undertaken by between 300-400 women from Kowloon City, then outside British jurisdiction. On 4th March 1885, twelve "married women" appeared before Mr Wodehouse charged with carrying "noxious waters" through the streets during the day.[59] They

---

59 *China Mail,* 4th & 6th March 1885.

turned a reasonable return by collecting the human waste of the various better European and Chinese houses every day. They took it in covered buckets back to Kowloon City, whence it was sent as manure into China. The collection of 'night soil' was a regular feature of life in a colony whose granite base did not easily permit of a subterranean sewage system and survived to the 1950s and beyond.[60] The 'official' system at the time was for liquid waste to be thrown into the surface drains and solid matter to be deposited in the dust boxes. These were then emptied once or twice a week into carts belonging to the Sanitary Department.

It comes as no surprise that many householders preferred to avail themselves of the more frequent and hygienic services of the Kowloon women. Joseph Grimble, the (Police) Inspector of Nuisances, was very satisfied with the careful way these women carried out their trade, and thought it was a suitable alternative to the dust box. But they were still transporting their buckets down to the harbour at nine or ten in the morning, when they should have finished during the hours of darkness, and by 7.30 a.m. at the latest. Insp. Grimble explained that the problem stemmed from the unreliability of the boats that brought them over from Kowloon – they should arrive in plenty of time, in the small hours of the morning, but they were frequently late. The ferry service was a public one, so the women had no control over the times of sailings. Insp. Grimble reiterated that these women's work benefited residents but, yes, they were continually being fined for working beyond the permitted hours. These fines, he said, were merely seen as a tax or levy, and they factored them into the cost of their trade. However, Hugh McCallum, the head of the Sanitary Section of the Public Works Department, did not share his junior's commendatory view of the women.[61] In his eyes they were simply plying their trade and had to observe the law as anyone else. There were enough of them, he said, to charter a ferry or two to take them across the harbour at the appropriate hour, without relying on the public service. He saw no reason to allow them any special treatment and, anyhow, he believed the government system to be adequate without

---

60 https://industrialhistoryhk.org/?s=night+soil

61 It is perhaps relevant that Hugh McCallum and his wife lived on the spacious Peak, where noxious material could be deposited far from the houses.

their services. As Secretary of the Sanitary Board, reporting directly to the administration, Mr McCallum had the final authority. He held out no prospect of the regulations being altered in favour of these women. Time, on that day, was then pressing on, and the case was adjourned for two days. When it resumed, before Mr Wodehouse, the magistrate had some sympathy with the women.[62] Since they had already forfeited two days' earnings to attend court, he discharged the case although he had to warn them that a repeat of the offence would certainly result in a more substantial punishment.

62 Henry Ernest Wodehouse, b. 1845, d.1929, one of Hong Kong's earliest career civil servants, was a long serving magistrate and coroner. Fluent in written and spoken Cantonese, his decisions form the bench frequently show compassion and understanding for the less fortunate of those brought before him, both Chinese and western. His eldest son Philip Peveril served as Assistant Superintendent of Police for many years, but it is his third son who is best known, the comic novelist and librettist, P. G. Wodehouse.

CHAPTER 3

20TH-CENTURY WOMEN IN THE COURTS

The opening of the year was greeted in Hong Kong with just modest celebrations. The newspapers debated whether 1st January 1900 saw the beginning of the 20th century or the start of the last year of the 19th. And, after all, for most of the population the Gregorian calendar had limited relevance. For one young girl the dawn of that year brought no happiness at all.

A prisoner in a brothel in Ship Street, Tong Kui had suffered cruelly ever since she left her mother's home the previous summer to marry a seaman in Shek I, Hung Shan, near Macao.[63] Here the 17-year-old lived in fear, both of the man and his mother, who frequently beat her. In September 1899 they decided to dispose of her and soon sold her to Leung Wai, a 45-year-old procuress based in Hong Kong, for $120. The girl begged her husband to let her go home, but she was put on a boat with Leung and taken to Hong Kong. Tong's mother had visited soon after, but the pair told her that her daughter had died. Leung had taken her to a brothel in Ship Street, run by Leung Sze. Much against Tong's will, this brothel mistress had set her to work. There the situation would have remained: confined to the house, the girl had no chance of finding help. However, in July 1900, her male cousin from Macao was visiting Hong Kong and chanced to walk along that road. He glanced up and caught sight of his relative, standing on the second floor verandah. Knowing the story of her 'death' and that her mother had not seen her since the previous September, he sent word home. Tong's mother hurried to catch the steamer to the island, made her way to Wanchai and then angrily demanded entrance to the brothel. Here she was reunited

63 *China Mail,* 10th July 1900, *Hongkong Daily Press,* 11th July 1900.

The Central Magistracy. Photo credit: Richard Morgan.

with her daughter, but the brothel mistress refused to release the girl without payment of $100. Tong's mother only had $60 with her, so tried to negotiate. Leung Sze eventually agreed to accept $80. But she could only get a further $15 – not enough for the mistress. Eventually, on the pretext of going out to borrow more, the mother left and hurried to the Registrar General's office. She knew that the Hong Kong administration would help women in her daughter's situation. She had also realised that the second, older, woman in the brothel was responsible for kidnapping Tong. She was therefore eager to get to the government office as quickly as possible, before this woman left the building.

Her confidence in the efficacy of this department was rewarded. Police Inspector John Lee, attached to the department for just this type of case, took charge and accompanied her back to the brothel. He soon arranged for Tong to be taken to the Po Leung Kuk. Insp. Lee explained to her mother that there no accomplices of the brothel mistress could get access to the girl. He was keen that no attempts would be made to frighten or blackmail her into dropping the charges against her assailants.

The officer was justified in his caution. At the Magistracy the defence of the two women rested on a conflicting story of their own, whereby Tong's own mother had sold her, since her husband had thrown her out. They alleged that there had been a court case in Shek I, and afterwards the girl had come to Hong Kong and had applied to Leung Wai to help her find a place as a prostitute. The brothel mistress said that she had taken her in and treated her with kindness. Insp. Lee had investigated and shown the story to be baseless, so it cut no ice with Magistrate Hazeland. He told the pair it was a very serious case, both of kidnapping for the purposes of procuring and holding a woman in a brothel, knowing her to have been so procured. He gave Leung Wai, the procuress, the maximum sentence that court could impose, twelve months in gaol, while Leung Sze, brothel mistress, had to serve nine months. Both would have to do hard labour whilst in prison.

Women charged with kidnapping girls and young women, intending to sell them into prostitution still appeared frequently before the magistrates. With ready markets in Hong Kong, Singapore, the Straits Settlements, the Philippines and the USA, women thought the risks worth the potential gain. It is a little curious why Mr Hazeland regarded this as an especially serious case. It varies from many cases in that even though the abduction happened outside of Hong Kong, the police were able to bring all the parties to court. There had not been violence done to Tong during the kidnap itself, although setting her afterwards to work in the brothel with male clients was surely that. The suspicion lingers that it was her state as a married woman, the rightful property of her husband (in Chinese custom and still somewhat in English law) that was more significant. An assault against her was, in its way, a type of theft from her husband, no matter that he had had his part in selling her. Presumably after the trial Tong Kai was restored to her mother's care, and they returned to Shek I – as usual, we hear no more.

Mui tsai and the treatment of children

As the century wore on, the treatment of children and young women – particularly *mui tsai* – improved only gradually. The *Women's and Girls' Protection Ordinance* had been used to prosecute the Ship Street women and continued to be one of Hong Kong's most oft-cited ordinances. In July 1920 Sub-Insp. James McKay, Insp. Lee's successor, had spotted a little eight-year-old girl, a servant to a woman living on Hollywood Road.[64] Insp. McKay became suspicious of the bruise on the child's jaw and what appeared to be some little burn marks. He took the child, who was doubtless terrified, to his superior's office. The Chief Assistant to the Secretary for Chinese Affairs decided that there was enough evidence of mistreatment to have the girl medically examined. Dr Moore, the head of the Civil Hospital, was frankly puzzled by the multitude of burns, blisters and sores all over the little body. She had no disease or skin condition to account for these – the burns appeared to be from lighted tapers or similar. The bruise was not compatible with any bump or fall, but had, in his opinion, been deliberately inflicted. The child was in evident pain. However, whether through fear of these huge men who asked her questions, or from even greater fear of the mistress, the child would not speak. Her mistress was arrested and represented in court by a solicitor, who brought up a neighbour of the woman's. She testified that she had never seen the child ill-treated, supporting the claim of the defendant that she had been as kind to her as if she were her own daughter.

The woman said that the child was sickly and had a skin condition which required the application of Jeyes Fluid, a strong caustic acid, to clear. She had also got a proper medicine for her from the Alice Memorial Hospital, but had not taken her to see a doctor. The defence lawyer put up as much of a case as he could for his client. Finally he had to attribute her continued use of the corrosive to "the ignorance of the class of people (to which) the defendant belongs." But Dr Moore's testimony prevailed. The magistrate thought even 'ignorant people' would not continue 'the treatment' when there was no improvement and that this was a case of cruelty. The newspaper heads the report "Child Tortured". But the scale

---

64 *China Mail*, 16th July 1920.

of fines that magistrates could impose for such offences were unchanged from years ago. The fine the woman had to pay was $50. This child's case was no isolated incident. Inevitably, there were many instances of cruelty to children from their birth parents or other blood relatives, and the Society for the Protection of Children, which was formed in Hong Kong in 1930, would investigate many cases. But from the 1920s onwards, the *mui tsai* system was subject to public scrutiny, particularly through the activity of local groups, both Chinese and western, with support from anti-slavery activists in Britain, who had questions raised in Parliament. Thus, cases of the abuse of young *mui tsai* girls featured with sad regularity in the press until the Japanese occupation. A year after the Jeyes Fluid incident, papers gave details of a ten-year-old child who, tied to a bedpost, had matches applied to her face.[65] The abuse came to light when visitors to the house reported their concerns to the police. The girl, so small that she had to stand on a chair for the magistrate to see her, had been beaten repeatedly over the previous months with bamboo canes, the prosecution displaying some of these sticks in court. She was still undergoing treatment for her injuries when her mistress, a "well-dressed young Chinese woman" appeared before Mr Lindsell.[66] He granted her bail, setting the sum at $1,000, while the police completed their enquiries. Unfortunately the trail for the modern reader then goes cold, and we can only hope that she served a term in prison and the S.C.A. and the Po Leung Kuk found the child a kinder home.

Another cold trail, this time when the defendant skipped bail and forfeited the $2,000 she had paid for that, dates from 1935.[67] Articles appeared during the late 1920s and early 1930s reporting that the Russian dancers at Shanghai nightclubs were being joined, and even replaced, by young Chinese women, to some acclaim. Such was also the case in Hong

---

65 *China Mail*, 19th August 1921.

66 Roger Edward Lindsell, b. 1885, d. 1940. Another of Hong Kong's career civil service cadets and lawyers. His first ten years in the colony were mostly spent in as Assistant to the Secretary for Chinese Affairs, thereafter he was appointed Police Magistrate. His dealings with the many who came before him in this capacity shows understanding and often compassion. Later he rose to be Puisne Judge and Acting Chief Justice.

67 *Hongkong Telegraph* and *China Mail*, 26th September 1935.

Kong, it seems, as Alice Luk was a regular performer at the Majestic Dancing Hall. Aside from her income from that, she had a comfortable flat at No. 46 Morrison Hill Road as the kept woman of an American seaman. At the Central Magistracy on 26th September, little Tung Hing, aged twelve but looking much younger, made a pitiful sight. She had bruising and scars on her face, over her eyes, all over her hands and arms, and on the insides of her legs. Her arm had been cut open in places by a bladed cane, and there were clear marks of bites. Luk claimed that the child was her niece, daughter of a sister who had died when the child was still a baby. She had brought her up and treated her as her own, even paying for her to go to school. But the girl told Mr Schofield that she was born in Shanghai and had been sold to Luk as a *mui tsai* when she was eight years old. The woman made her sleep on the floor, next to her bed and kept her working all day. The inspector in charge agreed that her aunt/mistress had sent her to school, but only for a week, after which the marks on her body were too noticeable. The woman admitted that she had bitten and hit her, but only because she had been naughty and stolen things to eat. "I find that very hard to believe," responded the magistrate. The state of the child had shocked Insp. O'Connor, who, when asking for a week's adjournment, also requested that Mr Schofield set bail high, as Luk's connections might mean that she could easily leave the colony.

It would appear that this is exactly what happened. A week later she failed to appear for the hearing and a warrant was issued for her arrest. Since there is no further mention of the case, we may presume that she was out of the reach of the Hong Kong courts. Unfortunately, neither do we hear what arrangements were then made for little Tung Hing.

Not all cases that came to court resulted in the child being removed from the mistress. A 15-year-old girl was the *mui tsai* of a woman whose husband kept one, perhaps two, concubines, all living in the same apartment. One day the girl answered back to the ill-tempered, sulky concubine, So King-sau, and found herself rewarded with a slap round the face.[68] She was still reeling from that when So used a piece of firewood to strike her over the eyes, first on the right, then on the left side of her face. Bleeding and sobbing, the girl fled to her mistress, who

---

68 *Hongkong Telegraph*, 12th June 1933.

carefully treated the cuts. But, living in the congested area of Circular Path, near Ladder Street, there was no way the incident would remain a family secret. Soon a woman who was part of the Anti-*Mui Tsai* Society visited, and said that she would report to the S.C.A. The mistress was not worried because the child's registration was in order. Sub-Insp. Fraser of that department was a fair-minded man, and could see that the girl was well cared for, and that the mistress seemed genuinely fond of her. He believed the child when she said that she was happy and wanted to stay with this lady. However, he explained it was his duty to protect *mui tsai*, and the concubine So would have to explain herself to the magistrate. He would also have to take the child to the Po Leung Kuk until the trial. Two days later, Mr Wynne-Jones heard the case and after hearing from Insp. Fraser, bound So King-sau over with a bond of $100, to keep the peace for twelve months.

As it gradually became harder for women in Hong Kong to keep *mui tsai*, ways around registration were frequently sought. The commonest way of achieving this was by claiming kinship with the child, as in Tung Hing's case. The use of another 'customary practice' served in the case of Lai Kan-hing to evade prosecution of the 'mistress'.[69] The means used here were sufficiently unusual to merit reporting in all the papers, and, unusually, the reports provide different aspects of the story, allowing a fuller picture to appear.

On 2nd February 1930 a man was hurrying down Western Street, on his way back to work after a meal break. All of a sudden, a girl stumbling along in the same direction but on the opposite side of the road caught his attention. He looked again – surely that was his daughter. He dodged across the road, through the rickshaws and motor lorries, to catch up with the girl. He was certain now that it was his Kan-hing, but there was blood streaming down her face and she was weeping – wailing, in fact. She blindly pushed her way through the crowd and did not seem to hear him calling to her. She seemed to be following someone, for she abruptly changed direction and tried to cross the road. As she let traffic go by, he caught up with her. "Where are you going, daughter? What's happened

---

69 The English-language papers report this case on 11th February 1930.

to you?" The fifteen-year-old pointed at the police station, just fifty yards away, and clutched at his sleeve to pull him along with her.

Inside No. 7 Station, the girl's 'mother-in-law-elect' was standing at the desk, talking volubly to the Station Sergeant, and pointing to her. The man then understood, and his blood boiled. He had feared something like this. "What have you done to my daughter," he roared. "She's not yours now, don't you remember? You sold her to me. I can do what I like with the lazy so and so." At this, the sergeant sent a constable for the first aid box and put through a call to the S.C.A. This was a matter for one of their inspectors. When it came to court the next week, Mr Butters, the Chief Assistant to the Secretary for Chinese Affairs, charged the woman on two counts: with assaulting a *mui tsai* and being in possession of an unregistered *mui tsai*. The woman had bought the girl on 19th December the previous year, when her family's desperate situation meant that her father could not make enough to feed them or pay off their debts. Lai's price had been $110, and she was eventually to marry the woman's young son. The woman did not consider her a *mui tsai*, but a *san po tsai* – a daughter-in-law-elect.[70] And yet, as she told the magistrate, the woman had treated her just like a *mui tsai,* and had talked continuously about selling her on. Lai had asked the woman whether it would not be best if she returned to her father and had later left the apartment and set out for her home. But the mistress sent a young *foki*[71] to find her and drag her back. She then instructed him to hold the girl down, while she hit her repeatedly about the face with a wooden clog.

The woman's solicitor represented her in court and produced the go-betweens who had arranged the original transaction and attested that it was as the woman claimed. Therefore, the solicitor said, the second charge should be dropped as the girl was no *mui tsai*, but that his client would plead guilty to a charge of common assault in place of the first indictment. Neither the Chief Assistant nor the magistrate were happy at the turn this case had taken. "There has been an elaborate camouflage

---

70 *San po tsai* is also transliterated as *sum po tsai* e.g. *Hongkong Daily Press,* 11th February 1930.

71 A *foki* is a male employee, usually in businesses but occasionally, as here, as an outdoor servant to a household.

to conceal that the girl is a *mui tsai*. If she is a *san po tsai* she must have the rights of a wife," said the latter. Common assault of this type carried a lower penalty than assaulting a *mui tsai*. Thus he could only impose a fine of $25 or one month's imprisonment with hard labour on the woman, and a five dollar fine to her *foki* for assisting in the attack.

Family life in Hong Kong, whether natural or adoptive, came, of course, in all degrees of functionality. This case, in May 1934, serves as a reminder that the *mui tsai* system, although it left defenceless children open to the widest range of abuse, could function to their benefit. A Lady Inspector attached to the S.C.A. stopped a young girl on Nathan Road and questioned her.[72] She appeared to be running errands, and the woman wanted to know whether her mother had sent her. She replied that she was doing jobs for her mistress, which led the inspector to accompany her back home. The mistress proved to be the concubine of a popular Chinese actor, Chiu Lai-cheung. The Inspector asked Pun Lai-fun whether the child was a *mui tsai,* and if so, whether she had the correct documentation for her. Finding that she did not, and that the girl had been with her for three years, she told her she would have to come to court. But she could see that the girl was healthy and well clothed and seemed to have a happy relationship with Pun. The court fined the woman $25 for neglecting to register her, but the Lady Inspector confirmed that she had no concerns for the child's well-being.

In so many cases the child's situation had arisen because of the desperate poverty of the birth parents, who contracted a debt and had only a daughter to offer as security. Sometimes a transaction was made which does really seem to have benefited the child, but because money changed hands, it lay outside the law, and had to fit into the category of *mui tsai*. Such was the trouble that came to Mr Wynne-Jones' court at the end of the same month. A married woman, So Wun, had, three years earlier, lent $50 to a certain woman.[73] Having nothing else of value, she had given over her small daughter to So. When the woman's husband died two years later, she had to borrow a further $15 from So to pay for his funeral. Now she wanted her daughter back, but told the magistrate

72 *Hongkong Telegraph,* 3rd March 1934.
73 *Hongkong Telegraph,* 30th March 1934.

that So Wun was demanding $2 a month for the three years as the child's upkeep. The accused had come to court to defend herself, and brought the child with her. She denied that she had asked anything extra, she just asked for the actual amounts borrowed. She had treated the child exactly as her own, she wasn't a *mui tsai* at all. She – So Wun – bought her the same sort of clothes as her other children and she had eaten the same food as the rest of the family. Sub-Insp. Fraser of the S.C.A. said that the child was, indeed, very well looked after. "And she doesn't want to return to her mother!" burst out So, whereupon she and the child dissolved into tears.

But the magistrate was unmoved. So was charged with keeping an unregistered *mui tsai*. Just calling the child by another name would not make her change that. She was not a relative, a paid servant nor an adopted daughter, and must therefore be a *mui tsai*. Mr Wynne-Jones fined her $100 with the option of two months' hard labour. It appears that So Wun opted for the fine, as she seems to have left the court with the child, both still sobbing. There is no record in the newspaper accounts of the child's opinion of what was happening to her.

But nor was it just Chinese children who lived in what might now be called dysfunctional families, even if the 'kidnapping' recounted next was more at the wish of the child than otherwise.[74] Here the victim of the alleged assault was a little boy of ten years, George Melhuish. He lived with his mother Mrs Anna Melhuish at the Criterion Hotel, Pottinger Street, which she managed along with her husband. On 10th July she appeared as the complainant, to accuse her daughter, Kate Mordy, of his kidnap. The mother told how she had to send for him to be brought back from Mordy's house in Wanchai. She gave the boy a whipping – perhaps for being 'kidnapped' – and then arranged for him to go to St Joseph's college as a regular boarder. Mr Hazeland declared that he could not see where the evidence of kidnap came into the tale, but suggested that the child should speak for himself. George Melhuish had a straightforward story – he had gone to his sister's home of his own accord, Mordy had not made him go there. He was happy there, and he had gone because he loved his sister. He did not want to go back to his mother – she was

---

74 *Hongkong Daily Press*, 11th July 1900.

always beating him. The magistrate had stern words for that woman, telling her she had wasted the court's time and should not have fabricated such a story. "But," he concluded, "I think it is very likely you have been treating this boy with cruelty."

The start of life – a perilous journey

Childbirth was a dangerous time for women and their offspring wherever in the world they might find themselves. In Britain, towards the end of the 19th century, infant mortality counted as those dying within one month of birth, was well over 20%, although this had halved within thirty years.[75] At this time in Hong Kong European babies had about the same chance of survival as their British-born siblings. However, the neo-natal death figure for Chinese infants was 74.5%.[76] Moira M. W. Chan-Yeung's *A Medical History of Hong Kong 1842-1941* provides a long-needed window into the state and development of women's medical services in the colony.[77] She explores some reasons for this shockingly large statistic and charts the beginnings of midwifery training there.

Chinese women were attended either by their relatives or by a *wan po* – a Chinese midwife – who had learnt the mechanics through watching older women. The practices she used dated back decades, if not centuries. The midwife here had no access to any western scientific or medical information on infant and maternal health. In many ways the same could be said of the midwives of rural Britain and Ireland, until the latter part of the late 19th century. But the different cultural understandings of the human body in the two places produced widely varied customs. Earlier in the colony's history, European women would

75 https://www.statista.com/statistics/1041714/united-kingdom-all-time-child-mortality-rate/ For comparison worldwide in 2010 this latter figure ranges between 0.4% in the most affluent countries to 14% in parts of the developing world.

76 *Report by the Medical Officer for Health for 1896,* 19th March 1897, Sessional Papers. This figure includes the very high mortality within the two orphanages of the convents, the sisters of which regularly received moribund children brought from the mainland. Additionally figures were already revised upwards to account for the under-reporting of Chinese births.

77 Much of the information in this section on infant mortality and midwifery in Hong Kong comes from this book and the author gratefully acknowledges her debt to Dr Chan-Leung.

attend and support each other through their frequent pregnancies, whilst those whose husbands could afford it would travel home as soon as they could. As the Government Civil Hospital developed, wives of working-class men would go there for their delivery. More affluent families would engage a private nurse to stay in their home for the duration.

In the Chinese community some of the children who did not survive were those born to desperately poor, undernourished mothers, often riddled with disease themselves. The primary cause of infant mortality, though, was *trismus*, now known to be a tetanus-related condition. This was introduced into the baby's system through the practice (administered by the midwife) of 'sealing' the umbilical cord with a powder that often contained a high proportion of earth or animal dung. These babies would lose the ability to suck after two or three days, then lock-jaw set in and they could take no fluids. Death usually occurred five or six days after birth.[78]

We do not hear about these sad cases in the courts, but just occasionally a charge of manslaughter (i.e. of the mother) was made against a midwife. Relatives were legally obliged to notify the police when a death occurred, and it was usually followed that, when officers had suspicions about the cause of death, they made an arrest. But in the earliest instance to come to light, it was a doctor who raised the alarm. The story started when relatives called in Dr Harston to look after the 22-year-old Lavidia or Leocardia Francisca da Cruz Roza, the dangerously ill wife of a clerk employed in Amoy.[79] Dr Harston could not prevent her death, which occurred a few days after she had given birth. For her confinement she had been attended by a midwife from the Portuguese community. Aged 80, Clara Cordeiro came from Macao but in 1901 lived in Shelley Street. Her methods were probably similar to those of the many untrained midwives in Britain. On 11th February, Det. Insp. Hanson charged her with having caused the death of the young wife, and Cordeiro appeared at the Magistracy the next day, when her case was remanded for a week. The court granted her bail, but since the amount required was $2,500, it is more than likely

---

78 Chan-Leung, *op. cit.*, p.188.
79 *Hongkong Telegraph*, 12th February 1901, *China Mail*, 12th, 19th February 1901.

that she spent the week in prison. On the next occasion the indictment was changed to one of manslaughter. Two doctors, who had examined the mother's body, gave evidence, as did the dead woman's sister and her mother-in-law. Cordeiro, who had engaged a solicitor to represent her, pleaded "not guilty". The doctors believed that the woman had died because of the midwife's "incompetence or malpractice". A careful search of the papers has yielded no further information. There is no mention of the case at the Criminal Sessions reports of the time. However, a note in the Captain Superintendent's Report for 1901 records that she was discharged, presumably through lack of corroborative evidence.

The unnamed woman who died in Tung Wah Hospital on 6th September 1911 had given birth a week earlier.[80] She arrived at the Hospital with atrocious wounds to the pelvic area and sepsis through her body. The lady had lived with her husband in No. 26 Battery Street, Yaumatei, and a Chinese midwife, Chan Wai-kwan, stayed there with her during her confinement. According to the statement of this woman, she had been anxious about the delivery, and consulted Dr Lee Yin Tze, asking for assistance, but he refused. She had to return to her patient and delivered the baby by forceps. The reports do not mention whether the baby survived. Chan left, but soon the husband realised that his wife was unwell, and took her to the Hospital. They were unable to save her. The medical staff there raised their concerns with the police. They, in turn, tracked down the midwife and took a lengthy statement from her. However, when they contracted Dr Lee, he knew nothing of the mother and had received no visit from Chan. The husband told police how she had returned to his home with a pair of forceps wrapped in dirty old newspaper. These she had used on mother and baby straight away, with no attempt to clean, let alone sterilise.

When Chan came before the police magistrate, the Crown solicitor explained that the charge was one of involuntary manslaughter, since she had performed an operation which she had no right to undertake. European midwives were not allowed to use forceps and the fact that she had not sterilised them showed negligence at the very least. From trial accounts, both magistrate and lawyers were unsure about the legal

---

80 *China Mail,* 28th September 1911.

standing of Chinese midwives. After enquiry, the magistrate found that anyone could set herself up as a midwife, for there was no law in the colony against doing so without a licence. But, surely, he said, such a person should behave with care, take every precaution and avoid negligence. The prosecution would produce witnesses, including two doctors. He perhaps also brought a midwife to speak about the usual practice. The doctors would give their diagnosis of the case, and if they suggested that there had been negligence then the woman must, said the Crown Solicitor, be sent to jury trial. However, if there was no suggestion of malpractice then Chan must be discharged. The magistrate adjourned the trial – which is where the story ends for us. To date, searches of the newspapers have not yielded the 'what happened next'. The only hint comes from the Report of the Captain Superintendent for that year. Under the heading of Manslaughter, he records:

> Fifteen cases were reported to the Police during the year as against 5 in 1910. In all of these cases arrests were made, but in only two cases were convictions obtained.

It seems, therefore, most likely that the case against Chan Wai-kwan collapsed.

But times, sensibilities and medical health provision were changing. The Enquiry in to the Causes of Infant Deaths, which the Governor, Sir Henry Blake, commissioned in 1903, had raised the issue of training Chinese midwives. In 1904 the medical authorities launched a programme at the Alice Memorial Maternity Hospital, which could instruct six candidates per year.[81] In 1911, a proper training institute was established there, now able to produce 24 qualified midwives each year. Whilst many Chinese women were still reluctant to submit to western methods, especially if they thought that a male doctor might be involved in the delivery, better hygiene and safer procedures were now more readily available.

---

81 Moira Chan-Yeung, *A Medical History of Hong Kong*, pp. 189-90.

Robbery and violence towards women, by women

Violence (as opposed to cruelty) was not a common feature of women's crime in Hong Kong – aside, of course, from those times when tempers and passions were high and a woman had access to a meat chopper. When an offence was committed with the use of undue force or brutality, there was usually a man involved somewhere, although he was not necessarily the one perpetrating the violence. Highway robbery was not something that the Hong Kong public associated with a woman. The highway robbery case of October 1927 when a Cheung Chau amah was robbed of her jewels saw a man and a woman come to court. Two other men, unidentified and uncaught, took some part in the crime. However, it seems clear from the reports that the female defendant, Wong Ho, directed the attack on Lo Ku, even though she ended up with the lighter sentence.[82]

The two women had known each other for about three years, although Lo Ku rarely came over to Hong Kong and was not familiar with Kowloon. Wong Ho had written to her at the beginning of October, telling Lo Ku that she had found a job for her – a friend of hers needed an amah for a child. What she did not explain was that the friend was a man, whose wife was not about at the time to care for the child. Wong and the man, Hoi Tak, met the woman from Cheung Chau off the ferry, and took her back to his flat in Tai Nan Street in Shamshuipo. She was not happy about staying in the same flat as the man, but eventually her acquaintance persuaded her that she would be all right. She acted as amah to the child for about a week before returning to Cheung Chau. However, they prevailed on her to leave a rattan basket with her clothes at the flat. She returned to Hong Kong on 27th October, this time being met by the man alone. Later that evening, Wong joined them and they decided to go out to the pictures and then have a meal. Reluctantly, Lo accompanied them. On their return, at about 12.45 a.m., they took what seemed to her a very long, winding route. As they reached that street, two other men jumped out of the shadows and pulled at her wrist bangles. Wong and Hoi seized her and held her fast, telling her to give

---

82 *Hongkong Telegraph,* 11th November 1927, 22nd December 1927, *Hongkong Daily Press,* 23rd December 1927.

over her jewellery, otherwise these men would kill her. The robbers took the bangles and a ring, together with $36 in her purse, and ran off. Back in the house, Lo became suspicious about her companions, especially when they started contradicting the other residents of the flat, who said that the police should be informed. Then they told her that they "didn't know where to go". But Lo persisted, and eventually they all went out. However, once out they told her that they were taking her to the robbers in Yaumatei, where she could get her belongings back. But then they led her on another long and convoluted walk. When they got to a railway tunnel near Hung Hom, at the end of Gascoigne Road – at least an hour's walk from Shamshuipo – Lo refused to go into the tunnel, which was very dark. At the tunnel mouth they both attacked her, pushing her to the ground and taking her remaining rings. They then pushed her over the steep embankment, obviously meaning to kill her.

Fortunately, Lo's fall was broken by a ledge, not visible in the dark, just a few feet below the path level. Here she waited until the pair had gone, then scrambled up. She cowered down as a man approached, until she realised he was a policeman. He took her to Hung Hom Police Station, and the police in the area were alerted. An Indian constable, making his hourly report, noted that at 4.10 a.m. he had passed a couple, hand in hand, near the railway sidings, a very unfrequented road by night, especially by pedestrians. Mindful of the recent alert, when the same constable saw a woman walking in the opposite direction at 5.40 a.m. he stopped and questioned her. Noticing that she was wearing bangles on her wrist that might well be the stolen ones, he brought her in to Hung Hom Police Station. She was soon identified as Wong Ho, so they transferred her to Shamshuipo Station where she was searched. Her story was that the bangles were lying on the road and she just wanted to give them back to their owner. But the search revealed that she was also carrying all the rings taken from the unfortunate amah. Wong came before the Kowloon magistrate later that day, when the case was remanded until police had time to arrest her accomplice and perhaps the other robbers involved.

They did not establish the identity of the two robbers, but Hoi Tak was eventually run to ground, although not without difficulty. It was not until 11th November that, on a tip off received by the police, he was captured at Shek I Junk Wharf. On that day Wong's case started at the Magistracy, but since the police needed more time to prepare the case against Hoi, it was again remanded. When they had arrested Hoi, he had initially admitted being concerned with the affair. But at the following hearing he disclaimed all knowledge, saying that he had not seen the statement he gave previously before he signed it. Wong reserved her defence, having been told that they would be both appearing at the criminal sessions a few weeks hence.

Before Mr Justice Wood, the prosecuting counsel, T. S. Whyte-Smith noted that the pair were fortunate not to be facing a murder charge. They did not have a barrister representing them, but were able to speak for themselves after the Crown's case had been presented. Hoi Tak maintained that he did not know Lo Ku at all, he had never met her in fact, but that she had a grudge against him. The police had forced him to sign a confession, but he had nothing to do with the case. The woman, Wong Ho, admitted that she had known Lo Ku – some seven or eight years, she now said, but the woman had imagined the whole story. She suggested that it was too ridiculous to believe: "Does anyone in the world believe that a woman would join with robbers?" she asked. But the police had produced sufficient evidence of the man's initial admission to convince the jury that his change of plea was just that, and doubtless both the judge and jury knew of instances where women did, indeed, throw in their lot with thieves and robbers. Lo Ku's testimony was convincing, and they took just fifteen minutes to declare both defendants guilty. Both were given sentences with hard labour, Hoi Tak for five years and Wong Ho for three.

Sometimes it was not always clear on which side the various parties in these robbery cases stood. On 12th August, 1923, Tse Siu-sang, a young woman, probably still in her teens, who wore semi-European dress in the very latest mode, called on friends in Connaught Road West.[83] She was quite an able painter and had executed some scenes in traditional Chinese style which the elderly friends, a commission agent with an insurance firm and his wife, had agreed to buy from her for $21. When she arrived that evening the lady suggested that she and the girl went to the theatre.

---

83 *Hongkong Daily Press,* 29th August 1923.

The girl was rather surprised, as the old lady rarely went out, but she was pleased, and suggested that they go to the Chinese Y.M.C.A. Theatre on the junction of Ladder Street and Bridges Street, not too far from where the couple lived. Tse had heard that an American girl who was appearing there was an excellent actress, and she was keen to see her. They hired a rickshaw and took a little seven-year-old child with them, who was perhaps the old lady's *mui tsai*. Soon, though, the woman dismissed the rickshaw and they started climbing up the hill, but not, Tse claimed, in the direction that she had expected. They walked on for some time, and found themselves passing the Helena May Institute on Garden Road and then taking the dark, unlit road that led up to the Governor's residence. It was in this road that a man suddenly appeared in front of them and robbed Tse and the old woman of jewellery and took the $60 that Tse had with her. They were not harmed, but the man had thrown pepper into the face of the old woman, which had blinded her for a while. Tse found a couple of sedan chairs to take them all back to Connaught Road.

But the story that the police heard and that was told at the Magistracy two weeks later was rather different. Apparently the elderly commission agent had become suspicious when his wife had been out so long, and when the party returned and he spoke to his wife, he called Tse in and accused her of planning a robbery on his wife. He went to the police the next morning and on the basis of this, she was arrested on a charge of feloniously procuring an unknown person to commit a robbery on the old woman. According to the agent's wife, Tse had arrived at their house, claiming to have won $150 on the lottery. She suggested that they both went to the theatre to celebrate. It was a long time since his wife had been on a trip out and did not know her way around. Having discharged the rickshaw, perhaps somewhere on Queen's Road, they kept climbing. The old lady claimed that they walked for over an hour, although that was admitted to be probably an exaggeration. The agent believed that Tse had hired a man to steal his wife's jewellery, since the lady usually wore a number of valuable pieces, a fact the younger woman knew. The little girl who was with them told him that no pepper was thrown into Tse's face, nor had this man taken anything from her. She also said that Tse had not cried out or tried to help the old lady. Back in their home that night, when tackled with the matter, Tse denied that she had engineered it in any way, saying that she also had been robbed. However, finally, when the man started talking about going to the police in the morning, she begged him not to, and said, "Conspiracy or not, I will make good." Both the couple and Tse Siu-sang were represented by their solicitors and the charge and the defence were explained at length. Having heard the stories, and with only the word of a seven-year-old as evidence, and no prospect of catching the actual thief, the Magistrate, Mr Wood, dismissed the case.

Poverty and the pursuit of fortunes

For the story of women's relationship with the courts and the prison, the 1930s surely mark a low point. The number of women in prison spiralled to an unprecedented level. The years 1933-39 saw, on average, seven times as many women serving terms of imprisonment as in 1923-29. But Hong Kong was hardly unique in this. The Great Depression in the USA, Britain and continental Europe saw marked increases in petty, opportunistic crimes, crimes of desperation and poverty, rooted in a need to feed starving families. The same held true in Hong Kong, although here, whilst suffering the after-shocks of the western stock-market crashes, the colony was receiving tens of thousands of refugees each year, fleeing Japanese strikes on southern China. Now, far from being a rare occurrence, the newspapers carry almost daily reports of thefts committed by women. Some were domestic servants, stealing from their employers, other were women without jobs, but in the right place for a tempting opportunity to present itself. Jewellery, usually only of a few dollars value, or amounts of money up to about $100 were the usual plunder, and rarely was any of this recovered. Almost without exception, they went to prison for between two weeks and two months. The number of people who paid the fine option, never large anyhow, now became quite negligible.

The police and court reports categorised as revenue crimes the wide variety of offences which saw government coffers depleted in some way. Aside from opium, duties were payable on many pastimes, both Chinese and western, such as alcohol, gambling at the races, tobacco and lotteries (where permitted). However, most of the latter were generally classed as common gambling. Hong Kong had fought a long and largely unsuccessful battle against the population's predilection for games of chance. In common with Britain at the time, betting on these, or on animal fights and some sporting events, especially by the lower orders, was outlawed. It is only very occasionally that a woman appears in court connected with a gambling case. No such case where the woman was the principal agent has come to light to date. But the selling of perennially popular lottery tickets was a chosen occupation for many a woman needing to make a little more. *Po pui* tickets were around for many years, for lotteries organised and held in Macao and Canton. An agent would come back with upwards of 50,000 unmarked tickets for a particular month's draw. These were then given in small batches to secondary agents, who had to put their chop or mark on each straight away, before selling the tickets in their 'patch' of a road, market or district. The tickets had no validity until this agent's chop was on them, so the primary agent had a hold over the sellers, since those unsold could not be returned. After the draw, winning ticket-holders had to find their seller and claim the prize money, given from the ticket takings. The sellers then settled up with the agent, who in turn returned to the source for the next round. Although tickets only cost a few cents each, the volume of sales was such that tens of thousands of dollars were involved each month. And all of this money was going out of the colony, filling coffers other than those of the Hong Kong government.

Those of the women who came to court for the offence of selling these tickets were inevitably the secondary agents. Typically their received gaol terms between six weeks and three months, with hard labour.[84] The fine options were often set high, e.g. the woman caught with 748 tickets had to find $500 if she wanted to avoid a three months term. Perhaps the family of the married woman, Li Mui, who had hidden 62 tickets in her stockings were able to find $75 to avoid losing her for six weeks.

---

84 *Hongkong Telegraph,* 21st June & 14th September 1933.

Rising temperatures – rising tempers

Fights and brawls involving women did not frequently come to public attention. The occasional such fracas that make it to the *Police Courts* columns of the newspapers were reported with jocularity, except when the case became rather more serious, as in that where one woman severely burnt her opponent by throwing vitriol over her in September 1913.[85] But from the 1920s on, incidents became more frequent. These squabbles might merely have been jostling for places in a queue, but that queue was for no mere frippery. Water was always a precious commodity in Hong Kong. With no natural watercourses of any size on the island, reservoirs were an early and urgent priority for the colonial administrators. Gradually the capacity of these increased, but struggled to keep pace with the demands of a rapidly growing population and a modernising society. When rainfall was low, water rationing had to be brought in, as happened throughout the 20th century until as recently as 1982.[86] In the 1930s the majority of people got their daily water from standpipes or street fountains. Some of these had been around since the previous century and were leaky and wasteful, so a programme of installing efficient new fountains had recently commenced. In the summer of 1932, houses connected to the mains and the old fountains had supplies turned on from 7 a.m. to 8.30 a.m., and from 4.30 p.m. to 6 p.m. only.[87] The new fountains were fed water between 7 a.m. and 6 p.m.

Long before the supplies were turned on, winding queues of people would form, especially in areas with only the old fountains. Each would have large water tins and barrels, and these were often left there to mark their owner's place in the line. Inevitably, perhaps, disagreements and fights broke out. Sub-Inspector McWalter, who looked after West Point Police Station, had reports of scuffles and squabbles almost every day at the fountains in his district. On 9th June he arrived at the Station at 1 p.m. to find a huge crowd, mostly women, intent on making their grievances heard. Whether the problem had stemmed from the morning

85 *China Mail*, 10th October 1913.

86 David Bellis, *Hot and thirsty: the struggle to supply Hong Kong with drinking water*, Gwulo, 2018. https://gwulo.com/comment/44509#comment-44509

87 *Hongkong Telegraph*, 2nd June 1932.

session, or they were an early part of the afternoon queue was not made clear, but a fight between five women, somewhere in the middle of the line, had spread, domino-fashion, in both directions. His constables and district watchmen reported that clogs were thrown, water tins were used as battering weapons and insults and obscene language was flying. One woman had her finger bitten, another an earring torn out and a third a vivid black eye. The police and watchmen had needed to physically separate the pugilists, then dragged them to the Station, with thirty or forty others coming along to watch. Eventually, sorting out the stories, Insp. McWalter charged five with brawling. The next morning, two were fined $5 and all were bound over for $50 apiece to keep the peace for one year.

Opium – the old offence

Although the trade in opium to China dwindled as the century progressed, the number of prosecutions for possession or smuggling of illicit opium did not show a similar fall. Women continued to appear before the magistrates on both counts, such as the mother who had hidden a little in her baby's clothes, then swaddled the child onto her back in the usual fashion.[88] With no information given in the papers, we are left to imagine how the detectives came to suspect her or know where to look! She may well have had to take her baby to Victoria Gaol for a month rather than try to find the $75 fine. The imposition of a $3,000 fine or six months in gaol for smuggling on an elderly, sick woman, lately arrived from Saigon, seems disproportionately severe.[89] This defendant had been found with 30 taels – just over three times the amount bundled up with the baby. The woman's solicitor pleaded with Magistrate Wood for leniency for his client, bearing in mind her frail state.[90] She had apparently been given it to carry by a man in Saigon – but Mr Wood felt that its concealment in some coconuts more than suggested that this was a case of attempted

---

88 *Hongkong Daily Press,* 18th February, 1916.

89 *China Mail,* 28th August 1923.

90 John Roskruge Wood, b. 1877, d. 1953. A Civil Service Cadet who passed most of his career in the courts of Hong Kong. After almost 20 years as a Police Magistrate, he was called to the bar and subsequently was appointed Puisne Judge and Acting Chief Justice.

smuggling. Such cases rarely made the large type headlines in the papers, and are often buried amongst minor pilfering cases, earring snatching and unlicensed hawking in the 'Around the Courts' paragraphs. Boatwomen quite often found themselves in court, having wittingly or unwittingly carried quantities of the drug into Hong Kong waters. Rarely were their protestations of ignorance of what they had on board given any credence. For example, two were given six month sentences in 1915 when 650 taels were found in the bottom of their sampan.[91]

Opium-related cases were so ubiquitous amongst the men appearing at the Magistracy that few received much in the way of investigation, but one that did occurred in March 1934. But there was rather an obvious reason for the English newspapers paying it more attention. Magistrate Wynne-Jones must have been taken by surprise when into the court were led two well-dressed women, a Mrs Leung Ying and a westerner, Mrs J. Boys, of Waterloo Road, Kowloon Tong.[92] They were both charged with being in possession of 300 taels of opium. On 25th March the European woman disembarked from the train at Tsim Sha Tsui Station, carrying a suitcase. Leung was in a stationary taxi at the front of the station. For reasons not stated in the reports, Revenue Officer Browne had become suspicious of Boys and followed her out of the station. When he approached her, she explained that she was being met by Leung, and went over to that woman's taxi and climbed in. Insp. Browne demanded to see the contents of the suitcase, and, observing the opium there, arrested both women. At the court, Leung was represented by her solicitor who explained that although she knew Boys, there was confusion as to whether there had been any arrangement to meet, the implication being that Boys had happened to see her, and clutched at the excuse to get away in the other woman's taxi. However, Police Inspector Lane intervened at this point. He knew that Boys had, some years earlier, been certified as feeble-minded, and asked Mr Wynne-Jones to order an examination into her mental state. When she had been read the charge, Boys replied, "The opium does not belong to me. I did not know it as opium, otherwise I wouldn't have

91 *Hongkong Daily Press,* 26th August 1915.
92 *Hongkong Telegraph,* 26th March & 3rd April 1934.

carried it." Insp. Lane was of the opinion that she had been duped into carrying it.

The magistrate acceded to the inspector's request, and placed Boys under medical observation for a week in the hospital at Lai Chi Kok Prison. Meanwhile, Leung's solicitor agreed bail of $5,000 for his client. Boys forfeited any arrangements she might have had for Easter that year. On Easter Tuesday, Dr Mackie, in charge of the prison hospital, and with a private practice in Kowloon, told the magistrate that he had known the woman for the past year. Having kept watch on her mental state and had various conversations with her over the last seven days, it was his opinion that she was not able to understand "the nature and results of her actions." She was promptly discharged and since there was no evidence against Leung but from Boys, this lady, too, was pronounced free to leave.

Nothing more has come to light about Mrs J. Boys from a trawl through the various records of the time. Where did she come from or what happened to her? Was there a Mr J. Boys? And what did she make of her rather sad story being made so public? Ignorance of what she was carrying did, indeed, protect her from prosecution, but, in the small expatriate world of Hong Kong, at quite a price.

Forgery
Alongside offences involving gambling and opium, another crime could strike more directly at the stability of the colony. Money, both coinage and notes, had always been a complex matter, ever since the early colony had adopted the silver 'Mexican' dollar as its currency. This coin was widely accepted throughout the east and beyond. The major banks had warrants to print paper money from the government and these were the only notes that were legal tender in Hong Kong. But since the average male annual wage for a labourer or similar was between $90 and $140, coins were the money of the ordinary people – foreign as well as Chinese.[93]

---

93 For example, in 1920 a messenger in the Imports and Exports Dept was paid $11 a month but those in the Colonial Secretary's Office just $9 a month. A good wage for a trained, but lower grade clerk in Government service was from $40-60 a month, and there are many examples of Chinese, Portuguese and western men employed at this wage.

Until 1912 Chinese coins – including the very low denomination 'cash', were widely accepted. But in 1911, with the revolution in China and the overthrow of the old order, this currency had fallen dramatically in value and Governor May had to suspend its use within Hong Kong. But aside from the problem of the circulation other jurisdictions' currencies, coins, especially the lowest value ones, as well as some Chinese banks' notes, presented another problem – they were just too easy to copy.

One of the earliest forgery cases involving a woman was that of nineteen-year-old Chan So when at her Magistracy appearance on 20th October 1913 she was charged with the possession of and uttering (putting into circulation) forged Kwangtung (Guangdong) five-dollar government bank notes.[94] Infuriatingly, the accounts of the trials – for this case went to the sessions – give detail about the jury empanelled, but little about the way the investigation had been conducted or the nature of the evidence called. This young woman had been caught selling a few of the 110 notes in her possession to another woman by a Chinese police sergeant. However, she was unaware that the notes had been marked and their journey had been traced. At the Magistracy she claimed that she had been given them to dispose of as best she could by a man of her acquaintance. The trail, though, proved that the notes had been passed on by a series of women before coming to her. No one else with any involvement was called, and there was little evidence presented, if the reports are to be believed. The prosecution considered that she certainly knew them to be duds, since she was trying to sell them for just fourteen cents each. Yet, when the jury returned after a short absence, they declared her to be not guilty of the crime.

Perhaps they felt that the girl had been taken in by others, a defence frequently put forward. Li Hang-yee, who went to gaol for six months after being found with rolls of forged ten- and five-cent coins had told the magistrate that she had been given them by a man she did not know, and asked to carry them.[95] Ng Wai-fong had the same story when a Chinese detective stopped her in the street in Shamshuipo.[96] He had her under

94 *Hongkong Daily Press,* 21st October 1913.

95 *Hongkong Telegraph,* 29th November 1932.

96 *Hongkong Telegraph,* 5th February 1936.

observation and noticed that she had arranged a shawl to rather obviously conceal something she was holding under her arm. This bundle proved to contain 210 rather crude zinc forgeries of ten-cent coins. She had been promised a few ten-cent coins by her 'unknown man' for carrying them to a certain Kowloon street: instead she had to do hard labour in Lai Chi Kok for four months.

Others were a little more devious. Three married women tried to go on a shopping spree with their ten-cent forgeries.[97] The owner of a sweet shop refused to accept the coins, so they went into a cake shop, unaware that the confectioner had followed them, and then alerted a constable. As they emerged – reports did not say whether they had acquired any cakes – the policeman arrested them. On their way to the Station, Leung Ying tried to throw away a bag with nine more such coins, but the officer intercepted her. There was only direct evidence against this one woman – she had tried her luck in the sweet shop – so only she was sent to prison for a month. The next year Tae Kee had two forged Straits Settlements notes and one dodgy ten-dollar Chartered Bank note when the police raided her flat in Hollywood Road.[98] Tae had no intention of making the constable's life easy, and put up a spirited struggle for the notes, biting his hand at one point. The accounts make no note of it, but part of the five months' hard labour she received was surely for her assault of the policeman.

Towards the end of the 1930s the Magistracies in Central and Kowloon were knee-deep in such cases. The papers carried news of only a fraction of those prosecuted, so it can be assumed that, almost daily, women were charged, if not convicted, of such offences. This helps account for the huge rise in prison population during the decade. The Japanese had overrun much of southern China – Canton would fall in October 1938 and Hong Kong was already flooded with refugees, many in piteous states of destitution. As the head of the Police Force had written in his 1936 report, "…unemployment was high …Hong Kong [had] a large number of persons desperate for a means of livelihood. Sheer poverty drove many

---

97 *Hongkong Telegraph,* 7th December 1932.
98 *Hongkong Sunday Herald,* 26th November 1933.

to theft".[99] As the situation deteriorated, all crimes increased, including that of forgery. Many such cases involved just a few counterfeit five- or ten-cent pieces – deception just to make ends meet. But some saw the possibility of larger-scale ventures, masked by the mass of crime going on around.

A former Canton tax collector, 59-year-old Ip Fook and his 35-year-old concubine, Lau King, lived at No. 17 Wanchai Road in November 1940.[100] Various information the police received led Det. Insp. W. N. Darkin to raid that flat and a cubicle in nearby Canal Road. He found a suitcase in the second flat, containing a large number of forged notes purporting to come from banks in the USA and China, as well as Hong Kong. At first each tried to put the responsibility and blame on the other, then both denied any knowledge of it, then finally the woman said that a friend they knew from Canton had left the suitcase. By the time of the couple's Sessions appearance later in the month, the police had uncovered nothing more. Believing that the woman was probably under the influence of the man and thus less culpable, Sir Atholl MacGregor sent her to prison for eight months but her husband received twelve months' hard labour. Both would have completed their sentences just before the fall of Hong Kong and the beginning of its occupation by the brutal Japanese forces.

Throughout its history, Hong Kong's position as the fastest-growing international commercial centre in the east had inevitably brought detriments alongside the many benefits. One such was that it had attracted more than its fair share of large-scale fraud cases. Usually these were directed against the banks or insurance firms. None have yet come to light which feature women in active roles – the nearest to such is perhaps the Monteith case, which appears in Chapter 10.

New times, new crimes

Throughout the years before the Second World War, the magistrates' days continued to be well-stocked with charges specific to Hong Kong and

---

99 *Report of the Inspector General of Police for the Year 1936,* Administrative Reports, 9th April 1937.

100 *Hongkong Daily Press,* 5th and 21st November 1940.

its situation. Often no criminal intent – they had just been caught out blocking roadways or pavements; for selling wares from a tray or box at the roadside, but without either enough time or profit to get a licence; for mooring up their sampan in a prohibited area; or for setting their rickshaw down to have a rest in the midday heat at a place that was not an authorised stop. But other infractions, that Hong Kong had not seen but were common in western cities, began to appear on the courts' case lists. One such was the offence of soliciting. The nature of prostitution in the colony meant that sex-workers were not on the streets, and any journey a brothel inmate might make beyond the house was purely private, as she went for a walk or visited shops or friends. This crime only appears on the annual *Police Statistics* from the 1920s and, although the numbers were always very low, reports occasionally appear in the press.

Mary Howard, who hailed originally from Spain, was well known to the police in Wanchai during the mid-1920s, for being too frequent a visitor to its hostelries.[101] Wanchai had always been a mixed area, with both working-class British, Portuguese, Americans and others living there, along with many Chinese – shopkeepers, small business people, craftsmen, clerks, etc. The area naturally had its share of brothels and bars, but this was long before the days of Suzie Wong and the nightclubs. Neither was it the main magnet for sailors of many nationalities freshly disembarked from their ships and with money to burn. The police had recently convicted two seamen of assaulting a respectable lady in a Wanchai street, and were being particularly vigilant to stop this becoming any norm. It was unfortunate for Howard, therefore, that the nice gentleman she offered her services to was plain-clothes officer, Sgt Hallam. Seeing his opportunity of securing a conviction, he allowed her to incriminate herself, so it was not until her hand encountered his revolver that she realised his identity. She called out to warn her amah, who was close by. This woman took revenge on the man for tricking her mistress, making quite a mess of his face with her nails and even pulling out some of his hair. At the Magistracy the next morning, Howard had to pay a $30 fine for soliciting and another of $10 for her amah's assault on the policeman.

---

101 *Hongkong Telegraph*, 1st April 1924.

Such decoying of potential suspects was routine during these decades, and they targeted women of non-British appearance.

In another case, nineteen-year-old Mercedes Garcia, who said that she was from Mexico, met a lance corporal from the Somerset Regiment in Queen's Road East.[102] That Monday evening she had proposed "a little walk towards Happy Valley" and told him that this would cost three dollars. The soldier, in civilian clothes, had no doubt of what she meant, but was recognised by some members of the Military Police before the couple had gone very far. At the Central Magistracy the next morning, Garcia, charged with soliciting, had brought a witness with her, but this woman contradicted her story at almost every point. Whether the military authorities fined or punished the soldier is not recorded, but the magistrate was not interested in sorting out the woman's story, and swiftly imposed a month in gaol or a $50 fine on her. She paid the latter immediately. Most of the small number of cases found of this nature involve a European or American woman.

This next example, with a Chinese protagonist, suggests that these women came off rather worse than their western counterparts. At about 11 p.m. one evening in October 1933, Yeun Kam approached two soldiers of the Lincolnshire Regiment in Nathan Road.[103] Private Johnston continued walking back to his barracks, but Private Allenby got into conversation with the woman and allowed himself to be led to a piece of rough ground. The newspaper reports are unsurprisingly reticent about the details of events, but the man realised that his partner was removing money from his purse. He pushed her roughly. He denied having hit her, but her lip split and started bleeding. However, Yeun had prepared herself for this eventuality and blew a police whistle. A constable arrived and took both to Mongkok Police Station. The soldier claimed that she had stolen 60 cents, but could not prove this. At court the next morning the magistrate dismissed this part of the story, but fined Yeun $50 for soliciting. Allenby did not incur any penalty, even though the constable confirmed that Yeun's mouth was bleeding when he found her, and the soldier was running away from the scene.

---

102 *Hongkong Telegraph,* 17th September 1929.
103 *Hongkong Telegraph,* 23rd October 1933.

The justice meted out to Mary Johnson, if it was that, was equally rough.[104] Described as a "coloured girl", she had met a plain-clothes police sergeant, William Hillyer, on the Praya East one June evening in 1922. Each said that the other had spoken first, asking where they were going. Johnson admitted that she had been a prostitute, but had given that up some ago and had made application to work for the Telephone Company and was living with her mother meanwhile. She had spoken to the policeman because he had addressed her by name, "Where are you going, Mary?" Why did she reply to that? "Well, I couldn't be rude. I didn't know he wanted to 'fix' me!" The pair had, it seems, led each other on, each suggesting various hotels, until they had reached the Post Office, where Sgt Hillyer told her to get off the tram, and then arrested her. The magistrate did not give her any assistance to change her life, by fining her $25 or giving her the option of 14 days in gaol.

Other new offences seen by the magistrates had to do with social developments that had been debated with a good deal of heat. Hong Kong was never behind in the adoption of new technology, and early car ownership was led by the governor himself, when Sir Henry May acquired one of the first cars, while there was still less than five miles of road suitable for such vehicles.[105] Private cars soon became a regular sight, and garages did a good trade in hire cars, with or without drivers as Chinese and westerners alike embraced the possibilities of motor transport with enthusiasm. Another period of energetic road-building followed, but in the wake of all this, the list of casualties and fatalities grew rapidly, as a population used to man-drawn vehicles as the norm, with the trams as the apogee of fast transport encountered vehicles that might move at reckless speeds – even as fast as 25 m.p.h. on occasions. Licensing, both of drivers and vehicles soon followed, and it was not long before

---

104 *China Mail*, 9th June 1922.

105 Sir Francis Henry May, b. Dublin 1860, d. Canada, 1922. Henry May was another Civil Service Cadet, one of the few who became fluent in both Cantonese and Mandarin and the first to become Governor of Hong Kong. His lasting legacy was as head of the Police Force, from 1893-1902, which he purged of corrupt elements and put on a professional footing. As Governor, he battled with Colonial Office opinion, but was viewed with approval by most in the colony, where he developed infrastructure and negotiated the difficult relationships with unsettled China.

women joined the ranks of drivers. They do not feature prominently in the numbers convicted of driving offences. Those that do appear are often learner drivers, stopped for being on roads – such as those around the Peak and Pokfulam that were prohibited to them, considered unsafe for inexperienced motorists. More occasionally, as happened to the woman who turned into Waterloo Road apparently without giving way to a car already there, a charge was brought by a fellow motorist for some breach of driving etiquette. Miss Jorge caused actual harm, putting a Chinese workman in hospital for a week, with severe bruises and shock.[106] He was spreading sand at one side of a Kowloon road when the woman lost control and swerved across the carriageway and into him. Her excuse was that a toy yacht, on the passenger seat, had fallen down and she was trying to put it back. Jorge incurred no fine for driving without due care but had to compensate the man by paying his wages for the days he had spent in hospital. Had she been a Chinese male defendant, the punishment would have been a substantial fine.

STUDEBAKER's NEW COMMANDER EIGHT REGAL SEDAN — *Six wire wheels, folding luggage grid, hydraulic shock absorbers and ball-bearing spring shackles, standard equipment.*

Studebaker sedan in Hongkong Sunday Herald, *7th July 1929.*

An earlier traffic accident had found the police displaying distinct partiality towards a western woman and of her receiving very light treatment at the Magistracy. Not long after midday on Wednesday 29th February 1928, Miss Grace Gale was driving her open-topped two-seater

106 *China Mail,* 31st August 1934.

car on what were still quiet country roads.[107] In itself, this would have been a sight to make the locals stop and stare – only a handful of western women, mainly police wives, lived this far north. Gale, accompanied by her amah, had left her Hollywood Road home and crossed the harbour on the Yaumatei Vehicle Ferry. Now she was bowling along, towards the junction of the Tai Po Road and Nam Cheong Street, where she needed to turn.

Soon, though, they became even more of a 'sight'. Traffic was very light on these roads, and no witnesses came forward to explain what happened next, but the two women found themselves some five or six yards off the road and in a small, muddy pond. Unable to back out of it, and with water seeping in, they both got out and tried to push the vehicle, with unfortunate results. The amah got a certain amount of mud on her clothes, but Gale apparently lost her balance and went down. By the time she regained her footing, she was fairly well covered in mud and pondweed. Fortunately for the women, the Governor's A. D. C, Captain F. G. Sillitoe, R.M., passed by, perhaps on horseback or motorcycle. He could not find out from them if there were any injuries, but told them that he would send the police along to help. The new Shamshuipo Police Station was less than two miles away, so he had soon reported that a European lady had suffered a motor accident and might be hurt.

Gale was sitting at the wheel of the car when Sub-Inspector Hoare arrived on the scene. Perched on the hood, the amah sat with her feet on the seat, since the floor was submerged. Insp. Hoare asked Gale if she was hurt, wouldn't she like to go to hospital? But the woman insisted that she was uninjured. She did want the police to get the car out of the water though. More officers were arriving, including Sgts Baysting, Mair and Tyler. Gale repeated her request to Sgt Tyler, but the accident had broken one of the front wheels, and the car would have to be hauled out by a garage. She then instructed the officer to send a message to the Peninsula Garage to come to attend to it. Noting that her speech seemed "unusual" – suspiciously thick – he returned to the station to call them. Insp. Hoare asked her how it had happened. "I haven't the faintest idea," she answered.

---

107 *Hongkong Daily Press,* 13th & 21st March 1928, *Hongkong Telegraph,* 21st March 1928.

"Please, Miss Gale, won't you let us take you to hospital or at least back to the station," he suggested. "Don't be so damned officious," was all the reply he got. But eventually she allowed herself to be taken back to the station in Sgt Baysting's sidecar. Two men had to assist her into it and then support her at the other end. She gave the police the impression of being unsteady and confused. The English papers ignore the fate of the amah who, presumably, followed her mistress. Five European officers and more would not have turned out to rescue even a high-born Chinese woman.

Insp. Hoare and other officers had privately thought that Gale was the worse for alcohol. But she was obviously also upset and shocked. She was mumbling incoherently all the while and did not seem aware of her condition. Sgt Tyler escorted her into the station and thought her condition "pitiable". When asked later what he meant by this, he said that she seemed to be under the influence of drink. However, he asked his colleague, Sgt Mair, if it might be advisable to give her some brandy to steady her. They decided to see if it improved things, and she seemed a little better after it. The spacious new station had married quarters apartments on the top storey. One of the wives was called upon to help, and the woman was shown upstairs, where the inspector's wife ran a bath for her. This lady put her clothes in the drying room and arranged for clean clothes to be brought over from Gale's home. She was given use of a bedroom until these should arrive. Meanwhile, officers had called Dr Newton from Kowloon Civil Hospital, and he arrived at 3.30 p.m. and spent about 30 minutes with the woman. Gale was in bed and refused to either be examined or to go to hospital. She insisted that she was uninjured, although the doctor could see a large bruise on her arm. He found her very emotional and her speech very thick and indistinct. He had the impression that she was intoxicated, certainly to an extent that she would be incapable of driving safely. He could smell alcohol on her. Clutching at his sleeve, she repeatedly thanked him, and "everyone". As he left the bedroom, he found Sub-Insp. Smith waiting in the corridor for him. Had she been injured, he wanted to know? After more discussion, he phoned through to Central Station for instructions, this outlying station being unaccustomed to hosting intoxicated European women.

He was told that he should warn her that the police would charge her with driving while under the influence of alcohol.

It was fully two weeks before the case was heard, but the papers made no reference to the unusual delay. At the hearing, Gale's solicitor, Mr D. H. Blake, was determined to have the charge quashed. Insp. Smith led the prosecution and had six colleagues give evidence about the events of the afternoon. But Mr Blake continued to insist that his client had no case to answer – the police had not seen her driving, nor had they brought any witnesses to that effect. The doctor had not mentioned smelling alcohol on her as part of his evidence-in-chief, but just in his explanation of her condition. The solicitor maintained that the confusion she displayed would be quite consistent with a nervous woman who had experienced such an accident. He snapped down any attempt of the officers to say that Gale was hysterical. "All the witnesses have put in a lot of irrelevancies, which are all to the detriment of my client," he told the magistrate at the Kowloon court. Insp. Smith reminded the court that either Gale or the amah must have driven the car at some point. It was registered in Gale's name and she had a licence. The magistrate sided with the police for a considerable time. The fact that they found the woman sitting in it, and in the driving seat, showed that she was in charge of it. But Mr Blake continued to argue, and eventually won the day, the magistrate reluctantly agreeing that there was no proven case against her. The papers recorded that the solicitor had not even had to produce a defence.

CHAPTER 4

THE CHANGING FACE OF CRIME, 1920-1941

The world was changing around Hong Kong in the early part of the 20th century and the role of women was shifting from passive recipient to actor. In many countries women were asserting the legitimacy of this through suffrage and equal rights campaigns. Since it had no elected governance, it was not surprising that this British colony saw no such demonstrations. Trade unions might be getting more vociferous but the work that women in the colony did was almost completely un-unionised. Equal pay was not even on the agenda. Hong Kong's share in the changing status of women might be very modest, but it nonetheless displays some little kinship with developments elsewhere in the world. Women in the USA and Ireland were leading the way in active support of other political aims and were unafraid of direct action. In Hong Kong some of the support given to the revolutionary aims of the activists was coerced, but some was willingly given. Arguably, their involvement in such subversive plans challenged the judiciary's established patriarchal response to most of the women who stood in the dock before them. The courts witnessed a small but growing number of cases where women were found in possession of weapons of various types and number.[108] But, with arms flooding into southern China, they were as available to political agitators as to those with 'purely' criminal intent, so it is usually impossible to tell if these women were attached to revolutionaries or gangsters.

---

108 Cases of this natures were prosecuted under the *Arms and Ammunition Ordinance, No. 2 of 1900* and its various amendments. Possession was here seen to presume guilt, and it became that the burden was more on the defendant to demonstrate innocence than for the prosecution to prove nefarious intent.

The Supreme Court, Library of Congress collection.

Arms, ammunition and bombs

One of the earliest such cases concerned the woman fined ten dollars in 1912 for possession of 500 rounds of ammunition.[109] Presumably this had not been a random 'find' by the police, but the papers give no further details, nor is there comment about the relatively small punishment. Such cases were common, although more usually with male defendants. The unsettled state of China meant that the colony, whilst not awash with unregistered weapons, had far more than in the previous decades. Information uncovered by the Chinese detectives attached to Wanchai Police Station had led Inspector Sim to search No. 4 McGregor Street, near Wanchai Market on 30th March 1917.[110] Here he found a large quantity of potassium chlorate, which, if mixed with sugar, would make enough explosive for four or five bombs. Insp. Sim and his men also found bomb cases and a large bullet destined for an explosive device, hidden in various bags and cupboards in the house. The woman whose home it was and who was ultimately charged, claimed first that the cook from the *S.S. Ecuador* gave her these bags, then that she did not know who had put them in her house. The next day the woman was committed to stand trial at the next sessions – but there the trail ends. It seems that

109 *Hongkong Telegraph*, 22nd November 1912.
110 *Hongkong Telegraph*, 4th April 1917.

the case was not pursued, with no mention of her at either the April or May sittings.

Later that year, Mr Melbourne heard the case of two boatmen and a boatwoman, in whose sampan a rifle, two pistols and 500 rounds of ammunition hidden in burlap bags had been found by the Water Police.[111] The three had hired a defence lawyer, Mr F. X. d'Almada, who explained that they had taken these bags on board in good faith, not knowing what they contained. Magistrate Melbourne was satisfied that there was no criminal intent and discharged the men, but the woman, who held the licence for the boat, he fined $50 for having neglected to ascertain what she was agreeing to carry. In most cases a woman's possession of weapons did not imply that she had any plans for using them herself, but that she was a convenient depository for their owner, who remained uncaught. The women always claimed not to know their donors, and there were too many such cases for the police to watch the houses for the visit of the weapons' owners. It was all that could be done that the police removed the arms from circulation and made an attempt to instil into the population – especially that afloat – that it was not worth the risk to hide a package.

By the early 1920s anti-British action by groups in Canton and southern China had escalated and these cases were appearing at the courts on a near-daily basis and further measures were called for to address the problem. The powers available to the Imports and Exports Department helped the police efforts here. The Revenue section of that, formed in the first years of the century, employed many former police detectives and had as part of its remit the discovery and confiscation of illegal drugs, smuggled coins and notes, and arms and ammunition. Ensuring that dutiable cargo went through the proper channels when landed helped ameliorate the loss of government revenue when it finally had to relinquish the sale of opium to China. Its officers had the power to search any vessel coming into Hong Kong waters. Former policeman, now Chief Preventative Officer, Samuel Clarke had rather a successful Sunday evening in February 1927, arresting two female sampan owners

111 *China Mail,* 7th May 1917.

amongst others.[112] The lowest regions of one boat had yielded four brand new Mauser pistols with accompanying magazines and 700 rounds of ammunition, whilst in the other he had found no less than 12,000 rounds, stowed away in five bags and well hidden from view. The first (unnamed) woman had engaged a solicitor to speak for her at the police court. Hers was the usual defence: she had not known what was in the bag when a man gave it to her to keep till he returned for it. She had conveyed him from another boat to the shore and the man paid her eight dollars for this. The solicitor was keen to stress that she had lived in Hong Kong all her life and had had no brush with the law before. It was natural, he said, that she would not think to ask about the bag's contents. But the magistrate disagreed. Given that such a ride, even with a bag, would probably warrant a fare of twenty cents or so, she must have been at least curious when the man offered so large a sum. The woman from the second sampan also claimed to have no idea of the identity of the owner of the bullets or that she had been carrying anything illegal. Both were sentenced to six months' imprisonment with hard labour and not given the option of paying a fine in lieu.

Amongst the various reports of this nature, there are a few rare instances when the magistrate was prepared at least to give the benefit of the doubt to the defendant. Although the ordinance under which these cases were brought loaded the dice against them, sometimes the word of the person in the dock did have the ring of truth to it, in the judge's opinion. Such a case, which resulted in a forerunner of a suspended sentence, was that of a young woman, the second concubine of Tam Koon Lin, a member of the crew of one of the Empress Line boats.[113] At the end of May 1932, while she was walking along Nathan Road, the woman had met a man, Wong, known to her and her husband. He had asked her if she would have room in her cubicle in Chee Woo Street to store two boxes for him. "Boxes of what?" she had wanted to know. "Oh, nothing important," Wong had replied. "Just some medicines." She had agreed and a little later Wong and a friend of his had arrived with two boxes that slid neatly under the bed in her room.

---

112 *Hongkong Daily Press,* 19th February 1927.
113 *Hongkong Daily Press,* 11th June 1932.

She had thought no more about them until on 4th June, when she was with some friends in the nearby Nathan Hotel, the hotel manager and a senior-looking police officer approached her party. To her puzzlement, Detective Sub-Inspector Archibald Elston asked her to lead him back to her house, and to show him which was her cubicle. She led him up the stairs to the first floor and was still more surprised to find the door open and another British policeman standing in the middle of the room, apparently guarding the boxes, which had been pulled out. Insp. Elston, the older policeman, said to her in Cantonese, "If you do not want to speak, you do not have to speak." She wasn't too sure what he meant by this, but he seemed keen that she should understand, so she said that she did. He then asked her again if this was her cubicle. "Yes, it is," she replied. "And do you own everything in it?" "Yes, of course, well, apart from those two boxes. They belong to a couple of men I know, they'll be back to collect them soon, I think." Insp. Elston asked her more about the men and she told them what she could – not that she knew much beyond their names. The younger policeman then opened the boxes, and to her surprise, in place of the bottles and powdered herbs she had expected there were four pistols, a huge amount of ammunition – later counted as 1,050 rounds – and various parts and attachments for the guns. The policemen registered her real astonishment, but told her that she would have to come with them as they were arresting her because she had these guns and bullets in her cubicle.

She was allowed to contact her husband, who then arranged for her to have legal representation. Because of the grave view that the Administration took of this offence, there was no chance of her being granted bail and after a brief appearance before the magistrate she had a few uncomfortable days in Lai Chi Kok. Tam Koon Lin did well by her by securing the services of Mr A. el Arculli, a well-respected solicitor. At the trial on 10th June, he challenged the police inspector on several points. Why had he not taken an interpreter? Had he been sure that the defendant had understood the caution? Well, he thought so. Had she been open and frank with them throughout the time she was with them? Insp. Elston had to agree that she had. The door to her cubicle had not been locked – did that not suggest that she had no knowledge of what really lay hidden beneath her bed? Had the police tried to trace the men who she said had left the box? The inspector admitted that they had not.

The evidence given by Mr el Arculli and the demeanour and responses of the young woman herself had satisfied the magistrate, Mr Fraser, that this was no ordinary case. "Taken as a whole," he said, "I feel that although under the Ordinance as it is, I must convict this woman, but I do not propose to impose any penalty." "That is most unusual, Your Worship," expostulated the inspector. "It is unusual," responded Mr Fraser, and Insp. Elston had to be content with that. The magistrate then told the woman that she would have to find $200, and would be bound over for that amount for twelve months. He explained to her she would then come before him again, and that the case would be dismissed if there were no further charges against her. One imagines that the implications of this – together with the fact that the amount required had been set surprisingly low, given the type of offence – would have been made clear to her by her solicitor, once outside the courtroom.

But questions remain. The press reports give no idea of how Insp. Elston and his colleagues became aware of the presence of the boxes in the cubicle. They had come to No. 5 Chee Woo Street that evening and gone up to the first floor. The principal tenant of that floor, the woman from whom Tam's concubine rented the space, had led them to the right cubicle, but there was no suggestion that she knew of anything amiss. The defendant had given them the names of the men who had left the contraband, but the police had not followed this up. Surely, either Tam or perhaps the friends she was with in the Nathan Hotel that evening might have known more of those responsible. The case gives the impression of being one where the police felt that they were sure of a conviction and had confiscated a quantity of weapons so saw no reason to pursue the matter further.

A changing China

Strikes and boycotts, which often gained wide support amongst workers, were nothing new in Hong Kong. Following the plague of 1894, the enforcing of by-laws concerning lodging houses was seen as an infringement of liberty by dockworkers, whose strike brought the harbour to a standstill until the police and troops were called in to clear the backlog. In 1912-3, the labouring classes had boycotted the trams and other public transport when the Governor had asked the tram companies to refuse low-denominated Canton coins, because of the great devaluation of Chinese currency. It was not just supporters of the uprisings in China that felt this to be a slur on the new Republic, and the boycott was very severe. It was broken with the help of many influential men of the Chinese community, who saw the deleterious impact this would have on trade in both jurisdictions.

The growing strength of the revolutionary Kuomintang government in Canton saw renewed agitation against foreign trading within China.[114] What it regarded as the overly favourable conditions accorded to such powers, especially Britain and Japan, came in for particular assault. In June 1925, the armed response of British- and French-commanded troops in Shamian, Canton, to an anti-foreign demonstration, left over 50 Chinese protestors dead. After this, the general turmoil in southern China, the splitting of the leftist party, and support from Russian-led Bolsheviks finally spilt over into Hong Kong. Those working for westerners, dockworkers, students and Tram Company employees were amongst the first to down tools, and a general strike soon spread. Inspired in part by rumours of dire British retaliation, over a quarter of a million Chinese had left for Canton by the end of July 1925, and normal life had almost collapsed.

Once more, Hong Kong's efforts to maintain the fabric of colony life were supported and very substantially aided by the Chinese bourgeoisie (merchants, bankers and men of independent means) who built a volunteer force to counteract the subversive activity of the strike-leaders. The strike-boycott, which saw a sudden rise in the price of foodstuffs and threatened all trade, hit the labouring Chinese hardest. The small businessmen, unskilled workers and those with fewest resources were predictably the worst affected. The strikers used intimidation and extortion

---

114 An accessible and fascinating account of this lesser-known part of Hong Kong's history is found in Chapter 6, *Preserving Hong Kong: The Strike-Boycott of 1925-1926*, in Carroll, *Edges of Empire*, to which I am particularly indebted.

to prevent those who had fled to Canton from returning, but the Chinese city was awash with 'refugees', and many endured real hardship there. By the beginning of 1926, the tide was turning and Hong Kong was functioning almost as usual. There were strenuous 'propaganda' efforts made, trying to report truthfully events both in Canton and Hong Kong, whilst ensuring that the latter compared favourably, in terms of stability, prosperity and the rule of law, to the former.

The race-course bomb plot

To read the English newspapers of the day, it would appear that all Hong Kong only had eyes and ears for the Jockey Club Race meeting in the first days of March 1926.[115] As in other years, huge crowds attended, with all those who could raise the $3 entrance fee for the public enclosure crowding in. Those without sufficient funds secured good positions for themselves around the edges of the course or perhaps on the rising ground on either side. The Club allowed members to bring two guests into their sacred space and there was much polite manoeuvring for this privilege from friends of the fortunate few. Businesses shut their doors, courts sat in the mornings only, the Exchange closed and even that institution of Hong Kong life, Watsons, ceased trading for three days and was open only for the dispensing of prescriptions in the early evening. The highlight of the whole meeting was, of course, the Hong Kong Derby, on 2nd March, and the favourite, both with the bookies and the general public, had to be Glorious Dahlia, owned by Sir Paul Chater. He was one of the founding fathers of the Jockey Club – and so much else – and perhaps the most simultaneously powerful and beneficent man in the colony. This, though, was to be his last Derby, for he died just two months later, aged 79.

Unbeknownst to the thousands there to see Glorious Dahlia romp home to the honours, police intervention in the nick of time had prevented the ground becoming a scene of carnage, albeit not on the scale of the disastrous 1918 fire. Although later that month the papers held the story of how a terrorist attack had been foiled, perhaps only a fraction of the English-language readers of the trial understood what had

115 All the newspapers report this most important social and sporting event, e.g. *Hongkong Telegraph,* 2nd March 1926.

been averted, so little was this aspect stressed. The case attracted much wider interest amongst the Chinese reading public, however, aware of what they escaped.

The discovery, by Principal Chinese Detective Lai Shui, of two six- or seven-pound cast iron bombs, full of granite chippings and destined to be thrown into the Derby Day crowds, came as the strike-boycott was running out of momentum. Activist cells in Canton and Shum Chun (Shenzhen) plotted to start another major strike in Hong Kong, to begin on Chinese New Year, 13th February 1926. However, there was no longer sufficient appetite there, and it failed to attract support. Thereafter, more direct action was planned, with at least twelve bombs imported into the colony for detonation in various locations. But the Police Force, and particularly the Chinese of the recently formed Criminal Investigation Department were on their mettle, and had been aided and spurred on by the secretive Labour Protection Bureau. They were adroit at tracking down these threats, so much so that only one bomb, at Hung Hom, was thrown.[116]

The police were following the movements of many suspected activists and one particular man came to their notice during those Race days.[117] He had lived for many years in the colony, where his life had been the uneventful one of a fitter, perhaps in an engineering company. But at the end of December 1925, he was laid off, when his firm was struggling with the effects of the disruption to trade. He had taken himself off to Shum Chun and there fallen in with a group which included the 'leading spirit' of those determined to throw the 'foreign devils' out of China. Attached to that circle was a singing girl, who had formerly been betrothed to one member. She had lately been kept by a man in Canton, but now had to earn her living as best she could. It was this group who devised the plan to cause terror through sporadic bomb attacks.

The group acquired bombs with iron casings, multiple explosives and shrapnel-like contents. So volatile were these that they needed no detonator, simply throwing them from a height would be enough to

---

116 For example, the find reported in *The China Mail,* 13th March 1926.

117 The case is covered by *Hongkong Daily Press,* 22nd, 23rd & 31st March, 9th April 1926.

cause them to erupt. The Hong Kong man was shown how best to do this and practised on smaller, dummy, versions. But he could not hope to get back into Hong Kong with the bombs on him. First, there would be the picket line to get past at the border, where questions from the strikers might raise suspicions of any British troops watching on the other side. Then, passengers and their luggage, coming by train from Canton, were routinely searched by the Hong Kong Police. So they proposed that the young woman would carry them down in a suitcase. By dint of travelling with an amah and dressing conservatively, she would appear respectable. Surely the police would not search a lady? The suitcase, a sturdy, good-looking leather one, added to the desired impression. She packed it with some of her own clothes, then added some of her former lover's that he had left with her. She had, or was given, $30, which would cover her fare and be enough money to pay off the picket men. Her own amah, whom she shared with some other girls, was not free to accompany her, so she engaged an older woman for the purpose, without telling her about the arrangements.

It was early on Tuesday 2nd March that the pair set out, with the bombs nestling between the clothes in the suitcase. The journey down to the border was straightforward, and $20 ensured their passage into Hong Kong. Their luck held on the train to Kowloon: police manpower was stretched and their train was one of those not searched that day. She was unfamiliar with Hong Kong, but the man had selected as a rendezvous a prominent cinema in Yaumatei, some way inland from the terminus building, but easy to find. Here he gave her the address of the boarding house on Hong Kong Island, where he had already booked a cubicle, and directed her to the ferry. They arranged that she would call there later on, perhaps taking a meal beforehand. He had not dared ask if she had brought the bomb he was to throw with her – in the crowded streets that had not seemed wise. The amah's presence was a surprise, since the last he had heard, the woman was coming down by herself, but there was nothing to be done about it. Anyhow, the old woman seemed unaware of what was being planned. He made his way back to the World Boarding House, near the new Western Market on Des Voeux Road. He had with him a rattan basket containing some clothes. On reaching the lodging house and giving his name, the attendant took the basket from him, as was customary, and showed him up to Cubicle No. 10 on the first floor. Here he dozed and slept, not expecting the women for some time.

He was cross to be disturbed by their arrival at 11.30 a.m. "Why have you come so early?" he asked. "I was afraid that the police might want to search the suitcase," she replied. She had dawdled for a little but then, perhaps losing her nerve, had followed the signs for the Yaumatei Ferry and then engaged a rickshaw to take them to the address. In the house lobby she asked to see the visitors' book. Pointing to the man's name, she told the attendant that this was the person she wanted to see. They were shown up to the first floor, but when the doorman made to carry the suitcase, the woman insisted that the amah should keep hold of it, a fact that stuck in his mind. Once by themselves, the woman said, "I have brought two 'things'." "Two!" exclaimed the man, "I have only promised to accept one. Why have you brought two?" "The second is for a man who will call for it later, about 1p.m." was the answer. Again, this was news to him. It would appear that he was already having misgivings, which only increased with this information. However, they proceeded as had they had planned, and in low voices discussed how to best transport 'the thing' to the racecourse. They decided that a 45-cent resealable tin of oatmeal would be just the right size to hold it snugly, with a little meal at the bottom and around the sides to stop it from rattling. They sent the amah out to make the purchase and borrowed a tin-opener from the house. When the amah returned, the man told her to sit on the verandah, while they prepared the tin. The opening proved slightly too small, but by cutting away the rim that would usually hold the detachable top, the bomb could slide in. They poured the excess oatmeal into a large handkerchief from the woman's suitcase, and once they were satisfied that the bomb was securely stowed, placed it on the couch and covered it with a shawl. The woman took the second bomb took out of the suitcase and reached for the rattan basket. "Slowly!" warned the man, nervous of any false move, despite knowing that it would take some considerable force to make it explode. Once they had covered it with the clothes he had brought, they pushed the basket and the suitcase under the couch. The amah was told that she could come back in. The man's resolve, such as it was, now deserted him completely. He declared that he was feeling poorly and was going out to get some medicine. Leaving suddenly, he took nothing with him. He did not buy medicine but crossed back over to Kowloon on the Yaumatei ferry, where he apparently just loitered aimlessly.

But while the couple had made their arrangements, the police kept the cubicle and their movements under observation. Earlier that morning, Principal Chinese Detective Lai Shui had taken rooms in the World Boarding House, one on the first floor, and one above. He stationed himself and a colleague on the second floor and left two other detective constables in Cubicle No. 14 and settled down to await developments. They observed the man leave and arranged for him to be discretely followed through the rest of the day. Shortly after that, one of his detectives spotted a uniformed constable and an officer from the Revenue Department approach the house, preparing to do a routine spot-check. Det. Lai slipped downstairs and explained to the men what was happening. He could use this inspection as an excuse to get into the cubicle. The attendant was instructed to rap on the door and ask them to open up as the Revenue people were there to check the house. There was no immediate answer, but they heard things being pushed around. Eventually, after a second knock, the bolt was drawn. The two sought to give the impression of unconcern as Det. Lai came in. The younger had just sat down at a small table while the amah was reclining on the couch, with a shawl behind her. Both ignored the detective when he instructed them to stand, so he pulled them up. As he questioned them, his colleagues discovered the oatmeal tin, the handkerchief full of oatmeal and the rattan basket and suitcase under the bed. He told both women he was arresting them for having bombs in their possession without a licence. Det. Lai then left them in the charge of his detective constables and went out to telephone C.I.D. headquarters. He had given strict instructions that everything was to remain just as it was until an inspector arrived. Sub-Inspector Fallon was soon on the scene with Det. Insp. Tim Murphy not far behind. He started the questioning – the younger woman was saying little, but the amah just seemed very confused and frightened. Det. Insp. Murphy had the impression that she knew little, perhaps nothing, of the matter.

The understated report of the arrest of the parties in the local English press might have attracted little attention, but the same cannot be said of the terror unleashed the following Wednesday.[118] The lunchtime crowds were dense near Hung Hom Market when the attack came. Just as dockworkers were making their way back to their jobs, an unknown hand threw a bomb into their midst. There had been no warning, and the dockers who were closest suffered the worst from the actual explosion. Splinters of hot metal came from the bomb and flew everywhere, with shards of sharp stone peppering faces and arms. Women going to the market and people who had just alighted from two motor buses nearby were hit and ran with bleeding faces away from the scene. Everywhere there was consternation and panic. No one could be sure which direction the bomb had come from as this had caught everyone off-guard. Both police and ambulance were soon on the scene and nine of the most severely injured were taken to hospital. The legs of one dockworker were so badly mangled that doctors had to amputate one. Despite their efforts he succumbed to his wounds the following day.

In the days that followed, extensive enquiries revealed little hard information. Posters appeared everywhere advertising large rewards for information – $1,000 if police made an arrest, or $250 if they found a live bomb as a result. But any intended victim or reason for the particular time and place remained a mystery.

The unrest in 1922 had prompted the Administration to issue a catch-all *Emergency Regulations Ordinance*.[119] Under this, temporary measures could be enforced to, for example, control sedition, censor the press, close the borders, prohibit trade union activity etc. This was still on the statute book in 1925, when the strike-boycott erupted, and it was further bolstered to meet the rising need. A regulation made by the Governor in Council on 6th July 1925 empowered two magistrates, sitting together, to impose punishments up to ten years with hard labour and floggings for breaches of the *Arms and Ammunition Ordinance*.[120] Thus they were

---

118 *Hongkong Telegraph,* 10th March 1926.

119 *Hongkong Government Gazette,* 28th February 1922, *Emergency Regulations Ordinance, No. 5 of 1922.*

120 *Hongkong Government Gazette,* 6th July 1925.

given the same powers as held by the Supreme Court in these cases. This allowed for swifter disposal of such volatile cases and obviated the need for such thorough evidence as required by the upper court.

Two magistrates, Mr R. E. Lindsell and Major C. Willson, heard the case in three sittings, spread over some seventeen days. On 22nd March the man's case was taken first, as the police had indicated that he would plead guilty. On that day only the amah had legal representation, and the unfamiliarity of court procedure to the other two was obvious. When Mr Lindsell, asked the man whether the bombs were in his cubicle with his knowledge and consent, he replied, "That is so," which the magistrate declared to be a guilty plea and they sentenced him to five years' imprisonment with hard labour. He was dismissed from the court. The prosecution, in the hands of the Director of Criminal Intelligence, Mr T. H. King, would, according to the press reports, later note that the man "had arranged matters so that the bomb did not explode." Whether this was known by the magistrates during their sentencing is unclear.

Then the case against the younger woman commenced. To the charge of being illegally in possession of bombs, she replied that she knew nothing about any of it. As the police's principal witness, the man returned and gave his account of events. The hearing was adjourned for a week while the police continued their investigations. The English-language papers had made little of the case, beyond reporting the trial. It had, however, attracted more attention amongst the Chinese community, and it may well have been through popular support that, at the second hearing, the young woman also had the services of solicitor Mr H. J. Armstrong.

At the opening of this session, the male prisoner was cross-examined by Mr Armstrong, but he threw the case into confusion by retracting all he had previously said which implicated the first woman. Yes, he did know her, but she had nothing to do with it. He had brought the bombs to the cubicle in the rattan basket. When asked why he had said that the woman brought the bombs, he replied, "I made the statement which implicated this woman under compulsion. She had nothing whatever to do with the bombs. I was the only man responsible for them. I implicated her because at that time I was under threats of assault." These threats, he said, had been made by the police. "Can you suggest why the police would want to get this woman into trouble?" asked the magistrate. The man could not enlighten him. Mr King, though, wanted to know more about these threats. " I would like to ask a question about 'assault'. I think he said the word 'beat'." The man came straight back. "No they did not beat me, they merely threatened to beat me if I refused to make a confession and as I could not stand the agony ..." Here he was interrupted by Mr Lindsell, and this line of questioning ended. When at the previous hearing he had been asked by Mr King if he had been afraid that the bombs might go off unexpectedly, he replied, "No, I don't dread death, but I had promised to carry out that job." He had then gone on to explain how the bombs were designed to explode only if thrown. There followed much discussion about the trail of events and the legitimacy or otherwise of the man's retraction of his statement.

The prison warders then returned him to gaol and the young woman now stood before the magistrates. She repeated that she did not know of any part of the plot. She had merely been on her way to Macao from Canton and had to stop a night in Shum Chun. If she had travelled directly she would have missed the last boat to Macao. At Hong Kong Station she had been met by a man, not the prisoner. This man had invited her to visit the prisoner, who was an old acquaintance, and he gave her the address of the boarding house. How was it he knew to meet that train? Well, they had arranged it some weeks earlier, and decided which train she would travel on. At the boarding house, she had not seen her amah leave the room at all, nor had she noticed the handkerchief with the cereal in it. She did not know that there were any bombs in the room, and she had not sent her amah out to buy oatmeal. The amah then gave evidence, and although the reports suggest that she was not asked very much, she did confirm that her mistress had sent her out to buy the tin of oatmeal, and that she had been out of the cubicle for some time, sitting on the verandah.

The magistrates were unconvinced by the man's retraction, although they admitted that a ruling on the case would be necessary. However, they believed that there was enough evidence to proceed against the first woman. On one point, though, all parties were agreed: that the amah had no share in any guilt here, and they discharged her at the final sitting, on

8th April. By that time she had spent over five weeks in gaol on remand. It seems more likely that well-wishers rather than official channels supplied her with her fare home and picket line money. The younger woman's solicitor, Mr Armstrong, tried to argue that she had no case to answer, since the evidence against her was primarily from the man's testimony. But there were other, albeit small, points against her, aside from the amah's testimony. The police had found a handkerchief, matching that used to hold the excess oatmeal, in her suitcase. The attendant confirmed that she had come with that suitcase, and she had keys that fitted it on her when she was taken into custody. The court found her guilty of being in possession of bombs and sentenced to four years' imprisonment with hard labour.

How far was she a knowing and willing accomplice? If the man's second testimony was true, and neither women had any share in this, how had they been 'set up' to go to very boarding house where the bomber had just engaged a room? How had he then explained the presence of the bombs to them? Was his retraction borne of a sense of guilt from leaving the women there with the bombs, to face the music alone? On the other hand, political action by women was being seen in China as the new Republic gained hold. Was her involvement with the activist cell in Shum Chun more than just a former attachment to one of the members? Did she share their conviction that the 'foreign devils' in Hong Kong needed to be driven out? Her accounts were fairly consistent but do not adequately explain her presence in the cubicle or her behaviour there. Or is the truth more prosaic, that she had, indeed, planned to go to Macao, and the fare and picket money had been in return for acting as courier. She had no connections to Hong Kong, it would be nothing to her if the bombs were used. She just had to meet up with two men, hand one over to each and then continue on her journey, taking advantage of a free passage to a new life in Macao.

In the tense atmosphere of the time, we should, perhaps, not be surprised to find a somewhat unrefined justice applied in the trials of politically motivated crimes. Equality before the law, that proud tenet of British justice, had a chequered history in the eighty-year history of Hong Kong's courts. It is fair to say, though, that it was more frequently seen in the rulings of career magistrates, with knowledge of the situation of local people born of long experience and usually a fluency in Cantonese, than from the bench of the Supreme Court. Mr Lindsell was one such, but these were strange times for the colony. Their sentencing of the man seems proportionate – he had, by his own admission, been part of a plot to wreak destruction on many people for political ends. He had thought better of his share of this, and "so arranged matters that the bomb did not go off", simply by leaving it in the cubicle with the women. He was a long standing resident in Hong Kong, but the women were strangers to Hong Kong. The police, even with what investigations they could make in Canton and Shum Chun had not found out who they were, and, of course, we do not learn their names. This 'otherness' may have set them apart and in the case of the younger woman, made her seem less deserving of the consideration that her gender and youth had given many in the lower courts before. The Hung Hom bomb was still fresh in everyone's memory, and the magistrates needed to send clear messages to activists in Canton and elsewhere in southern China. Those plotting to inflict injury on Hong Kong should not assume that the use of women accomplices and actors would mitigate punishment.

Whatever the woman's motives had been, spending four years in the cramped confines of the Women's Prison had not formed part of her plans when she travelled to Hong Kong. Perhaps the only relief she enjoyed was that as the prison's sole long-sentence female, she would occupy a cell to herself and have slightly increased rations. She would also be one of the very few women to benefit from the remission scheme, which was rather more generous for women than men. Her good behaviour throughout her sentence could earn her a reduction of eight months.

Heroin production and smuggling

Judging by the number of cases appearing before the courts connected with heroin, both the possession and smuggling thereof, its prevalence and popularity were a few years in arrears of the USA or Europe. But by 22nd March 1927, when the *S.S. Atsuta Maru* docked at Kowloon wharf, carrying Polish woman Helena Rogovi-Kumin, Hong Kong was becoming both a conduit for and a consumer of the drug.[121] The 32-year-old mother-of-two lived in Paris as Mrs Kamien and had a long-held ambition to see Japan. She had told some friends of this, and they had introduced her to a man there who had a proposition for her. She could have a free second-class passage to Kobe and fifty pounds sterling if she would take a particular trunk with her. This piece of luggage, she was told, belonged to a George Stanigross, who was in Japan and was anxious to have his possessions with him. There was nothing to worry about, the man assured her. All that it contained were just ordinary things, clothes, books, ornaments etc., but this was the easiest and safest way to get the items over to him, and he would meet her there. A letter then informed her of the arrangements made. The ship sailed from Marseilles, and she had to go there just before it was due to leave. She would meet a Japanese man, Mr Mansuri, in the Café Louvre-paix. How would she recognise him? Well, that would be easy. He was a small man and would wear blue spectacles and a blue suit. The meeting went smoothly. He handed over her ticket and came on board with her. In her cabin was the wardrobe trunk, of which Mr Stanigross would relieve her in Kobe. Mansuri agreed that it would be quite safe in the baggage room and be out of her way there.

Presumably the woman had a pleasant and unexceptional voyage. At Singapore she was surprised to receive a message that the Romanian, Stanigross, would be waiting for her on the quayside when they docked in Hong Kong a few days later. But this man, who had recently arrived in the colony from Shanghai, was the subject of some international police information, and was being kept under observation during those days. On the evening of 21st March, the ship dropped anchor in the harbour and he boarded the launch that went to meet it. Either then or earlier he booked a first-class cabin for himself for the rest of the voyage to Kobe. He met up with Kamien and took her arm for a stroll to a quiet part of the ship. He returned to shore later that evening but was on the quayside when the *Atsuta Maru* docked the next morning. It was the ship's officers, warned to watch and report on the movements of the couple, who saw

121 *China Mail,* 23rd March 1927, *Hongkong Telegraph,* 29th and 31st March 1927.

them meet and then return on board. Two Revenue Officers, Messrs Watt and Lanigan, as usual both former members of the Detective Branch, went first to the man's cabin and searched that. Stanigross, who had nothing there to conceal, was courteous and accommodating. Senior Revenue Officer Watt then went to Kamien's room, leaving his colleague to finish his search. When he asked her to open her cabin luggage, the woman said that she had handed over her keys to Stanigross, although no explanation of this was offered. Once he had the keys, R.O. Watt made a search and discovered a receipt for the wardrobe trunk in the baggage store.

Both were arrested upon suspicion of smuggling and taken, along with the trunk, to the wharf-side office of the Revenue Department. On the way, Stanigross tried to jump into the harbour, but accompanying police officers prevented his escape. The Revenue Officers had seen trunks of this description before, and went straight to the false back, which, when removed, proved to contain 700 taels of heroin, in 80 small packages. The main compartments of the trunk revealed a small set of carpenter's tools, presumably to allow for the removal of the back. The other contents explained how it was proposed to evade any closer examination of the luggage. The plan had been that the pair would carry the drugs off the boat on themselves, Kamien carrying the majority. Then, if checked in Kobe, the trunk would have had an innocently empty false back. She would wear four petticoats, one over the other, each of which was provided with small pockets, just large enough to fit one of the heroin packs. Those responsible for packing the trunk had left nothing to chance: even an unopened pack of safety pins had been slipped in, so the pockets could be secured. There were also two belts, described as girdles, which could be worn by either of the pair. Again, each came equipped with small pockets. If Kamien was unaware of the drug's presence, as seems likely, all this suggests a reason for Stanigross' apparent change of plan. He had to ingratiate himself sufficiently with her, so that she would agree to the subterfuge and wear the required costume.

The Government Analyst valued the heroin at $5,600 and he estimated there to be sufficient for 100,000 doses, each strong enough to kill a new or infrequent user. The pair were brought before the magistrate the next day, charged with possession of the drug and of importing it without a licence. The police had already encountered the problem of communication with them, especially with Stanigross, who had little English. But Hong Kong was an international port, and had a Russian-speaking solicitor, Mr F. G. Vaux, who was understood by both the defendants. He asked for an adjournment of two days, since there had been insufficient time to interview them properly. But the Police, Revenue Department and the Crown Solicitor would need longer to prepare the prosecution, said R. O. Watt, probably about a week. Mr Vaux discussed bail with the magistrate, although he suspected that neither client carried adequate funds, and so would pass the intervening period in prison. The severity with which the courts viewed the case can be seen in the amount required for bail – $10,000 each.

The following week, the case was heard over three days. During Stanigross' hearing, the solicitor raised many points of law, regarding whether his client could be said to be in possession of the drug. Magistrate Lindsell was inclined to agree on some points he raised, but considered that there was, nevertheless, a case to answer. Kamien had engaged Mr Leo d'Almada to defend her, and feeling that her own story would be her best defence, he put her straight into the witness box.[122] Under cross-questioning by the Crown Solicitor, Mr Whyte-Smith, she presented a consistent picture of a rather gullible woman, who acted in good faith, and, motivated by self-interest (the free trip) did not bother to ask questions. Mr d'Almada rebutted the near presumption of guilt which the Ordinance under which this case was being heard put on the defendant. He said that the woman's statement showed that she did not know that the drug was in the trunk. Mr Lindsell was not prepared to accept this, and convicted her on both counts – possession and unlawfully trying to bring the heroin into Hong Kong, but asked Mr Whyte-Smith if he had

122 Leonardo d'Almada e Castro Jn., b. Hong Kong 1904, d. Portugal, 1996. Having been educated at St Joseph's College in Hong Kong then Exeter College, Oxford, Leo d'Almada became the first Portuguese barrister in Hong Kong and the first to be appointed King's Counsel. He was a gifted defence barrister and an impressive orator. During the Japanese occupation he made a daring escape from Macao with the British Army Aid Group, then returned to the colony after liberation to assist the British military court.

any comments about the sentencing. Fortunately for Kamien, this man told the court that the Crown regarded the woman as a carrier, rather than a principal actor in the case.

Mr Lindsell, who had already found Stanigross guilty on the two counts, fined him $4,000 or six months' hard labour, with a further three months without the option of a fine for the second offence. Upon Helena Kamien, he imposed a fine of $500, or three months' hard labour. On the application of her solicitor, the magistrate agreed to a 'stay of execution' for a week, in order for her to telegraph to her husband in Paris to send the money. When Mr d'Almada asked if Mr Lindsell could reduce the penalty against his client, he responded sharply. "Certainly not. She has got off lightly as it is."

Helena Kamien's trip to the east had not taken her as far as Japan. She had spent a week getting to know the inside of Hong Kong's gaol and doubtless had another week there before the money came through from Europe. She had not received her £50, and now she was down by the equivalent of a further £75 due to the fine. And she had to find her passage back home. The case drew a lot of attention in Hong Kong, partly because of the nationality of the defendants. They were not Chinese, so this was no usual case. But nor were they British, so the colony's English-reading public could enjoy it without feeling that their country had been brought into disrepute. It was also one of the earliest large hauls of this drug.

By the late 1920s and 30s, heroin offences were becoming almost as frequent as opium convictions had been in earlier days. Of the many cases that filled the courts, some were similarly for smuggling the raw material, whilst others concerned the making up of pills in the little 'heroin factories' that popped up in the less-frequented villages, mostly in the New Territories. These pills were then traded, and more prosecutions resulted from this. There are at least a few dozen occasions when women were involved in these activities, and some where they were the only people arrested. One such case, where they were, for once, named, was when Wong Yee was sentenced to a year's hard labour or a $2,500 fine for possession of 11,500 heroin pills.[123] She lived in No. 152 Wellington

---

123 *Hongkong Telegraph*, 26th September 1935.

Street, where Revenue Officer Grimmett found 3,500 such tablets, hidden in false panelling in her cubicle. He had acted on a tip-off given him and had already cautioned the woman when her amah, Wong Sik-lam, came in, unaware of the officer's presence. She was holding something, and when R.O. Grimmitt asked her what it was, she gave him the package, saying that she did not know what these tablets were. Her mistress, Wong Yee, then told her to take off her belt, and concealed in that the officer found a further 8,000 pills. It was clear both to the officer and then to the magistrate that Wong Sik-lam was not involved except in so far as she had followed her mistress' instructions, and so merited her discharge.

Chief Justice Sir Atholl MacGregor, one of Hong Kong's most compassionate and socially involved judges, was determined to eradicate the scourge of heroin from the colony.[124] In a case at the August sessions in 1939, he said, "I am not going to make any exceptions. Anyone in Hong Kong knows what to expect when you are found taking a hand in heroin traffic."[125] The Revenue Department had sent a party of officers, disguised as potential purchasers, up to a hut in Nan Nei Wan village near Shek O. There they had arrested three women and three men for possession of 154,000 pills. At the court, one woman, Chan Ching, stated that she had just arrived at the hut since she was visiting her relative. The judge accepted this and freed her, but the five others were each gaoled for three years with hard labour, without the option of paying a fine. Then just the next month three men and a woman received the same sentence from the judge for running a heroin pill factory at Sha Po village.[126] Here six people had been arrested, but two had escaped custody whilst being taken to

---

124 Sir Atholl MacGregor, b. Edinburgh 1883, d. at sea 1945. A prominent colonial lawyer, who served in Nigeria, Kenya and Trinidad, in the latter two as Attorney General, he was appointed as Chief Justice for Hong Kong in 1933. Sir Atholl won great distinction and respect for his measured, insightful work on the bench. He was also very involved in local concerns, especially those that benefited people on the margins of society. He was interned in Stanley Civilian Camp during the Japanese occupation, where he was instrumental in establishing a camp court and continued to act as Chief Justice for the community. He contracted beri-beri and died shortly after liberation during the journey back to the UK.

125 *Hongkong Daily Press,* 25th August 1939.

126 *Hongkong Daily Press,* 29th September 1939.

Yuen Long. The other four each had a story about why they were in the house – one claimed to be the cook, another the 'boy'. The woman said that she was the wash amah. The following year, when trying yet another such case, with the men and women involved being prosecuted by R.O. Grimmitt, Sir Atholl said, "For a matter of years now I have made known to the public that I have no mercy whatsoever on those who, for personal gain, are willing to poison their fellow men."[127]

127 *Hongkong Daily Press* 19th March 1940.

CHAPTER 5

FEMALE PRISONERS AND THEIR MATRONS

The very first case heard in Hong Kong's just-opened Supreme Court in October 1844 was against a married couple, Laong-awa and his wife Laong Kwok-shi.[128] It was alleged that they had lured two young boatwomen onto their vessel, moored in Victoria harbour, bound them up and then taken them up the Canton River.[129] In a village there they kept them prisoners and intended to sell them into prostitution, for $90 each. News of the abduction reached the brother of one of the girls, who went to Canton and secured their release by paying a ransom of $220. All the parties returned to Hong Kong, where the police arrested the Laongs. At court the couple were unrepresented by counsel, but Laong-awa spoke for himself and his wife. He told the Chief Justice that there had been a serious argument between the brother and themselves, resulting in this man making the case against them in revenge. Although this may well have been the case, Laong was given short shrift by the Attorney General, who appeared for the prosecution and the jury were ready to assent in finding the couple guilty. Laong-awa was sent to prison for eighteen months with hard labour, while his wife received the same length of sentence, without hard labour but would be publicly exhibited every month in a cangue – the Chinese version of the stocks.

The prison in Hong Kong, although hailed as one of the first two stone structures erected in the emerging town of canvas and grass-matting, was a rather insubstantial structure hurriedly put up in 1841. The recent arrivals

---

128 The opening of this chapter – both information on the case recorded here and its initial structure – owes much to Christopher Munn, *Anglo-China,* ch. 4. The case quoted here appears on p. 160 and is also in James Norton-Kyshe, *The History of the Laws and Courts of Hong Kong,* vol.1, p. 65.

129 Now more commonly known as the Pearl River.

saw this and the Magistracy as the priority and had them completed just months after the British occupation of the island. With the house for the Chief Magistrate, Major William Caine, placed nearby, both were on high land.[130] They overlooked the harbour, with the prison close to the end of Pottinger Street. But the colonists expected only to bring to trial and then imprison British and western men. From the description quoted by Norton-Kyshe, it emerges that, of the three blocks of the first prison, it was only that for the Europeans which was purpose built and was the one referred to in early reports.[131] This was a building 64 feet by 30 feet, being two rows of six cells, divided by an eight foot passageway. They had not anticipated that the Chinese should go through the British judicial process and so a prison for them was an afterthought. These prisoners were kept in two buildings, linked by an open courtyard, and marginally more robust than the usual mat-shed type. It seems that these were requisitioned sheds which had to serve until 1844 or 45, when permission to spend a little more money was sought and obtained, and two more permanent stone structures were constructed on the same site. The larger of these, with a total area of 2,260 sq. ft. (about 210 sq. m.) had two dormitories to hold men under hard-labour sentence, the smaller had rooms which could accommodate those awaiting trial, and was equipped with a verandah and (stone) beds.

So, the police marched the couple away. Laong-awa went to the three-year-old shanty-prison, but where did his wife go? The early administrators had little experience of prison management, but they knew that they must keep the sexes segregated. In Britain, Sir Robert Peel's *Gaol Act* passed in 1823, along with other legislation by that reforming prime minister, had received copious press attention over the years, and so they soon realised that they needed to find accommodation for women too. But there was

130 William Caine, b. Maynooth, Ireland, 1799, d. Lewisham, England, 1871 was Hong Kong's first Chief Magistrate and had a profound impact on the early development of the justice system of the colony. Essentially a soldier, his military career was primarily in India, but had come to China with the campaigns of 1839. He was versed in military rather than civil or criminal law, and the severity with which he treated defendants often reflected this.

131 James Norton-Kyshe, *The History of the Laws and Courts of Hong Kong*, vol. 1, pp. 30-31.

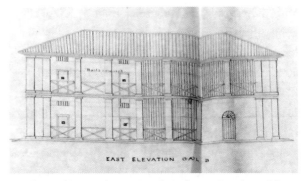

EAST ELEVATION GAOL B

1847 Prison (East elevation), National Archives, London, CO 133/4 1847.

no discussion at Laong Kwok-shi sentencing about where she would be confined, from which it seems safe to infer that she was not setting a precedent. The first women the magistrate imprisoned have passed into obscurity: the earliest newspapers, published weekly, do not always report cases. Later records show that a room had been made available in the Magistrate's house which could hold any women prisoners. This house, built in 1842, had replaced the mat-shed that had served for the first year. Since the sentences of these trail-blazers were short, perhaps a few weeks, or less, and they could be counted in single figures, the situation presented no particular problem. Now there was to be a longer term inhabitant of this room. The Magistrate had also been required to make over a room for another class of previously unconsidered prisoner, the debtor, who had not been tried for a criminal offence and therefore could not be confined alongside convicted men. The law entitled this class of inmate to a better style of life and he could arrange to receive his own food from outside. Perhaps Laong Kwok-shi, and the other earliest incarcerated females, received meals from an amah serving in Major Caine's house, and the Jailer, Mr J. Collins, occasionally 'checked up' on them.[132]

The early judicial system
In many parts of the British Empire, the early administrators adopted the pragmatic solution of assimilating as much of the local law and legal practices into colonial law as would keep the recognisable status

---

132 Mr Collins is so designated in the early *Blue Books*, but subsequently the spelling *gaoler* was adopted.

quo for those they now sought to rule. English law was reserved for the management of the colonists themselves and fellow westerners. Captain Charles Elliot had proclaimed this, when he assured the resident population that they would be "governed according to the laws and customs of China, every description of torture excepted".[133] The fisherfolk, boat-people and farmers of the island, so distant from Chinese centres of power, would have had little idea of the judicial practices of the Qing empire either. In this southern tip of China the people already in and around Hong Kong would be familiar with a social order based around head-men, clan and village allegiances, with the local temples seen as the regular places of arbitration and dispute settlement. Early plans included the handing over of those Chinese found committing crimes in Hong Kong to a Chinese magistrate based in (then Chinese) Kowloon. British judges would oversee the trials conducted there, but would not intervene, except regarding the use of torture.

However, British Hong Kong needed to protect its business enterprises and did so by stamping evidence of its sovereignty onto the life of the place. In this way, it was hoped, they would not have to rely solely upon the presence of their military and naval powers. But from the outset, it had to guard against the flood of 'undesirables' entering the territory. Of these, it was the western rogues and scoundrels who most alarmed the administration, rather than their Chinese counterparts. Thus, establishing the Magistracy, for the trying of British subjects by Major Caine, had been such an early and important consideration. But the Government in London, which was ambivalent about the value of Hong Kong, set its face against two legal systems in such a small territory. In April 1843, Sir Henry Pottinger, Elliot's successor and first Governor of Hong Kong, received instructions from the Colonial Office to proclaim that all residents would henceforth be subject to English law and sanctions.

The local administration may have had its eyes on western ne'er-do-wells, but it soon found that the Magistracy was inundated with offences committed by the Chinese arrivals. Elizabeth Sinn notes that Chinese Imperial law made emigration an offence and branded those doing so as

---

133 Norton-Kyshe, *op. cit.,* vol. 1, pp. 4-5, 2nd February 1841.

traitors during the Opium War period.[134] Thus many of those arriving on the island were already on the margins of their own society. The majority might be law-abiding enough, concerned primarily with making some money, but the attraction for the criminally minded was clear. The two Chinese prison buildings were soon full, primarily with men serving sentences of a few weeks or months, but also with about 50 imprisoned for a year or longer.[135] With criminality throughout all sectors of the population showing no imminent decline, it was obvious that the colony urgently needed a higher court, with greater sentencing powers. The Supreme Court opened for its first cases on 2nd October 1844.[136]

Early governors and prominent western business-owners volubly defended the 'benefits' of British justice, now applicable to all on the island. A judicial system blind as to race, creed or station in life and enshrining the presumption of innocence and trial by jury was obviously superior to all others. This, they believed, must surely be immediately apparent to all right-thinking Chinese. But failures in the working of the court often undermined these noble ideals, so the 'right-thinking' rarely saw the merits of the system in practice. It was the Chinese, rather than noisome westerners, who provided the bulk of its work, outnumbering European defendants more than ten-fold. The judiciary was unprepared for the challenges of implementing justice on a people little acquainted with the Chinese court system, let alone the very different English method, and the administration had done little to help the local population understand it. In addition, the hearings were conducted in English with interpretation that was, at its best, faltering and often utterly inadequate. The all-western juries were loath to assume that any Chinese defendant might be innocent and accepted evidence that was frequently scrappy. The lawyers took no account of the prevalence in Chinese practice of instigating 'revenge' cases, and there was little consistency in sentencing.

---

134 Elizabeth Sinn, *Power and Charity*, pp. 9-10.

135 James Norton-Kyshe, *The History of the Laws and Courts of Hong Kong*, vol. 1, pp. 30-32.

136 Unlike Britain and other countries, there was no Court of Assize or Quarter Session courts in Hong Kong. Instead, the two tier system of the Magistracy and the Supreme Court prevailed until the introduction of the Court of Final Appeal in 1997.

Allegations, many well founded, were made of bribery and corruption in the conduct of cases at the Supreme Court, both of the senior officials and of the interpreters and clerks. Such was the general dissatisfaction with this court that after a few years that it was used only for the most serious of crimes, and its tally of cases diminished. It was well into the 1850s before it managed to re-establish its integrity and gain public confidence. Nevertheless, some of the early governors still cited its very existence as one of the main attractions of the colony to respectable and affluent Chinese merchants looking to do business there.

Laong Kwok-shi is a rare example of a woman who stood trial at the Supreme Court in its first ten years. Nor were they commonplace during the following ninety years. Some of these rarities have already been encountered and the stories of those with more complex trials, often facing capital charges, will appear in subsequent chapters. For the overwhelming majority who entered the doors of the courts at all, it was for a swiftly conducted case at the Magistracy. But lest that suggests a Hong Kong seething with thieving and vicious women, it must be borne in mind that, throughout the 19th century, less than one percent of the total female population stood before the magistrate as defendants in any year, with perhaps a few more than that as plaintiffs.

The people of the prison

The earliest records of staff employed and convicts kept in the gaol appear in the *Blue Books*, from 1844 onwards.[137] During that year, 53 European and 196 Chinese men were held, and three women: two European and one Chinese. Most would have been 'inside' for just a few weeks, and were supervised by just one man, the Jailer. The next year he had two turnkeys (warders) working for him and an executioner. Major Caine held oversight of the prison, in his role as Sheriff, and, as Chief Magistrate, was responsible for putting most of the convicts into the gaol. European and Indian police acted as guards, patrolling by day and night the enclosed compound and the other prison buildings. In 1847 these were at capacity: designed to provide accommodation for 12 in

---

137 Norton-Kyshe, *op. cit.,* vol. 1, p.30. The report, reproduced here, was written by the Chief Magistrate (Major Caine) on two years of the prison's operation (between 1841-3) gives some idea of number of prisoners held.

individual cells and 170 in large wards – during one week there were 186 men being held. The two European and five Chinese women sentenced that year were held in the designated room in the former Magistrate's House. Although only five years old this was already in poor repair. The magistrate had moved out two years earlier and it now served as the jailer's residence at the front with the debtors' prison and the women at the rear.

In 1851 the Governor reported how unsatisfactory and insecure was this building as a prison, writing that in 1845 "it was perfectly impossible to arrange anything satisfactory …on account of the unsuitableness of the plan and the insufficiency of the materials and workmanship, which to correct would have involved the reconstruction of the greater part of it."[138] Whether the conditions had anything to do with the sickness of one of the British women, who died before her sentence was through is not known. The sentences of most of the men, of all nationalities, included hard-labour. For the Chinese this involved being shackled into chain gangs and put to build the first rough roads, while the Europeans were probably stone breaking. None of the cases involving women in this period refer to hard-labour, but this probably had more to do with a lack of suitable work and a place in which to do it, than with any less severe sentencing. Compared to their male contemporaries, the women imprisoned in 1847 for tree-cutting at Wong Nei Chung and West Point passed their sentences in comparative ease, if not in healthy conditions.

The first *Blue Book* gaol report, in 1844, included a copy of the single-page handwritten regulations.[139] The prison systems in Great Britain were, at this mid-century point, in something of a state of flux. Large, state-run convict prisons co-existed with local town and county gaols and village lock-ups. Transportation was soon to be a thing of the past, as were the hulks: decommissioned, end-of-service naval ships used to hold prisoners before despatch to the penal colonies. Prison reform had been a subject for public discussion for many years, crossing party lines when Whigs and Tories disagreed about much else. It was led first by John Howard in the late 18th century, whose work persuaded the government to legislate

---

138 CO129/38 pp. 89-95, 27th November 1851, Correspondence between Governor Bonham and Earl Grey, Secretary of State for War and the Colonies.
139 *Blue Book, 1844,* CO 133/1.

B

Regulations for the Government of Her Majesty's Gaol on the Island of HongKong.

An European Constable will be ordered for duty at the prison daily, he will never leave his post unless by orders of the Magistrate. He will keep in his possession the key of the door of the prison yard, which door must never be opened unless in his presence. One sub-inspector and four privates of the Native Police will constantly attend at the prison — this Guard will furnish a sentry day and night, to be stationed in the verandah.

On occasions of alarm the constables will instantly accoutre, two will remain to guard the Gaol, and the others will proceed to the Magistrate for orders.

The keys of the Gaol will be under the charge of the Senior Non Commissioned Officer, and must be always at hand.

1 Each prisoner must be searched before he is locked up and knives and other cutting instruments taken from him.

2 No clothes, food or any thing else will be allowed to enter the gaol without being previously inspected by the constable on duty.

3 No prisoner will be allowed to quit his cell, unless to labour, or to obey the call of nature, without the Magistrate's permission.

4 No prisoner will be allowed to receive visitors, unless by the sanction of the Magistrate, and in the verandah. Prisoners so receiving visits will be searched after their friends shall have left them.

5 Permission to purchase tobacco, fruit, and other harmless luxuries will be given to well behaved prisoners.

6 No unnecessary communication to be allowed between Prisoners and Policemen.

7 The Senior Non Commissioned Officer will visit the cells morning and evening, and satisfy himself of the safety of his Prisoners. He will recollect that the preservation of their health will mainly depend upon cleanliness of person and abode, to which he will particularly direct his attention.

8 The Constable on duty will see that no prisoner leaves the prison unless under the special charge of a Policeman.

Frederick W. A. Bruce

1844 Gaol Regulations, The National Archives, London, CO 133/1 1844.

for some order and method to be brought to the hell-holes that were the gaols. Thereafter, the Quakers, especially Elizabeth Fry, kept the concept of the redemptive, reformative value of imprisonment to the fore.

With no national system or set of standards in the mother-land, Hong Kong had little on which to base the organisation of a convict prison. Thus Victoria Gaol appears in some ways more resonant of a huge village lock-up than a state prison such as Millbank, Pentonville or Brixton. There were no guidelines from the Colonial Office for the Hong Kong authorities to follow, and few of the men involved in this venture would have had contact with prisons in England on which to draw. The primary concern of the regulations was the responsibility of the police guards to remain alert; to supervise those who needed access to the gaol and to impress upon the Jailer that he was responsible for the safety and health of the prisoners. It only mentions discipline in the observation that unnecessary talking between guards and prisoners was discouraged and the guards had to ensure that no prisoner left his quarters for reasons other than work, exercise or the call of nature, unless with permission. Well-behaved prisoners could purchase tobacco, fruit and other 'harmless' luxuries (excluding opium or any liquor).

The *Blue Books,* which now asked very specific data about the operation of the colony, included pre-printed forms for the gaol. These give us some of the most detailed information we have about day to day life there. For example, in the 1848 forms for 'Gaols and Prisons' we hear that the Jailer, Mr J. Collins, lived with his wife and family in the front of the former Magistrate's House. There is no female turnkey, but any females were attended by the Jailer himself, exclusively. That year twenty-one women were sent to gaol, all of them Chinese. But with their numbers growing, it was obvious that the prison required a female turnkey. In 1850 the return records that this unnamed person was paid £12 10s. per annum. This, about $5 per month, was one third of the lowest European turnkey salary and similar to what a Chinese labourer could make. We can be reasonably certain that this first female employee was a gaol officer's wife, and likely Mrs Collins. After all, it was probably she who had provided most of the care for the women until that time.

A small improvement, long delayed

The 1851 report from Governor Bonham mentioned previously also addressed the need to rebuild the Debtors' Gaol and sought permission to allocate money to this. It was planned to use virtually the same site, but to create a discrete building, with the rocky outcrop below what would become Chancery Lane being removed. The rough land to the south of the Chinese gaol buildings was to be levelled and a separate Gaoler's House built there. Plans were attached in the 1853 *Blue Books* of both the site as it was and the proposed new buildings.[140] A retaining wall had earlier been put around the Chinese and European prisons: now, one side of the Gaoler's House had access into the compound so created. A boundary wall, equipped with watchtowers, was built along Arbuthnot Road, Chancery Lane, Old Bailey and parallel with Hollywood Road, opening for access via Pottinger Street. As can be seen from the plan of the intended new Debtors' Prison, the women would occupy the rear portion, but have to access it through the main door, as the whole building was encased by a wall. Their accommodation only amounted to an enclosed yard, 28 feet by 20 feet, a dormitory, bathroom and small porch, and the corridors between. The female turnkey – shown here as 'keeper' – would have a room and a bathroom for herself, but the rest of the building, including the verandahs, were for the male debtors. The kitchen was in the yard, thus food would have to be brought to the connecting door, opposite the porch, leading into the women's area, and then eaten outside in their yard or in the dormitory. But there is no evidence to suggest that this was built immediately.

Prison management in England now dictated that convict prisons kept different classes of prisoner separate.[141] Hong Kong did not have the space to observe all the fine distinctions of English gaols, especially as it had to separate European and Asiatic prisoners. Although the magistrates were soon sentencing men from India and other parts of Asia, there appears

---

140 CO 133/10, *Blue Book for 1853, Gaol Report.*

141 Local women's prisons in Britain existed from the first years of the 19th century, but it was not until Peel's Gaols Act of 1823, requiring the separation of male and females, that convict prisons just for women started to appear, the first such being at Millbank, Brixton and Fulham (all now within Greater London) in the 1850s.

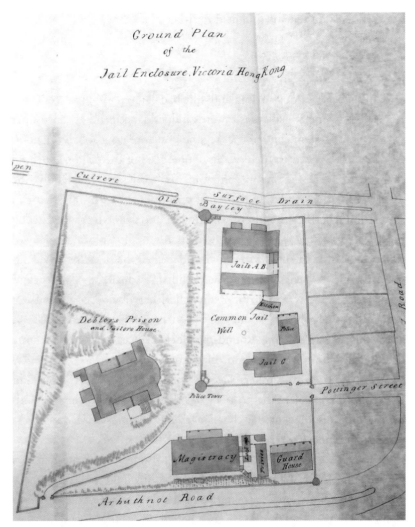

The 'Jail Enclosure' in 1853 showing original Debtor's Prison (former Magistrate's House), The National Archives, London, CO 133/10 1853.

to be no further segregation, except in relation to the diet provided for them, It aimed to accommodate in distinct groups:

Those condemned to death;
Prisoners held for penal servitude (hard-labour);
Simple misdemeanants (convicted of crimes but not sentenced to hard labour);

Prisoners on remand and held for trial;

Debtors;

Women.

Whilst local prisons in England still had large communal cells, the trend in the convict gaols was towards individual cells for each prisoner (the 'separate system') and a strict regime of silence imposed throughout. Aside from the need to preserve discipline, part of the rationale behind this was to avoid the 'moral contamination' of lesser offenders by the worst. The concerns that underpinned prison reform in Britain were not simply about curbing the excesses of brutality and depravity that existed in the 18th-century gaols. Protestant Christian morality informed many of those advocating the new systems, and advocated the breaking of vicious criminal spirit. Then they could be rebuilt into docile and industrious workers from the wrecks of humanity that they obviously were. There was nothing 'lily-livered' about the measures considered appropriate to effect this transformation. Round-the-clock silence, ten hours or more of mind-numbing labour, bland, inadequate food and most of the day spent in isolation from others was designed to subdue the resistance of the criminal character. The prisoner was then moulded by the 'fire-and-brimstone' preaching of the chaplain at the religious services all were forced to attend.

In Hong Kong very few of the Chinese prisoners were considered in any way the responsibility of the British, and nor would the Chinese have welcomed such a view. The majority of such prisoners would make no claim of Hong Kong as a home and the administration clearly did not wish to see any troublesome Chinese settling in the colony. Sentences longer than a few months usually culminated with banishment, for a term of years or even life. Premature return would attract even more punitive sentences. With their attitude to the Chinese being one of bemused ignorance, the British were content to leave any attempts at reformation of character to the missionaries, and, in any case, did not have personnel with sufficient language skills to attempt any communication with the men, beyond the most basic. Imprisonment here was for purpose of punishment and containment alone. However, this also applied to the majority of Hong Kong's western and Indian prisoners. This more limited approach to imprisonment fitted in well with the administration's reluctance, and inability, to spend more money than necessary on the gaol. Thus whilst some level of separation between different classes of miscreants could be achieved in the European gaol, there was insufficient space and little official will for such in the Chinese/Asiatic gaol.[142]

Yet all the time, numbers grew. Thus towards the end of the 1850s the cells designed for one European held four men, whilst the 'wards' of the Chinese had become so overcrowded that they were unmanageable by any turnkey. He could only peer in through the grill at an unlit room some 70 feet by 30 feet, using his oil lamp to shed a little light. The crumbling state of the buildings was reflected in the escapes, fights and general ill-discipline of the gaol. Aside from the female turnkey, there had been only a slight increase in the staff during the decade. In 1856 it consisted of just of a jailer and his assistant, two turnkeys, a chain-gang overseer and the debtors' turnkey.[143] Six Indian and one Chinese guards patrolled the perimeters of the buildings and compound. Theoretically they were all managed by the Sheriff and Deputy Sheriff, but there was little the western turnkeys could do to keep any order in the overcrowded rooms. As the Colonial Surgeon mentioned in his reports of 1855 and 1856, the men were eager enough to keep good discipline, but were given scant authority over the prisoners so they could achieve little. The chain-gang worked only slowly and those prisoners not sent out slept, gossiped and fought their time away, refusing to do any work. A commission was established and reported on 5th March 1857; the result was a wholesale turnout and reorganisation of the staffing. Andrew Lysaght Inglis, a former Registrar General with a good command of Cantonese, was appointed to the new post of Gaol Governor, at the reasonable salary of £300 per year. Under him was a Warder, one Chinese and four European turnkeys and six guards, two Indian and four Portuguese. The debtors' turnkey, Mahommed, and the two Indian guards were the only men retained from

---

142 The call for such separation comes more regularly and forcefully from the various Colonial Surgeons, responsible at this time for both the overall health of the gaol and that of individual prisoners.

143 *Blue Book, 1856,* CO133/13.

the previous team.[144] The female turnkey became the Matron, and was, for the first time, named in the *Blue Book*s – Elizabeth Cox. If Inglis' salary was excluded, the administration could congratulate itself that the wage bill was some £50 less per annum than before. Inglis soon proved his worth and had the prisoners engaged in many repair works around the gaol and the chain-gang were building roads with new vigour.

Although it was not possible to fully separate the various categories of prisoner in the early gaol, the segregation of males from females was rigorously maintained. Such separation only appears in print with the *Blue Book* questions, but in the early years the Governor (later Superintendent) could assure London that no male prisoner was allowed sight of a female prisoner. At some time during the mid-1850s the women came back into the main gaol, probably because their former accommodation was now so decrepit and a danger to health. According to a note in Dr J. Carroll Dempster's report of 1856, the "women are confined in cells in the same corridor with the men and further, there is no means of their taking exercise, in their cells they must remain."[145] The administration could be thankful that they did not have the same magnitude of problem that some English and Scottish prisons faced. During the mid-century years in England women made up almost 25% of the total prison population, and the proportion in Scottish gaols was 37%. It was unusual for Victoria Gaol to hold even half a dozen women at any one time during the 1850s and 1860s. About a quarter of those admitted were there awaiting trial or in lieu of paying bail, but with no record of how many or the type of cells (individual or association) given to them *pro tem* in the main gaol, the extent to which separation of classes amongst the women was achieved can only be speculated upon.

The only evidence that suggests any separation in practice is from correspondence between the Governor, Sir John Bowring, and the Colonial Office regarding prisoner Chun Cheong-she.[146] He records that she was held in a cell 8 feet by 10 feet. However, this woman, whose story

---

144 Mahommed – no second name was given – had been employed at the gaol since 1844.

145 CO133/13, *Report of the Colonial Surgeon for 1856.*

146 CO129/52 pp. 334-40, 13th December 1855.

is recounted in Chapter 7, was rather unique. As far as it has been possible to ascertain, she was the first woman to be sentenced to death in Hong Kong, a penalty commuted when she was found to be pregnant. There was an obvious need to separate her from the normal run of women, serving a few days or a fortnight.

Finally, in 1857, the government found the funds to rebuild the Debtors' Prison. The plans that had been sent to London four years earlier seem to be those used, since the same ones would be sent in subsequent years. The women were apparently moved into this building. However, there were no facilities here for an individual cell, whether for a long-term prisoner or as a punishment cell, but fortunately numbers were still low. In most years there were less than 50 women committed to gaol, and their crimes still rarely warranted sentences in excess of a month. But there was still the anomalous situation of convicted criminals held in a building other than the convict gaol. In 1859, the Justices of the Peace, having inspected the female prison, recorded that they "desire to express an opinion that, as soon as possible the present plan of confinement of Female Criminals be altered to a suitable place within the walls of the Criminal Prison, it being desirable to preserve the separation between Debtor and Criminal prisoner".[147]

Staffing the Gaol – turnkeys and matrons

A statistic frequently repeated about the Hong Kong Police in the 1850s and 60s is that the average term of employment for a European constable was three months. Many were recruited from the men that the British Garrison or the Royal Navy had 'let go', or from sailors with the mercantile marine who could not get a ship. A few had just pitched up in Hong Kong in the course of their ramblings, having found the gold rush was over. The lure of the cheap (often adulterated) grog and easily available women, ample opportunities for a little 'free enterprise' in the way of bribes and 'hush-money', minimal training and low wages were the downfall of many. Aside from a very aggressive form of malaria rampant in these early years, both venereal disease and typhus were on

---

147 *Hongkong Government Gazette,* 19th November 1859, report on Special Meeting of the Justices of the Peace, 16th November 1859.

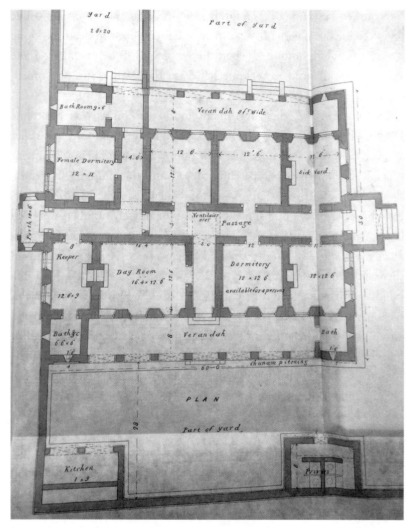

Proposed Debtors' Prison with women's quarters at southern side,
The National Archives, London, CO 133/18 1861.

offer in the brothels although the *Venereal Diseases Ordinance* of 1857
and its successor checked disease in those frequented by western men.
If a man managed not to fall prey to disease, he frequently fell foul of
his superior officers and lost his job. A few left when they found a better
or easier place, but it was usually those who had purchased their own
discharge from the army who persevered in the job and would eventually
earn promotion to sergeant or above. Men below the rank of inspector

were not recorded in the *Blue Books*. The records of Victoria Gaol are rather more complete, but suggest that the pool from which the turnkeys and guards were recruited was little different. Perhaps because there were, in the first fifteen years, only a small number employed there (no more than twelve until 1861) individual names appear in the annual records and would continue to be listed thereafter. Successive editions of the *Blue Books* frequently give an almost entirely different set of names to the previous year, and it may well be that these hide an even greater turn-over of men within the year. It is not apparent where these men lived: maybe a senior European turnkey, especially if married, was accommodated in the gaoler's house; some in the guard room and perhaps others in the gaols themselves, but all did live on-site. There were reports of misdemeanours by the turnkeys, particularly of escapes of prisoners permitted because these men were drunk, just as there were reports of nefarious activities of police constables from all contingents.

The unnamed Female Turnkey of 1850 was the first woman that the Hong Kong government employed. Although her duties were often light, the requirement to attend at every meal and to check her prisoners during the night meant she had to be close at hand. The wife of the gaoler or a senior turnkey would therefore be ideal. The earliest such, known from the government *Authorities for Payment* records rather than the *Blue Books*, was Mary Goodings, whose story is recounted by Hoe.[148] It amply shows how fragile and precarious was the life of a European woman of the working class. In 1855 Mary Goodings, who had formerly been married to turnkey James Roe and had one surviving child by him, appears in the records as acting matron of the gaol. Soon after Roe's death, in 1855, she married his colleague, Robert Goodings, the gaoler (or keeper). He too died, succumbing to dysentery, one of the principal killers of Europeans, just thirteen months after their marriage, in April 1856.[149] Their child followed him to the grave a few months later, but Mary maintained her role, earning her $5 per month. She then married for the third time, to

---

148 Susanna Hoe, *The Private Life of Old Hong Kong*, pp. 80-81.

149 Dr Dempster, in his 1855 report, noted that this man's health was very broken down, and not helped by having to walk a considerable distance between his house and the gaol in all weathers. CO133/12 *Report of the Colonial Surgeon for 1855*.

Goodings' successor, Robert MacKenzie. He, however, was one of those who lost his job in 1857 in the reorganisation of the gaol, and with him, of course, went his wife.

The matrimonial career of her successor, Elizabeth Cox, was hardly more propitious. As the widow (Elenor) Elizabeth Sanders, she married Robert Cox at the Registrar General's office on 28th January 1857. Robert then secured the post of warden of the gaol in that reorganisation, probably in May or June of that year. His wife, although more than five months pregnant, became matron on 1st August. Their son, Robert Charles James, was born on 27th November and baptised on 20th December. But Warden Cox did not live long enough to attend the baptism, dying on 10th December. The details come from Revd Dr Carl Smith's invaluable cards, from the registers of St John's Cathedral. In the *Blue Book* page for the gaol in 1857 Robert Cox does not appear, not being on the staff at the end of that year, but the most recent European turnkey was appointed on 11th December, and the other turnkeys moved up a step in seniority, the previous head turnkey taking Robert Cox's post. Elizabeth left her post on 25th January 1858. During her half-year at the prison she had charge of perhaps 15 Chinese inmates in total.

In the thirteen years between 1857 and 1869, there are no less than eleven different women listed as matron. From 1858 through to 1866 the six names that appear suggest that the post-holders were Portuguese. Although there were Portuguese guards, none appear to be related to any of these matrons. These women, probably born in Macao, may well have spoken Cantonese, and while the women occupied their new quarters in the 1857 Debtors' Prison, she had her own room. The women appear to have been kept in this small area from late 1857 (at the earliest) until sometime in 1862 or perhaps a little later; once again, the low numbers of prisoners made this feasible. For example, in 1858 there were usually just three or four women held, and never over eleven. For comparison, the rest of the gaol typically held 60 European and 240 Chinese men on any day. From this point there is no mention of the ethnicity of the female prisoners in the records, but both western and Chinese served sentences there, as the court reports in the newspapers reveal.

Of the many gaol matrons of the 1850s and 60s, the only one to stay over 18 months was Anneline, a woman not given any surname in the records. She arrived on 1st January 1859 and retired on health grounds on 1st May 1862 when the Colonial Surgeon, Dr J. I. Murray, reported that she was suffering from 'mental derangement'. Dr Murray, finding that Anneline was quite without any other means of supporting herself and had no home either in Hong Kong or Macao, made representation on her behalf to the Governor. The internal correspondence that then followed is in rather blunt language: "Anneline... whom you report unfit for duty. You will report length of her service, where she is to go when she leaves gaol, and what annuity is proposed for her. No longer fit in consequence of failure of her intellect, or in other words she has become crazy. Certified by Colonial Surgeon."[150] The government granted her a gratuity of $15 (about £3 1s.), being one month's salary for each year of her employment, and in his (retrospective) application for permission Governor Robinson reported that Anneline proposed living with friends in the colony.[151] In this letter he also told the Colonial Office that he had been quite unable to recruit any successor at the salary offered and had, therefore, to double the amount to £25 per annum. Happily, London raised no objections to this very slight increase in the annual expenditure. A comparison of this salary and the annual cost of the European prison diet, which was £9 2s. per man for bread, (probably poor quality) beef, vegetables and a little sugar, gives an indication of how necessary this increase was. The only other report we hear about the Portuguese matrons is in the gaol report for 1864, where the recently appointed Superintendent, Mr Francis Douglas, sent by the Colonial Office, noted that Mrs E. F. Remedios spoke Cantonese well and performed her duties to his satisfaction.

A bigger gaol – a better gaol?

The administration knew that it had to address the shortage of space and the dilapidated condition of the old prison buildings. On the progress of

---

150 *HKRS 275 no. 252,* 1st May 1862.
151 CO129/89, pp347-9, 4th August 1862, *Correspondence between Governor Robinson and Sir F Rogers, H. M. Treasury.*

this, the just-retired former governor, Sir John Bowring would write in 1860:

> There are few oriental prisons superior to it; and petty offences are frequent among the Chinese population, for the sole purpose of obtaining the comparative comforts it affords. But it has many defects, and I appointed a commission … [which recommended] to the home government (whose previous sanction is necessary), that a large sum should be appropriated for the reconstruction of the jail. That sanction was obtained before I left Hong Kong, and as the finances are in a most prosperous state …there is no reason why Hong Kong should not possess a model prison.[152]

The first thoughts had been to extend the current buildings, and Governor Bowring submitted plans to London at the end of 1858. But the arrival of the energetic young replacement, Governor Hercules Robinson, early in 1859 saw those change to a thorough re-build of the whole site, and he even procured a grant of £7,000 from the British Treasury to facilitate this. Fresh plans were submitted at the end of that year, and work commenced towards the close of 1860. Sadly, information on how such a radical transformation was effected has not come to light, even though it would eventually involve the demolition of all structures within the compound, including the recently complete new Debtors' Prison and gaoler's house.

The new gaol was designed as the upper half of the classic 'radial' system of prison building designed by a British architect in the United States and soon taken up in Britain.[153] In Hong Kong's version, wings ran in five directions, the greater part of the building forming east and

---

152 *Woolmer's Exeter & Plymouth Gazette*, 7th April 1860, letter to the editor from Sir John Bowring, in response to allegations that he had neglected to attend to the problems of the prison. The former governor was Exeter-born and had returned to that Devon town in his retirement.

153 Initial plans show that a complete circle of radii was at first suggested, but limitations of the site and the projected costs caused plans to be halved.

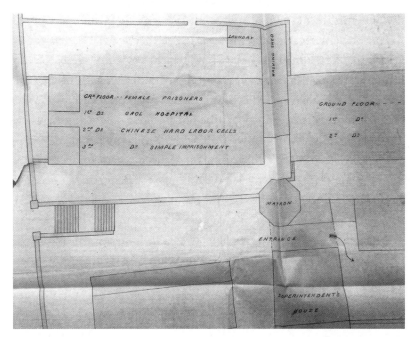

Section of the radial design for Victorial Gaol, showing Women's Prison and matron's quarters, The National Archives, London, CO 133/24 1867.

west wings, running parallel to Hollywood Road.[154] The building which housed the women's prison was a four-storey extension of the east wing, some 69 feet by 31 feet (approximately 21m by 9.5m). They also had exclusive access to a yard down the long south side of the building. The women were on the ground floor, the gaol hospital directly above them. Chinese hard labour prisoners and those kept in 'simple imprisonment' occupied the upper two floors. The plans were sent back to London and are preserved in the Colonial Office records held at The National Archives in Kew. These do not show the way the space was divided, but it was stated to include two large association cells, six individual cells and two punishment cells, along with bathroom facilities. The matron had separate accommodation: a two-room octagonal building at the end of the passage leading to the gaol entrance on Arbuthnot Road. This faced

154 For example, the plans submitted with the Gaol Report in CO133/21 in 1864.

the Superintendent's house, and connected with the main east wing of the prison via a covered passage about ten yards long.

The first years of the new building, which seems to have been fully in use by the end of 1862 or early 1863, did not go well. There were a number of escapes, put down to the defective workmanship of some parts of the structure and poor discipline among the turnkeys. There was also the disgraceful conduct of Charles Ryall, appointed warden in 1863. On finding that a former colleague from his seafaring days was one of the prisoners, he arranged for this man's wife to bring in his dress clothes, obtained a duplicate key for the man's cell and let him out late one evening, allowing him to change out of prison garb in his rooms. The two men and their wives then enjoyed a merry party, which came to an end only when the Police Magistrate, Charles May turned up as an unexpected and unwelcome guest. But part of the staffing problem must have stemmed from the poor conditions offered to the prison turnkeys. As Mr Douglas, the much-needed superintendent, noted in his 1864 report, it had only just been possible to build the accommodation for subordinate officers. Until that time some had to live as best they could in the corridors outside prisoners cells, while a few shared a couple of old association cells. With salaries between £35 and £82 10s. per year and such rough living, posts there had held out few inducements.

The women of the gaol

The turnkeys' accommodation was in a long narrow building between the prison and what was to become the central police station, but again the internal organisation of this building does not appear in the plans.[155] However, it is easy to imagine that the benefit of fully separate accommodation would have been an inducement for any gaoler's wife to take the post of matron. Although the pay for the role was still, at £25 per year, very meagre, when it supplemented the £82 10s. or £78 salary of a first- or second-class turnkey and meant their own front door, it gave the couple an acceptable standard of living for the time. From 1866 British turnkeys' wives were again employed, although, in the case of the first

---

155 Again, the plans were included in *Blue Book* reports, e.g. CO 133/24 1867.

married woman, Mrs Crutchley, there is no evidence of a corresponding husband on the staff list. We then learn a little more of the next occupants of the role, and their reasons for leaving. The turnkeys and guards were not infrequently dismissed for neglect of duty or misconduct, but for the women it was more likely to be the loss of their husband that saw them also lose their job and home. Mrs Gleison, the wife of first-class turnkey C. Gleison, took up the post on 3rd July 1867, but resigned just seven months later. In the intervening time her husband had died, and the records give her reason for resigning as that she wished to join her children in Singapore. The next matron, Mrs Mason, fared little better, and had to resign on the death of her husband. This staffing problem settled down a little when Mrs Payne became matron on 1st January 1869. She was the Portuguese wife of Chain-gang Guard Payne and had the advantage of speaking Cantonese. Payne had started in his job the previous year and by 1871 had been promoted to 1st class guard.

Soon after her husband's promotion they both left the gaol employment, and she was succeeded by twenty-five-year-old Mrs Mary Collins. She joined the staff in December 1872, just two months after her husband became a 2nd class turnkey. Like so many of her predecessors, she lost her husband a few months later, but managed to stay on at the gaol. Her work must have been satisfactory since, perhaps in recognition of her widowed status, her pay was increased to £32 10s. that year and to £50 per year in 1874. Whilst on the face of it this might not seem very significant, it was very unusual for the salary to change in this way, especially without it first being cleared with the Colonial Office in London. Incremental scales, based on years' of service, did not then exist in subordinate government roles, but this local adjustment was probably made after an application by the Acting Superintendent, Malcolm Tonnochy. Mary Collins repaid this consideration with 14 years' service as gaol matron.

From this period the records give more detailed instructions on the role and responsibilities of the matron. She was answerable to the superintendent and had sole charge for all women held, whether as convicts, debtors or awaiting trial. In this her position was the same as that of matrons in prisons in England. As Zedner remarks, "The responsibilities placed on the female staff were almost unparalleled at a time when men ran most institutions of comparable size."[156] At the conclusion of a new convict's hearing, the police involved in the trial took the woman to the report room in the Central Station to complete the Prison Register. Into this they inscribed her name, details of the offence and sentence, and listed any personal possessions she had. It was there that she would find out the number to which she would answer from now on. This officer then led her up to the gaol gates, where she would be met by the matron and taken the short distance to the Female Prison. The matron now searched her and saw that she bathed and dressed in prison clothes, afterwards reading (and explaining) the gaol rules to woman. However, one of the principal responsibilities of the of this post did not have to do directly with her charges. Rather, she had to ensure that no male member of staff, not even the superintendent, entered the 'female ward', unless accompanied by her. Naturally, no man was permitted to be present during the searching. She had to remove any prohibited items and deliver these to the superintendent. Her day-to-day duties included the supervision of mealtimes, the distribution of food and ensuring that every woman was seen by her at least twice a day. She set them to their work, which included cleaning the ward and saw that the rules were obeyed. By night she must visit their sleeping quarters at least once, at a time that should not be fixed.

The time most female prisoners spent in prison was, in the main, brief, but Superintendent Douglas stated that in 1864 there were seven women serving terms of between four and ten years. There are seven women listed as felons (i.e. sentenced for serious crime, here probably kidnapping, serious robbery or possibly manslaughter), and yet the same figures also give the maximum number of women held in gaol on any one day as five. Similar discrepancies in the figures exist throughout this period. In the case of the petty crimes, the magistrate's court still resembled a factory production line. Defendants found guilty in such were usually given the option of paying a fine or going to gaol. Yet although the fines required typically ranged between twenty cents and twenty dollars, at

---

156 Lucia Zedner, *Wayward Sisters. The Prison for Women* in *The Oxford History of the Prison*, p. 344. The women's prisons in England were, however, much larger than that in Hong Kong.

least three-quarters of those convicted chose or had to go to gaol. Thus the (male) gaol teemed. For example, in 1871 of the 5,000 or so men 'doing time', 4,200 were there for three months or less. Amongst the women this tendency could be even more marked – the same year, of the 284 imprisoned, 277 were there for less than three months. This pattern continued for the next two decades, e.g. 1885 was a quiet year for the Female Prison with only 46 convicted inmates, and six of these had sentences between three and twelve months.

Women were more likely to gain their only experience of gaol whilst awaiting trial. More than 25% of the women held were awaiting their appearance before the magistrate or, if the police needed time to investigate, were on remand. On the infrequent occasions when the magistrate had committed a woman to stand trial at the Criminal Sessions, she might have to wait two or three weeks. However, this cannot fully account for the relatively high number, compared with that for men, where about 10% were held on remand or in lieu of bail. Part of the reason must be women's poorer access to money for bail, along with the lack of facilities to hold female defendants in police stations.

Women's experience of prison life differed as much from that of men as it did for women in British or American gaols. Perhaps the most significant contrast was that of scale. For most of the 19th century, just one woman had charge of them. Until the move to Lai Chi Kok in 1932, the staff team was so small that the matron would know each inmate, insofar as the length of her stay allowed. She had received them into the gaol and then searched them and provided them with a block of carbolic soap with which to wash. If they were starting a sentence, she had provided them with the rough tunic and trousers that was the Chinese female prison uniform and then had a daily presence in their lives. In the men's prison, there was an average daily population of about 500 men and more than 200 warders and guards by the turn of the century. Thus warder and prisoner would only get to recognise each other should the man be inside for long enough or be sufficiently obstreperous.

Daily life for the women

However, in her conformity to prison routine, the women's lives resembled the rest of Victoria Gaol's prisoners. The new arrival, whether she was there awaiting her time in court or beginning her term had to fall in with this. All rose before sunrise, taking their first meal before work started at 6.15 a.m. in the summer and half an hour later in winter. The washroom had a cold water tap and a privy (toilet) but no flushing lavatories. In British female prisons one of the most frequent complaints of the wardresses was of women not keeping themselves clean. This was a concern of the medical officers with regard to Hong Kong's male prisoners, but not of the women here. In 1872 and 1876 there had been considerable discussion between London and Hong Kong on the subject of cutting women's hair, either routinely on entering as a convict or as a punishment.[157] In Britain this was standard 19th-century practice, and after it ceased to be routine admission procedure, the hair often had to be cut when the women were found to be crawling with lice and fleas. But in pre-1911 Hong Kong there was some understanding of the grave degradation done to a man by cutting off his queue, and women's hair was considered in a similar light. Dr Ayres, in one of his meticulous reports, said that the women in the prison almost always kept themselves, including their hair, meticulously clean.

The morning and evening meals, for those in the first fourteen days of their sentence, were eight ounces (225g) of rice cooked with a little salt, and water to drink. Any European prisoner could expect a similar weight of bread and water. At 11 a.m. a congee made with two ounces of rice was allowed. Thereafter, to the total 18 ounces of rice a few ounces of fish, fresh or salt, was added on five days of the week and a pound (450g) of vegetables on the remaining two. There were also small daily allowances of oil, salt, chutney and tea.[158] Before the day's work began, prisoners had to clean and tidy their bed-space in the association cells. The records give no dietary regime for female European prisoners, since they were a rare

---

157 CO129/156 pp. 277-80, 2nd February 1872, correspondence between Governor MacDonnell and the Earl of Kimberley, and CO129/174, pp. 306-7, 4th July 1876, between Governor Kennedy and the Earl of Carnarvon.

158 Taken from *Gaols and Prisoners Report for 1886*. Amounts given for female Chinese prisoners.

(but not unknown) breed. That given for western men was likely the fare offered to such women, perhaps somewhat reduced in quantity. Each man was allowed a daily ration of a pound each of bread and vegetables, half a pound of beef or pork, almost three ounces of sugar, and tea and salt as the Chinese diet.[159] Part of the allowance went to make soups or suet puddings.

Since they must stay within the two rooms of their prison, work for women was very limited. All but those held for debt or awaiting trial had to work. If sentenced to do 'hard labour', the 19th-century female convict would pick oakum all day: a mind- and finger-numbing task, where the strands of tar-encrusted ships' rope had to be separated. The harsh strands cut fingertips and got under nails, until hands were sufficiently hardened and calloused. For the others, there was coir (coconut fibre) mat-making, tailoring and mending, and, of course, cleaning the rooms. Mr Douglas noted that the seven long-term prisoners conducted themselves very well and were assiduous in their tailoring work, which was probably upon gaol officers' uniforms. Work finished at 4.15 p.m., after which the evening meal was served. Sometimes, during the remaining hours of daylight the women undertook needlework, but with no official reference to any cost of this, materials were probably supplied by the matron herself or by some of the church ladies' groups, which occasionally interested themselves in the prison. The women were expected to be in bed by 6.30 p.m. The *Blue Book* reports state that they had eleven hours sleep a night. This apparently early hour would not be unfamiliar to most. In the various detailed crime reports, up to the end of the period covered here, householders are regularly reported as having gone to bed by 7.30 p.m. or earlier, despite the presence of electric light in some homes by the 1920s and 30s. Individual and association cells throughout the gaol were unlit, although corridors and passages had oil lamps and, later, gas lighting.

---

159 The large quantity of meat permitted for each man was perhaps due to the cheap price of beef and pork throughout this century, just twice the price per pound of bread, for example.

Government employment of women

Following the appointment of the female turnkey in 1850, it was not until 1858 that another woman appears on the list of the Civil Establishment: the Matron of the Lock Hospital. As the name implies, this was a closed hospital where Chinese women coming under the 1857 *Ordinance for Checking the spread of Venereal Disease* were treated until, in the great majority of cases, they were cured.[160] The women here were patients, not criminals, but were not free to leave or to receive visitors. During the 1860s the Lock Hospital matron had charge of about twice the number of women held in the Gaol. In contrast to the gaol, the staffing here was stable, with husband and wife team, Mr and Mrs Noronha appointed as apothecary and matron respectively on 1st January 1858 and remaining in post until the middle of 1866. Mrs Noronha's salary, reflecting the special medical skills she required, and the importance with which the government viewed her post, was £50 per year. Only women from the brothels serving European clients had to undergo the routine inspections, and since the men using these houses were primarily military, naval and police, the administration put priority on keeping them as disease-free as possible.

It was during the 1870s that the very small story of female government employment in 19th-century Hong Kong really starts. As the number of women being treated at the Lock Hospital increased, it was necessary in 1868 to appoint a second matron, at the same salary. In 1874 two female (Chinese) nurses joined the staff, paid just £7 10s. per year, but soon increasing to £20. This was the first use of the term 'nurse' in the official records. The Civil Hospital employed cooks, coolies, scavengers and gatekeepers, but all the care for patients came from the three, later four, 'ward-masters'. One of the female nurses was transferred to the main hospital the following year. Here in 1877 the tally of ward-masters reduced to two, but six male nurses had been appointed. The Smallpox Hospital and the Asylum also had male nurses from this point, but the number of female nurses had only increased by one: Mrs Simmons of the Lunatic Asylum.

---

160 European prostitutes were granted the privilege of being both checked for disease and treated if necessary in their own homes.

Doubtless there were people whose behaviour around the town caused them to be thought insane, but the police would have scant reason to do anything other than bring the person to the magistrate as a vagabond or suspicious character. Sometimes he would send them to the Civil Hospital or the Gaol, but many of the Chinese were simply taken back to Canton. The Tung Wah rescued some – they were more fortunate as that Hospital would ensure that they did get back to their home village. There are intermittent reports of European 'lunatics' being sent back to Britain at the government's expense. But the new Colonial Surgeon, Dr Phineas Ayres, appointed in 1873, was a young man full of energy and reforming zeal, determined to make Hong Kong healthier for all its inhabitants. He realised that as it became a more settled community, the colony would need its own Lunatic Asylum where the mentally fragile could be cared for and relieved of their symptoms.[161] In his Annual Report to the Governor in 1874, he called attention to "the problems created by confining such people in the Hospital and the Gaol. Not only were the whole Hospital or Gaol kept in uproar, but the terrible cries from these unfortunate people became a public nuisance to the residents in the neighbourhood."[162]

However, before the authorities had even planned a building, the case of one American woman resulted in the employment of a Female Keeper. Sarah Jane Bennett, born in Buffalo, USA in the mid-1840s, had come to the China coast first in 1863 as a 20-year-old stewardess on an American barque.[163] Described as a Creole, illness had forced her to leave the ship at Amoy: from there she had gone to Shanghai where she had married an Afro-American soldier in the Chinese Imperial Army. When he was arrested and sent back to America, Sarah, left destitute, had come to

---

161 Reading the Medical reports through the century, the Asylum had, by its own account, quite a good record of curing or relieving patients, allowing them to be discharged. In this it did not resemble the huge institutional asylums of Britain or America.

162 Quoted in his Report of 1877, *Hongkong Government Gazette,* 6th July 1878.

163 *Hongkong Daily Press,* 30th January 1868 & 6th May 1873, and notes from American Consular enquiry. Her story occupies a few of Carl Smith's cards and it is from here and the newspaper references that this account comes. What became of her is unclear, unless she was the first female patient of the Asylum, to whom Dr Ayres referred when he mentioned that this woman was cured.

Hong Kong, apparently seeking help from the Consul there. This was refused, and she lived for some time with another American who in 1874 landed in prison for drunken brawling. Throughout her stay in Hong Kong she had repeatedly been gaoled for drunkenness, but during 1875 her mental health broke down. It was at yet another appearance in the police court that the magistrate sought the involvement of Dr Ayres and the American Consul. Whilst the latter made investigations about her background, a Mr and Mrs Simmons were identified as people who might undertake to have charge of her. Or rather, it was Mrs Maria Simmons that the government sought authority to employ as a female nurse at a salary of £75 per year, in July 1875. In a rare instance of convenience allied to compassion, it was noted that Mrs Simmons was an unfortunate but hard-working woman, with a drunken husband and who was therefore worthy of pity. The couple then took sole charge of Sarah Bennett in their own home, the 'generous' salary reflecting the need for Mrs Simmons to feed and clothe her patient. She did not appear on the Civil Establishment list until 1877 when the 'provisional and temporary' Asylum opened. The small hospital with just four cells, each about thirteen feet square and with plenty of windows, was away from the more populous part of the town in a requisitioned building. Here Sarah Bennett stayed for a few months until she was pronounced cured by the Colonial Surgeon and discharged. Although in 1878 there were no female patients, Maria Simmons retained her post, which she would hold until 1892, when at 56 years old she retired on a pension. She died some fourteen years later, aged 70, quite a remarkable age for a European who had spent a considerable portion of her life in the least hygienic parts of Hong Kong.

Not to deviate away from the Female Prison for too long, it is worth mentioning how these few posts fared and developed through the rest of the century. After the Noronha's at the Lock Hospital, other Portuguese matrons followed, including Mrs Guilhermina Assis, who held the post until 1883. In 1884 the government recruited Mrs Jane Ackers, qualified in both general nursing and midwifery, from England, at a salary of £100 per year She held the post until the rescinding of the *Contagious Disease Ordinance* and the amalgamation of the Lock Hospital into the

Government Civil Hospital, when she became matron of the Women's Venereal Ward. Here she provided very similar care for many of the same women who now voluntarily sought examination and treatment. By this time she was one of several female employees in the Hospital. In 1889 it employed French-speaking nursing sisters from a convent in Saigon, but this did not prove satisfactory, and they were replaced the next year with five trained nurses and a matron, Clara Eastmond, brought out from London. In 1897 a Lying-in Hospital was established, with two Chinese nurses, in an attempt to persuade more local mothers to avail themselves of western childbirth methods and halt the alarming levels of infant mortality in the colony (as recounted in Chapter 3). The following year a small Nursing Institute came into being, with two European nursing instructors. Meanwhile, Caroline Walker had replaced Mrs Simmons at the Lunatic Asylum, and whilst later she came under the matron, Clara Eastmond, it was she who was in charge of the female inmates here. All the hospitals were employing amahs (ward maids) from the 1890s, and although they were poorly paid, this did increase the number of women in the wards and provide some opportunities for Chinese women.

The only woman on the civil establishment list before the 1880s, other than those in the gaol and medical departments, was Ng Shi, the teacher of needlework in the Central School from 1870. We may assume that she is female when the level of salary the role attracted is considered. Paid just £15 per year, Ng Shi received the same as the school coolies and less even than the (Chinese male) pupil teacher.[164] Fifteen years later there were two teachers sharing the work and the wage. Then, on 1st March 1890, the small Central School for Girls was founded with (aside from the caretaker) an all-female staff including a headmistress. On 18th December 1893 this became the Belilios Public School (English Division). However, outside the government school system women had been teaching in Hong Kong since the very first days of British administration. Aside from the few employed privately as governesses, the two convent schools, St Paul's and the Italian Convent (later the Sacred Heart Canossian College), both

---

164 A pupil teacher was a senior student employed as an apprentice teacher-cum-classroom assistant.

received government aid and were staffed by teaching sisters, and so have a long tradition of educating girls and young boys that continues today.

One other female appointee must be mentioned, a woman who occupied a specialist role. The sister of the founding director of Hong Kong's Observatory, Miss Anna Doberck B. A. became, at 34 years old, the Assistant Meteorologist in May 1892. In an attempt to resolve the staffing problems encountered at the Observatory, chiefly through the Director, Dr William Doberck's somewhat cantankerous nature, the administration agreed to the appointment of the Copenhagen-educated woman. While her brother retired to England in 1907, she remained at the Observatory until 1915, when her role was abolished. The post had come with a salary of $1,000 per year, comparable to that of the matron in charge of the Civil Hospital. There is just one other type of government work, although unpaid and unacknowledged, undertaken by women. It was occasionally necessary for the police to search female suspects. It was not until the 1900s that Female Searchers were employed, and then first by the Naval Dockyard Police Force. Until that time, this was a function that European sergeants' and inspectors' wives had to perform at the various stations where they lived – a rather unsavoury duty.

Female wages were gradually rising, but part of this was within the government's general response to rising prices and the slide in the value of silver, to which the Hong Kong currency was linked. In 1879 it started recording all salaries in dollars in the *Blue Books*. The $300 that the Gaol Matron now received, which ten years earlier would have been worth £60, had fallen by 11% in its value, and would slide a lot further before the century was out. Coping with a continual shortage of money was a common experience for most working-class people in the colony, of whatever nationality. Their informal social support systems were all important, therefore. The British in Hong Kong bonded together in groups defined both by occupation and by social class. In the 19th century, this mutual support extended to the adoption of orphaned children and the marriage of widows and widowers. The Portuguese community, with their much deeper roots in the region, and relatively few members that were not Macao or Hong Kong born, had extended families and wide friendship groups to fall back upon. So as Anneline had friends with whom to stay after she left the gaol, Mary Collins and some other early matrons at the gaol would have been able to tap into the band of gaol guard wives, perhaps sharing servants as well as child care. The regulations permitted her to be away from the gaol with the permission of the superintendent and that when necessary, she could delegate her duties to the wife of a turnkey or guard or other suitable married woman. Mary Goodings must have had recourse to this both during the later stages of her pregnancy and confinement, and on the death of her second husband. Now that there was proper separate accommodation for the matron, Mary Collins, widowed early in her marriage, continued at the gaol until ill health forced her to apply for retirement in December 1887, aged 43. She was granted a pension of $116.66 per year, but died the following July and was buried in St Michael's Catholic cemetery in Happy Valley.

CHAPTER 6

THE WOMEN'S PRISON – A SCRAMBLE FOR SPACE

D isease, including dysentery, malaria, typhoid fever, tuberculosis and typhus, was a constant presence in the city. These illnesses flourished through the lack of adequate sanitation, great overcrowding and deficient nutrition amongst the poorer people. Standards of hygiene in the sale of food were fair, but the squalor in which many had to live caused problems thereafter. Gaol illnesses were largely those of the town: unsurprising, when so many men simply passed through for a brief period. There had been an infirmary room from the outset, although the first was situated so close to the privies and associated drains that patients frequently caught malaria besides the illness that had sent them there. The hospital on the east wing floor, above the women's accommodation, was more suitable and sufficed for two decades, although it had occasionally to annex communal cells. The large association wards of the mid-century were breeding grounds for disease, for example, when a prisoner entered during 1866, recently arrived from Macao with symptoms similar to yellow fever. Within a few months, the spread of this contagious disease had resulted in 373 hospital admissions and 40 deaths. However, as the 'separate' system of confinement in individual or, in times of over-crowding, three-man cells became the norm, such contagion became less frequent. Both the Gaol and Colonial Surgeon's reports gave details of the medical problems of the men, amongst which anaemia, malaria and malarial fever (then called remittent and intermittent fevers) and dysentery were frequently seen. Problems caused by the withdrawal of opium and contused wounds after flogging (all men flogged required medical treatment in the weeks after punishment) were those attributable to the gaol itself.

One notable absentee from the roster of diseases in the last decade of the century is bubonic plague. This devastating pestilence struck Hong Kong early in 1894, causing the deaths of over 2,500 in the colony, and many more who had already fled back to their home villages and towns on the mainland. About 80,000 people fled back to Guangdong province, whence the disease had come. Trade and normal life ground to a near standstill and the western part of the town had to be thoroughly cleansed. During the next ten years it claimed the lives of over 8,000 and outbreaks in 1912, 1914 and 1922 a further 5,000. Hong Kong saw its last cases in 1929.[165] And yet, through all of this, there was no outbreak of the disease in the gaol. Although unknown at the time of the initial outbreak, rats carried across the harbour and infesting the town were responsible for the spread of the disease. Presumably, the cleaning routines undertaken by prison labour ensured that the gaol was free of this vermin, and therefore, of the plague.

In the Colonial Surgeon's annual reports there are very few references to illness amongst the women, even though almost all lived communally. To some extent, as usual, their small numbers and close supervision doubtless helped check the spread of any disease brought in by a prisoner. Long-time Colonial Surgeon, Dr Phineas Ayres, who stoutly maintained that opium smoking *per se* was not a problem and that only its excess caused concern, paid special attention to prisoners who had been long-time addicts. He noted that one 60-year-old female prisoner, who told him that she had smoked for 25 years, was admitted suffering anaemia. This was treated successfully, but although she was not allowed any opium or given any substitute, she suffered no ill effects.[166]

Making way for the Gaol Hospital – to Wyndham Street

Although the general health of the gaol was good, and that of the women's prison caused no comment, by the early 1880s the hospital was straining at the seams. Dr Ayres frequently complained in his reports about the preponderance of vagabonds and beggars amongst those the magistrates

165 Chan-Yeung, Moira, *A Medical History of Hong Kong 1842-1941*, pp. 152-3.

166 Report of the Colonial Surgeon for 1878, *Hongkong Government Gazette*, 9th July 1879.

sent his way. Many on their admission, he said, looked "so seedy that they are put under observation for a time to make sure of their condition."[167] Thus, in July 1885, towards the end of Mrs Collin's term as matron, there was no option but to requisition the Female Prison as additional hospital space. Six Indian guards were then billeted in the octagonal building that had been hers, and a house, No. 47 Wyndham Street, was rented to accommodate herself and her charges.[168] The Rate Books, which list every property in the colony and the person responsible for paying the quarterly levy, records that this house was the property of one G. Carvalho throughout this time. The government spent $500 on its conversion from residential property into this more specialised use. Fortunately, that year there was only an average of six prisoners on any day, so it was a simple matter to take them the short walk down Arbuthnot Road to the house.

Unfortunately, to date neither plans nor photographs of the house have come to light. Wyndham Street loops uphill and round to connect Queen's Road Central, opposite the Post Office, with Hollywood Road, and until the mid-1920s the section which ascends from the main road was known as 'Flower Street'. The level road that ran beneath and converged with the descending Arbuthnot Road contained more variety of buildings, both two and three storeys, but predominantly in a European style. Gaol Superintendent Henry Lethbridge, bemoaned the fact that the house had only two association wards and punishment cells, and a small yard. It seems probable that the alterations had removed internal partitions on the ground and first floors to create the larger communal spaces, with some washing facilities downstairs and accommodation for the matron on an upper floor. The rateable value suggests that the building was not large. It usually held between 6 and 18 prisoners, with one exceptional year, 1892, when there was an average of 27 women on any day.[169] That year there were an unusually high number committed for sentences between three months and a year, and six were there for terms of up to five years. The period when the prison was outside the main gaol coincided with a

---

167 Report of the Colonial Surgeon for 1884, *Hongkong Government Gazette* 18th April, 1885.

168 *Hongkong Government Gazette*, 26th September 1885.

169 All figures taken from the annual Gaols and Prisoners Report in the *Blue Books*.

time when those held for civil offences (debt) was above average. While they never reach double figures, and were not there long, it doubtless caused friction that these debtors could not have the less basic facilities that they might expect.

Cramped as they were, the situation of the women was still better than that of their male counterparts. In the main building overcrowding was a continuous and sometimes dangerous problem. Writing in his 1890 report, the superintendent, Major-General Gordon, told how so many men had to be crammed into the association cells that, had Victoria Gaol been a lodging house in the town, and he its landlord, he would have been fined $50 per cell.[170] In all 95 of these cells the men had about one-third of the cubic airspace required by law in boarding houses. The men were packed together, lying on the floor covered by blankets. Any pretence at keeping the silence was a mere formality, and whilst the Colonial Surgeon worried about health and sanitation, he, Mj.-Gen. Gordon, saw much greater evils in immorality and the 'school of crime' thus created.

The matron had similar problems, segregating her charges. Keeping apart those held on remand from the women serving sentences was seen as of paramount importance by the gaol regulations. To achieve this, all others, bar the debtors, had to live together in one ward. In some years, where the numbers in both categories were low, this would not be too difficult for the matron. But other times, when the police turned up with a few women awaiting trial just as the twenty or so prisoners had been equably spread between the two association wards, it was doubtless a different matter. There must have been occasions when a lone woman on remand was put into a punishment cell, perhaps with a few more comforts added, just to prevent another upheaval. In any case there was no chance here of preserving different areas for those whose offences had and had not merited them hard labour; and the first-time offender from the gaol habitué (although this latter was rare).

Matron Nolan – a Hong Kong woman

Mrs Margaret Nolan, who was the matron for most of the time that the Female Prison was in the private house, was the wife of head

---

170 *Hongkong Government Gazette,* 11th April, 1891.

turnkey Nicholas Nolan, a long serving and well-trusted officer. She had succeeded Mary Collins upon that lady's retirement, and, for once, there was an opportunity for the two women to have some 'hand-over' of responsibilities. Indeed, since the regulations permitted a turnkey's wife to deputise for the matron, Mrs Nolan may well have been familiar with the role before taking it over on 7th December 1887. She had married in 1867 in County Wexford in Ireland, when Nicholas was a soldier, just back from wars in India. The couple came out to Hong Kong with his regiment in 1872, but soon Nolan left for a post as sergeant in the Naval Dockyard Police. From here he moved to the gaol and a post with better prospects. Taken on as a 2nd class Turnkey, his previous experience saw him promoted a year later to 3rd Head Turnkey. Within a decade of joining he was Head Turnkey and sometimes acting Warder, his salary having increased three-fold to $1,200 per year As an employee with such a responsible position the superintendent had no qualms about this couple occupying the quarters above the Female Prison, although, of course, Nolan would not have entered that unless on instruction from the superintendent, and accompanied by the matron. The family strengthened its ties with the colony's civil service, first when the eldest of their three surviving children married the warden. Then, in 1891, their eldest son, aged 16, was successful in the competition for one of the newly created student interpreter posts. Perhaps it was an upbringing in and around the very multi-lingual world of the dockyard and the gaol that gave Nicholas George Nolan a head-start: he later became Chief Interpreter of the Supreme Court and the colony's most proficient linguist in the 1910s.[171]

The years 1891-2 saw a pay increase for most of the roles occupied by westerners, and for the more senior Chinese posts, as the prices of foodstuffs and other imported goods rose. Nolan's salary, as 2nd Head Turnkey, had increased from $720 to $972 in 1891 and the next year that of his wife became $480, whilst his rose again to $1,080. The family's financial circumstances were thus improving, but there was further

---

171 This family was related by the marriage of Nicholas George, to the large clan of Newmarket, County Cork men who served in the Hong Kong Police Force from 1864-1950. More of the Nolan's story is given in the author's *Policing Hong Kong – an Irish History.*

expense to come. In 1895 they had to find a bond of $2,000, as a guarantee that their son, Nicholas George, would stay in Government service for a minimum of six years. Such bonds were usually required when the role held particular responsibility, or access to government funds. Here, the administration wished to defray the costs of the language education they had provided the young man, which included a time in Swatow (Shantou), should he leave for a commercial role. That year the salary of both father and son was $1,200 per year. Margaret Nolan's was increased to $600 the following year.[172]

The Wyndham Street house had bathing and clothes washing facilities, but apparently no kitchen, as meals had to be brought by prison coolies from the gaol kitchens. The area had buried drains, but of limited size, so the house would have utilised the night soil collection system that was standard in the colony, rather than flushing water closets. A pressing concern was that the women only had the enclosed side yard of the building in which to exercise. A space of 24 feet by 9 feet could only hold a few at a time, if they were to be properly supervised and prevented from talking to one another. Although so close to the main building, it was, of its nature, isolated. By the mid-1890s Government House, the principal departments of the administration and most of the police stations were connected by telephone, with the exchange at the Central Police Station. But not so the gaol: it would be many years before there was an internal telephone system. The house had one or two prison servants, and Indian prison guards watched over it, both day and night. Just occasionally a woman was obstreperous and even violent. How did the matron cope with this situation? She could call for aid from a guard stationed outside or send a servant with a message to the warden, and then one of the punishment (solitary) cells might be used. Few men would be seen by the prisoners, apart from the doctor. Aside from attending to any sick prisoners, he had to check each incoming convict's health and authorise the detention of any in solitary confinement. The matron answered directly to the superintendent. It would be he, accompanied by Mrs

---

172 *Hongkong Government Gazette*, 23rd May 1896, Ranks of Staff and Salaries, Victoria Gaol.

Nolan, who made any necessary checks on the building or the housing of the prisoners.

The women of Wyndham Street

Who were the women serving time in this little house? A cursory browse through the small columns of a few issues of *The China Mail* in June 1892 shows why the prison was so crowded that year. The magistrate gave two women six-month sentences for the unlawful possession of prepared opium. One had been found with 15 taels on her, the other, in Yaumatei, with one. They might have paid the $50 fine, but that was not usual. Inspector Baker had conducted a raid in Fletcher Street in Wanchai and caught a gambling den playing for money. Three keepers of the den, two men and a woman, were sentenced, the latter receiving the lighter sentence of a $25 fine or one month in gaol. Magistrate H. E. Wodehouse also heard the case of a female who brought in a kidnapped girl from Kwangsi (Guangxi) with a view to exporting her to Singapore to be a prostitute. The kidnappers had taken her from her uncle's house to Canton, where she had been sold for $250 to the woman. The procuress had told her to tell the harbour officials in Hong Kong that she was Annamese and going to join her husband in Singapore, but a Po Leung Kuk detective on the steamer persuaded her to tell the true story.[173] This was a good illustration of the kind of work the Society did for the colony, remarked *The China Mail*. The procuress was not given any option of a fine, but joined the other prisoners in No. 47 Wyndham Street for nine months. The prison also had to be a refuge or holding place, where the police could take women *pro tem*. A woman attempted to commit suicide by throwing herself off the Praya wall. She would not be punished, but at the time this was still an offence and she must appear before the magistrate who would decide what was best for her. Had she sustained injuries in the fall or been long in the water, the police would have taken her to the Civil Hospital for immediate treatment. But this woman had been hauled out straight away by a Chinese constable and so went to the prison, where the matron

---

173 Annam, the central region of what is now Vietnam, was, at the time, part of French Indochina.

had to get her dried out, ready to go before Mr Wodehouse the following morning. He then placed her in the care of her son.

It was imperative that Mrs Nolan had some assistance as it became apparent that the number of women held on any day was never again going to be in single figures. In October 1891 space had to be made for a 'Female Nurse', the first occupant of which post was Haū Chung, paid $144 per year, and living in the Female Prison. But as necessary as it was to augment the staffing of the little prison, the efforts of the gaol to find suitable women met initially with scant success. In 1893 the Superintendent had to dismiss two successive nurses for misconduct, and in the first three years there appear to have been six Chinese in that post. It would be no surprise to find Margaret Nolan had gained sufficient Cantonese for her role during her time in Hong Kong. She was also a gentle and careful matron: the 1891 report of the Medical Attendant to the Gaol, Dr L. P. Marques, praises her work, not only for the sick prisoners:

> The Matron, Mrs M. Nolan, who acts as a nurse whenever there is any sick female prisoner, is very attentive to her duties, and by her tact has been very successful in persuading the women to obey the rules of the Gaol.[174]

and again the following year,

> There were, amongst the female prisoners, some cases which required great care in nursing. Mrs M. Nolan, the Matron, has proved to be very trustworthy and kind to the prisoners.[175]

The arrival of the twenty-six-year-old Mrs Joanna Maria Raptis in 1894 resolved the staff problem. She was the Portuguese daughter-in-law of a long-serving turnkey who had retired just a few years earlier. About

---

174 Report of the Medical Officer in charge of the Gaol, L. P. Marques, attached to the Colonial Surgeon's Report for 1891 *Hongkong Government Gazette* 19th November 1892.

175 Report of Medical Officer, as above, *Hongkong Government Gazette* 24th June 1893.

four years' married, she had a period of absence when her fourth child was born in 1896, but then served as Wardress (as the post was then designated) until 1905. Unlike the post of matron, the regulations made no reference to any restriction on where the nurse/wardress might live, although the gaol undertook to provide quarters. Mrs Raptis' husband, who also had been a gaol turnkey but was now the storekeeper at the Taikoo Sugar Refinery, lived out at Quarry Bay, some four and a half miles from the prison. The woman's employment was just a little too early to benefit from the trams, which started in 1904, so she may have availed herself of the accommodation provided, especially as her duties would have involved her presence at night. In the meantime things were changing for Margaret Nolan. In June 1896, worn down by long hours, and never having taken leave from his work, her husband had to go into the Civil Hospital.[176] On Saturday 4th July he passed away and was buried the next evening at sunset in St Michael's Catholic Cemetery. He was 55 years old.

Margaret never really recovered from her grief, although she continued as matron until April of the following year. She retired eight months shy of the ten years required to earn her a pension, but received a gratuity of $597. Nicholas George helped her write a very elegant appeal to the Governor for an increase in this, saying how difficult it was to survive on just the salaries of her two boys, but the family was not in quite such desperate straits as she implied. With them, she used the $2,000 she inherited to complete the purchase of a large lot (plot of land) on Wanchai Road, where, in the next year, they built a pair of substantial houses, Summerville and Rockview. However, she did not live long to enjoy the relative luxury of these properties, dying four years to the day after her husband.

Working in Victoria Gaol

Mrs Nolan's last months as gaol matron had been busy ones. During the preceding decade plans had been prepared to increase the gaol accommodation, both for prisoners and staff. Superintendent Lethbridge

---

176 Unlike the police and most other departments of government. the Gaol did not offer half-pay leave to its employees until well into the next century.

had frequently urged the proper and adequate housing of the women, but it was not until his last year in the post that it was found possible to remodel the old women's prison, at the eastern end of the gaol, into something better fitted for their needs. The 1896 Gaol Report records that the women moved back into the main building on 31st October of that year. Once there, they found that they now had six individual and two penal cells, five association wards (although not as large as in Wyndham Street), along with a larger enclosed outdoor exercise area. The final years of the century saw the figures for female prisoners rise substantially, so that regularly there were 30 women there each day, and it was around this number that were escorted by their matron into their new quarters. Although these were not ideal, they were an improvement on No. 47. However, other buildings had been erected close by this block since the women's removal over ten years earlier. Now three sides of the women's prison was hemmed in by close walls, and since the remaining side faced Arbuthnot Road, and it was at the ground floor level, there were no opening windows there. In consequence the ventilation was poor, and, as Superintendent May was to report the following year, the temperature in summer became extreme.[177] This energetic man, already Captain Superintendent of Police, had taken control of the gaol that year and put in place a series of modifications. Using prison labour, these included the building of a new prison hospital where the officers' quarters had been. This hospital was to be altogether larger and more commodious than its predecessor, and would allow the female gaol to be extended, with perhaps an extra floor of space. However, although all the building work was completed mid-way through 1898, there was no swift change-around. Reminiscent of a child's puzzle, each piece had to take its turn. The work on the upper storey for the women could not begin until the hospital had moved into its new home. And that could not happen until the Indian warders, who were temporarily housed in the new building, could move into their new accommodation, in Wyndham Street, which was being erected by outside labour, of course. As of February 1899,

177 CO129/275 p.569, report of F. H. May to Governor William Robinson, 7th May 1897, in connection with Carew case.

the building of those quarters had not yet begun.[178] Problems with the supply of materials and disputes with the contractors meant that these were not ready for the Indian officers until 1902, when finally the big 'shuffle round' could happen.

During the absence of the nurse, Mrs Raptis, in 1896 there had been the predictable problem of finding a replacement, made rather more difficult as now there were to be two assistants. In line with changes in the men's prison that saw turnkeys styled as warders, they became 'wardresses' for the first time, but paid only $120 per year each. Another series of women were employed and dismissed or resigned, until, two months before Mrs Nolan's retirement, Filomena Lewis arrived, with Mrs Raptis returning a few months later. The salary for each was $240 per year. The *Blue Books* then have a few years where the staff of the women's prison are recorded only by their surnames. This is out of step with usual practice – European warders are given an initial and surname, and all the Chinese and the great majority of the Indian employees appear with their full names. The Portuguese Franco, presumably a Mrs Franco, was appointed matron at the same salary as Mrs Nolan on 15th April 1897. No man of that name served on the gaol staff then, although there were three others in government employment elsewhere. We know little more about the background of these women, except that Mrs Lewis' 14-year-old son died of the plague the following year. These three women set the pattern for the employment of predominantly Portuguese women that only changed when the prison moved to Lai Chi Kok in 1932. For the very small pay offered, and the limitations it imposed on staff, no British woman could be found who would accept the uncongenial post.

But where were the staff of the Female Prison now accommodated? There is no reference to the octagonal building they formerly occupied being removed, after housing some Indian guards in 1885, so it is possible that they returned there. However, the *Conservation Management Plan* for the entire site, published in 2008, states: "… a house was built for the Matron in the Prison Yard adjoining the Chief Warder's Quarters. The house consisted of two rooms with bathroom, pantry and cook house accommodation. This building cannot be clearly seen on any historic

178 *Hongkong Government Gazette,* 11th February 1899.

maps, and likely does not exist in any form today."[179] This report does not indicate the source of this information, and searches by this author have brought no such reference to light. However, the superintendent's report on the Carew case mentions that "The quarters of the matron which are now shared by one of the wardresses open onto the yard which is now used for these purposes" (exercise and labour).[180] Regulations published in 1897 state that "The Matron shall reside in the place allotted for female prisoners."[181] The wording seems almost to suggest that the current location of the women in their old quarters was not permanent. But three years later, a further revision to the regulations amends this to "shall reside in the prison."[182]

By retiring in mid-April 1897, Margaret Nolan had just missed having charge of perhaps the most notorious British woman in the region that the 19th century had seen. Mrs Edith May Hallowell Carew, after a long and tortuous trial in the British Consular Court of Japan, had been found guilty of the murder by arsenic poisoning of her husband, George Carew, in Yokohama on 23rd October the previous year. In a case that electrified the foreign community of Hong Kong almost as much as it did that of Japan, the attractive young widow was the recipient of much sympathy, and the 'guilty' verdict and subsequent death penalty the Judge, Robert Mowat, intoned stunned many, including, it would seem, the judge himself. The case has been extensively researched by Douglas Clark and his account makes lively and, at times, nail-biting reading.[183] Using the dubious excuse that Japanese prisoners condemned to death on the day of the Emperor's birthday (31st January) had been pardoned by proclamation, Judge Mowat declared that, in the case of this woman, she should thus be at least granted a commutation to life imprisonment. This was even more specious when it is noted that Carew was condemned on 1st February. However, London did not overturn the decision. After a

179 Purcell Miller Tritton LLP, *The Old Central Police Station and Victoria Prison, Hong Kong*, p. 32.

180 CO129/27., p. 570, as note 12.

181 *Hongkong Government Gazette,* 27th March, 1897, notes 70-78.

182 *Hongkong Government Gazette,* 7th April 1900, notes 72-80.

183 Douglas Clark, *Gunboat Justice, vol. 1*, pp. 344-365.

period in the Consular Gaol in Yokohama, where rumours abounded that Carew lived in high style, receiving guests and able to order in what food she pleased, she was transferred to Hong Kong to continue her sentence, arriving on 3rd May 1897. She had been escorted by a warder on the voyage, occupying a first class cabin and served second class food. When the ship docked in Victoria Harbour at 7 a.m. that morning, she wisely asked (and was permitted) to take breakfast on board before departing for Victoria Gaol.

Her transfer to the prison was discretely effected, but the arrival of a well-dressed woman with a small mountain of luggage must have caused comment amongst the various on-lookers always at the entrance to the Police Compound and the Gaol. Carew was affronted to find that she could not have her clothes and possessions with her, and distraught to learn that her caged canary would not keep her company in her solitude. However, soon anxieties were raised about the probable effects of any long-term confinement in the prison on her health. The Medical Officer considered that no European woman could tolerate the lack of ventilation, intense humidity and heat of the building for long, and thus it was imperative to transfer her to a prison in England. But for the superintendent of the gaol, it was the risk of the three Portuguese staff of the prison being tempted by bribes to favour the woman that was his principal concern. On 7th May 1897 he wrote, "The temptations placed in the way of such women enjoying as they do such small salaries by having in their charge a prisoner who has notoriously considerable private means, and a large number of sympathisers who believe in her innocence and are ready and willing to assist her in any way they can, is I must admit very great and such as to demand serious consideration."[184]

Meanwhile, the Home Secretary refused the application to appeal the sentence sent by Carew's solicitors. The various permissions and warrants for the transfer, alongside an extended discussion about who would pay for the removal, took a few months. Eventually, on 19th October, accompanied by Wardress Lewis and about-to-retire Police Sergeant

184 CO129/275, pp. 569-571, F. H. May to J. H. Stewart Lockhart, Colonial Secretary. May's rather notorious racial prejudice is at work here, but he was also making that point that the staff was so small that there were no checks on the women falling prey to such temptations.

George Phelps, she departed on the *S.S. Sumatra*. The expense claim Hong Kong submitted included one serge and three dungaree dresses and a straw hat, presumably for the prisoner. Once in Britain, they travelled to Holloway Prison, where Carew would stay pending the Home Secretary's decision on her future place of confinement. George Phelps, his work now done, found that neither the pension nor the bonus were waiting for him, although both had been agreed before he left Hong Kong. He had to find temporary accommodation for himself and his family, whilst the original correspondence from Hong Kong was located.[185] The treatment of Filomena Lewis was a little better. The Governor had requested that she receive an 'inconvenience allowance' of three shillings a day while in London, but since she had board and lodging at Holloway Prison and was to receive her regular salary at the very advantageous rate of four shillings to the dollar, this was considered unnecessary.[186] However, rather than waiting until she was about to leave London to give her this, it was decided to advance her sufficient to enable her to go sight-seeing and purchase things to take back with her. She had, the governor of Holloway noted, very limited English, so perhaps a wardress from the prison was allowed to show her round London during the two weeks before her return passage.

Hong Kong may have felt it had seen the last of Edith Carew, but she had more in store for the colony. It was, perhaps, at a routine visit to the prison by Justices of the Peace, when she was pointed out to one, Sir Algernon West. This career civil servant had been William Gladstone's private secretary until the elderly prime minister stood down in 1893. Now, maybe pausing to have a word with this rather unusual prisoner, he found himself listening to Carew tell him how male prisoners were regularly tortured in the Hong Kong gaol. She alleged that she had heard the screams of those undergoing torture, that it was quite a notorious thing throughout the prison, and that she had even seen the gaol doctor stand with his pocket-watch in hand, timing the length of the punishment. The civil servant communicated with Lord Selbourne, Under Secretary

185 CO129/280, pp. 426-434, correspondence from 2nd December 1897.
186 The prevailing rate that year was about two shillings to the dollar. Mrs Lewis received £8 for her two months' salary.

of State for the Colonies, and then had another interview with Carew.[187] He was convinced of her sincerity and sure that she spoke the truth as she knew it. His letters, unsurprisingly, caused a minor storm at the Colonial Office, albeit one that was conducted very *sotto voce*. At the time, the former Governor and Colonial Surgeon, William Robinson and Phineas Ayres, were both in England, as was the Colonial Secretary, Mr Stewart Lockhart, and all gave their opinion on the letters. In typically robust terms, Sir William Robinson opened his thus: "I am surprised at Sir Algernon West fathering such rubbish". The other two provided equally firm rebuffs, but with rather more in the way of evidence. There had been a very detailed enquiry into the excessive use of flogging in 1896, a year before Carew came to Hong Kong, resulting in moderating reforms. The doctor was of the opinion that the noises the woman heard might well have come from the patients in the gaol hospital, on the floor above the Women's Prison, some of whom were very severely ill. The Colonial Secretary was not at all surprised that Carew had bitter feelings about her time in Hong Kong's gaol, since it must have come as such a shock to her, from the comfortable life she had been allowed in the Consular Prison in Yokohama. There was anxiety that the story would reach the House of Commons, but it would appear that Sir Algernon received the strongest assurances that no such thing was ever permitted in one of Her Majesty's prisons, and was prevailed upon to take the matter no further. It was shortly after this that Carew was transferred to Aylesbury Convict Prison, until she was freed in November 1910.[188]

Having spent Christmas sailing through the Mediterranean, Filomena Lewis' great adventure came to a close as she returned to her post at the Prison in February 1898. It was three years later, when she and Joanna Raptis had been joined by a wardress named Dores that, for the second time in Hong Kong's history, a prisoner returned from her appearance at the Supreme Court a condemned woman. The story of Wong Po and her miserable end is recounted in Chapter 7, but the weeks of waiting for the decision of the Executive Council, then her descent into a malarial coma

---

187 The surviving papers are at CO129/289, pp. 440-447, commencing with Sir Algernon Wise's letter to Lord Selbourne, 19th May 1898.
188 *Los Angeles Herald,* 21st November 1910.

must have affected the women, both staff and prisoners, albeit that her death came after she had been transferred to the Maternity Hospital.

In the first decade of the 20th century warders took most of the male prisoners out to the yards for shot drill or stone breaking, whilst others worked in the print room or at bookbinding or shoe-making.[189] The prison used men with skills in the building trade in the building's upkeep, whilst others cleaned the prison or worked in the laundry, which took in sheets and bedding from the Civil Hospital in addition to dealing with prison clothes. Laundry labour was reckoned to be as physically exhausting as any crank-turning or shot carrying. Heavy loads of washing had to be turned and lifted in and out of the huge washing coppers, and then put through great mangles to rid them of excess water. Some men's labour was in their cells, including those on the crank machine, oakum picking or mat-making.[190]

All the Chinese prisoners received a clean set of clothes each week, with Europeans getting a weekly change of underwear, and outer clothes washed when necessary. Prisoners were not supplied with sheets, while their blankets (one or two per person, according to the weather) were washed as needed. The thirty women created, therefore, quite a volume of clothes to deal with, and the reports on the industry of the gaol record that, for example, in 1910 eight women were working at clothes washing each day. There is no evidence to suggest that part of the gaol laundry was reserved for females, and with the administrations' determination to keep them apart from the men, they would not have worked in the main washroom. The same unreferenced note in the *Conservation Management Plan,* referred to above, states that a drying area has been created in the yard for the women. However, it also seems unlikely that their clothes would be sent for the men to wash. In any group of women of the age most of the prisoners were, there will be some who are menstruating. In

---

189 Shot drill was the soul-destroying practice of requiring prisoners to move heavy cannonballs from one end of the yard to the other and then back again, either by carrying them against their chest or by passing them from one to another along a line.

190 The crank machine was another soul-destroying practice requiring the prisoner to repeatedly turn a crank that did nothing and whose resistance could be adjusted by a warder if they felt the labour was not hard enough.

most literature it is a subject shrouded by attempts to protect the delicate sensibilities of men. However, assuming that period protection here was similar to that in Britain (and, it would appear, other parts of the world), they may have simply bled into their clothes or used pads made of rags and linen 'clouts' held in place by pins or sewn into garments.[191] The latter were washed each day, but where the woman let her clothes absorb the menstrual blood, washing was left until the period had ended. The poorest may well have been so ill-nourished on entry to the gaol that their menstruation was erratic, but if prison diet had led to this, one or other of the Medical Officers of the gaol would have noted it (being made of sterner stuff). It is interesting that although there were, on various occasions, calls for a reduction to the female diet, partly because of waste, this did not happen.[192] All told, it would seem most probable that the Female Prison had its own washing copper, mangles and ironing boards. But because of Hong Kong's frequent rain, and the poor ventilation on the ground floor, the often humid conditions became more dank as the place was often festooned with wet clothes and cloths.

Washing was not the only work given to the women. Until the mid-1910s there would be a few engaged in oakum picking. This was considered hard labour, since the amount that was required of each prisoner meant little respite from the unravelling the tar-encrusted lengths of rope into individual fibre, without the aid of a metal pick or nail. In the first few weeks fingers would bleed, until callouses developed, which made the work harder, but at least less painful. However, in Hong Kong it was never as popular with prison authorities as in Britain, since, albeit with the help of a nail, it was often the occupation of young Chinese children, sitting at the quayside and unravelling piece after piece for payment of a few cents. This meant it cost the prison more to buy the oakum than the price for which they could sell the unravelled fibres. 'Hard labour' seems to have been more broadly defined here than in the rest of the gaol, mainly because of the absence of suitable tasks. Some convicts, therefore, undertook tailoring – making prison uniforms and those of the officers (a

---

191 Lecia Bushak, *A Brief History of the Menstrual Period.*

192 Report of the Gaol Committee, *Hongkong Government Gazette,* 10th March 1877, calling for a reduction by one-quarter of food allowed for the women.

harder job since the blue serge was much thicker and less yielding until it had been washed once or twice). Mending, knitting and cleaning of the common areas of their prison would occupy the rest.

Debtors and prisoners awaiting trial did not have to work, but, unlike the men in those categories, the women would often do so, to relieve the tedium of the days. On Sundays the only labour performed was the housekeeping and cleaning tasks. Good Friday and Christmas Day, and, from 1899, the first day of Chinese New Year were also rest-days. The gaol was, in theory at any rate, careful to respect the requirements of other faiths. Jewish prisoners could request to observe the Saturday sabbath and not work, whilst from 1911, Muslims in the prison who observed the Ramadan fast were on light duties only. In 1925 the Superintendent designated Saturdays as a half day – however, this seems to have more to do with staffing the men's gaol when the warders' conditions of service improved. Many of the women confined were no strangers to long hours and hard work. Perhaps for some, being relieved of the additional tasks of caring for the home or preparing food for others meant that life in prison was slightly easier for them than outside. Unlike their male counterparts, the women were never put to unproductive labour. In the 19th century most of the men were turning crank wheels, moving stones or, in earlier days, operating the short-lived tread-wheel. It was not until 1927 that all unproductive labour ceased.[193] The annual reports of work performed in the gaol detail not only how many prisoners were engaged at each task each day (on average) but what notional value was attached to this. In 1910 laundry work and tailoring were assessed at 15 cents per day, cleaning at 10 cents and oakum picking, which tended to cost the Gaol rather than otherwise, just 2 cents. Needless to say, no payment was made to the prisoners undertaking this work, but by accident or default, this is the first example of women's work being given equal monetary value, since the calculations were blind as to gender!

---

193 Printing and book-binding became some of the predominant trades of the male prison. By 1910 the Government had all its forms printed by gaol labour.

The unchanging routine in silence – or not

In the male prison, the chronic overcrowding frequently meant that there was not enough space for all the men to work, nor labour for them to perform. In the previous century, superintendents had complained that the Chinese prisoners would easily sleep and doze through the day if left unoccupied and resented being put to work. However, since outright refusal triggered a substantial drop in their rations – 'ill-conducted or idle prisoners' received just 12 ounces (350 grams) of rice, salt and water per day, for seven days – most complied. The behaviour of the women is mentioned only infrequently, and then always in favourable terms. Dr Marques had praised Mrs Nolan's tact in the matter of the women's observance of rules at No. 47 Wyndham Street, yet under the much closer supervision of their prison, only the most truculent could have disobeyed rules for long. But the existence of two penal – punishment – cells must show a need. Corporal punishment, which continued to be used on the men throughout the period of this study, could not be inflicted on women, thus the matron's only sanctions were a reduction in diet or solitary confinement, for which she had to first seek the agreement of the Medical Officer.

Whilst the women might have been quiet and compliant, that did not mean they were all content with their lot. In the hours beyond their enforced labour, there was only any recreational activity if the matron cared to supply it, and with the numbers increasing this did not happen in the early part of the 20th century. They were confined together, but barred from speaking to one another, with no books, games or other pastimes. So, as Bella Southorn, the wife of the Colonial Secretary, said in 1933, "Those people that comfort themselves with the reflection that 'stone walls do not a prison make nor iron bars a cage,' have probably never seen the inside of a jail nor the dejection of women prisoners given an hour's leisure with no means of occupying it."[194] Life was hard for many in Hong Kong, even without the added burden of prison. The presence of a conveniently deep harbour or the availability of cheap opium meant that suicide or attempts at it were a commonplace. During the 19th

---

194 *Hongkong Telegraph*, 24th May 1933, address sent by Mrs Bella Southorn to the organisers of the Hongkong Female Prisoners Industrial Sale of Work.

century in most years a small number of prisoners took their own lives, mostly by hanging themselves from their barred windows, some using their queue for the purpose. After the declaration of the Republic of China, and the outlawing of queues in 1911, and the better management and supervision of prisoners in the cells, these attempts became a rarity. Such desperate action would have been difficult for any women in the pre-1896 accommodation, but in 1897 the Medical Officer records that one woman hanged herself in her cell. Unfortunately, although an inquest would have been conducted, the papers contain no record of this and it seems to have been an isolated incident.

The rule of silence throughout the gaol was an import from Britain, but, as noted, lacking the same rationale, it was merely a matter of discipline. It receives far less official attention in the colony than in the records produced by English prisons, but infractions of this rule account for hundreds of the punishments meted out to the men in Victoria Gaol each year. Yet with the continued overcrowding, it must have been difficult for the warders to enforce this. There are no separate records of punishments given to women, so it is only possible to speculate whether the women's gaol was the place of quiet industry by day and silence at night that the regulations intended. There is nothing to show the amount of extra space the Prison gained – if, indeed, it did, when the floor above was eventually vacated. Small references to work carried out suggests that meals and labour for all took place in the association cells, aside from any in penal cells. In the English prison system, by the turn of the century, many were expressing concern for the fragile mental state of the 'weaker sex', and whether they could cope with isolation as it was practised there. Statistics were produced to evidence that it created a greater incidence of lunacy and mental instability in longer-term female prisoners. In consequence many prisons brought women out of their cells during the day, to work in 'silent association', often in the corridors in front of their doors.

Was the Female Prison, then, as silent as it was meant to be? From hints about the slightly less austere regime in place there, this was perhaps not quite the case. There was little chance of it when, as frequently happened, the women admitted had babies to care for. Regulations permitted a child to be admitted with its mother so long as it was still being breastfed, and the government undertook to pay for its clothing. This was initially interpreted as up to twelve months, but later reduced to nine months. Yet both magistrates and the prison authorities had licence to be flexible and often were. Children rather over one year accompanied their mother when no near relative could provide care, or when such relatives as came forward were 'undesirable'. The Medical Officer could decide that an infant was too sickly to be separated from the mother. These babies provided a welcome softening of the atmosphere of the prison. Women also arrived in various stages of pregnancy and until 1906, the *Blue Book* reports (rather erratically) mention births as well as deaths. Whether any of the additional space they may have gained on the first floor became a nursery is unknown, but one of the early improvements made when they finally moved to Lai Chi Kok in 1932 was the addition of a labour room and maternity section to the hospital ward. The focus of concern of the authorities was always on the child's welfare. With a matron and wardresses to support and advise, meals a little enhanced, as ordered by the doctor, and medical attention if required, pregnancy and birth must have been easier and safer for the mother than many experienced beyond the prison walls.

The babies and toddlers of inmate mothers were not the only children within the Female Prison. As will be seen in the section on Juvenile Remand Homes in Chapter 8, Hong Kong had no provision for wayward girls before the 1930s. Magistrates could send boys to the Catholic-run West Point Reformatory, but there was no such institution for girls. The 1892 Commission on the Po Leung Kuk mentions a few they define as 'bad girls'. From the context it appears these are not young prostitutes, but junior criminals.[195] The convents could occasionally be prevailed upon to readmit an errant runaway, but beyond these, the prison was the only recourse. The punishment usually given to boys was a birching, administered in the Gaol soon after sentencing, without admitting them there. Magistrates were reluctant to send young children to prison. From early reports there are hints that the gaol authorities were well aware that boys were subject to both physical and sexual abuse and received instruction

195 Report of the Special Committee on the Po Leung Kuk, *Sessional Papers 1893*.

in crime from the 'old hands'. Throughout the 19th century attempts were made throughout to keep boys under 16 separately confined. Girls could not be whipped or birched, and, in the minds of officials, there were no particular fears for their safety in prison. Hesitation to send them there reflected more the paternalism of magistrates than anything else. Yet some were, and from as young as nine or ten years, although only for days or a few weeks. How did the children cope with this strange world? They likely had to do their share of prison labour, but that would be little different to their home life. Presumably they wore their own clothes, as, along with European female prisoners, they were quite a rare occurrence and the prison was unlikely to have child sized uniforms, just as it may not have had western-style uniforms for European women.

Reliable women – the staff of the growing prison

The *Blue Books* through the first decades of the century show that the gaol authorities still had problems engaging matrons and wardresses. Mrs Franco left in April 1899 after just two years and Filomena Lewis took over the role, with Mrs Raptis and a second assistant on the same terms as earlier. For the next few years, the first two women remained, but a succession of assistants passed through. Mrs Raptis resigned in 1905 but returned as matron when Mrs Lewis was dismissed on 31st October 1907. The reasons for the dismissal remain unclear, and there is so little reported on the Female Prison in these decades it is difficult to even make any conjectures. Tamar Ai, a wardress appointed in 1905, was similarly fired in 1910, but again, there are no details. Joanna Raptis, whose post now brought her $720 each year plus accommodation, was invalided out in July 1909, perhaps with a gratuity. The next day her replacement, Mary Bredenberg, arrived. She then provided much needed stability, staying in post until she retired in December 1926, aged 49, through ill-health.

The challenges of researching people's histories in Hong Kong, especially those from large families or with more common surnames, means that relatively few of the gaol staff here can be identified with any certainty. But such a name as Bredenberg should, surely, be easier. However, the Carl Smith cards and the extensive *China Families* website give just one person, an employee of the China Maritime Services, Axel

Tycho Bredenberg, born 1853, listed variously as Swedish and American. He was a former seaman and worked first in Shanghai, then moved to Canton in 1885. In 1890 he married Mary Henrickson, an orphan of unknown parentage at the chapel in St Francis Hospital in Wanchai. This girl may have been the daughter of a German, Peter Hendrickson, who had been in the Hong Kong Police Force in the 1860s and later, and she was probably raised at the French convent orphanage. The problem here is that, if this is the future prison matron, she would have been only 13 at the time of her marriage, according to her pension records. However, in the days before ready access to birth records – especially those of orphans – she may well have been unsure of her exact date of birth, or conveniently lost a few years if it might have helped secure the position.[196] She would not be the first to do this in Hong Kong before the Second World War! But Mary Bredenberg was widowed in 1905, when they were still in Canton, which would tie in with her applying for the gaol post four years later.

Numbers in the Prison had eased in the first years of the new century, with a daily average of about 22 women most years. However, with the influx of people from neighbouring southern China, fleeing the unrest and violence of the early 1910s, Hong Kong saw an escalation in crime. Allied with this, British prisons were instituting slightly improved employment conditions for their warders and better supervision of inmates, a development of which Hong Kong's administration would be aware. In 1914, therefore, Mrs Bredenberg gained an additional assistant. After initial problems, the team settled down, and the Matron had a Senior Wardress, paid $420 and three others, receiving $300 per year They names in the Civil Establishment list are mostly Portuguese women, but with an occasional Chinese one amongst them. By the end of the decade most, including Mary Bredenberg, took brief periods of leave, something that had not occurred earlier. Fortunately, although Hong Kong's population had doubled in these years, the growth in

---

196 There is a discrepancy in Axel Bredenberg's age, too. The Chinese Maritime Customs records give his birth date as 7th May 1853, making him 37 at the time of his marriage. The records held by the Catholic Cathedral in Hong Kong state that he was 45. Such disparity between the bride and groom was not unusual, and suggests that he may well have come to the convent to find a suitable spouse.

female prisoners was not on quite the same scale, and the absence of one member of staff did not cause too many problems.

Year	In prison awaiting trial	Total convicted	Sentence > 1 year	Sentence > 3m < 1yr	Sentence < 3 months	Daily average no. prisoners
1899	24	114	6	12	96	21.9
1900	42	135	2	7	126	13.1
1901	37	140	2	7	131	13.2
1919	54	208	5	36	166	36
1920	59	211	7	44	163	35
1921	100	173	0	30	138	41

Imposing longer 'short' sentences for crimes such as possession of weapons and forgery, plus an increase in time needed to prepare cases for the magistracy hearing, resulted in crowded conditions the Female Prison during the 1920s. But, being only about 5% of the prison population, the administration was unlikely to worry about a group of docile prisoners. In the main gaol the situation was far more serious. Men were having to sleep in corridors, warders had many more problems controlling prisoners' behaviour, and there were frequent fights and occasional attacks on staff. After the 1914-18 war, the question of building a new prison had to be addressed. Part of the former Quarantine Station in Lai Chi Kok, a mile north of Boundary Street and then still close to the coastline, was set aside for this purpose.[197] By the end of 1920 this was open to accommodate 200 male short-term offenders in four 'association' halls. Although the buildings themselves were light and airy, there was little additional room, and thus no space to keep men occupied during the day. Some could create a garden around the prison, while mat-making occupied others. The juveniles, i.e. those under 16, were, at long last, housed separately from the adults, with a hall to themselves. A schoolmaster was engaged for a few hours per day. It was another five years before three further, much-needed, halls were built and the opportunity taken to construct workshops.

By the middle years of the 1920s, the situation in the female prison was becoming acute. Hong Kong's population had risen from 680,000 in

197 *Hongkong Government Gazette*, 19th March 1920.

1920 to 1,100,000 nine years later, and this time the prisoner numbers had grown in proportion. The unsettled, often chaotic state of southern China, and now the aggressive incursions of the Japanese into the region, were pushing ever more people to seek the relative stability of Hong Kong. Many of these were desperately poor, arriving with only what they could carry. Dire need motivated their crimes rather than malevolent intent. But inevitably, the influx also brought with it women skilled at pilfering, along with those who thought the situation would make the abduction and sale of a child easier and perhaps more remunerative. Thus in 1929, the wards and cells housed 71 inmates and the upward trend of prosecutions and convictions showed no sign of abating. Now, at last, the superintendent had to take note of the women's overcrowding in his report.

Yet as the numbers increased, each prisoner still had to be attended to individually, and the matron would be acquainted with the reason that each were there. In 1923 the day arrived that each matron had probably dreaded, but was commonplace in the men's prison. Chan Pak, convicted, along with a young man, of the murder of her husband in August 1923 was the first woman under the British administration to pay the 'ultimate penalty'.[198] As a prisoner on a capital charge, she was kept in a separate cell, and her legal representatives would be given access. Only a small minority of women appearing in the courts could afford this, so the presence of a solicitor in the prison was an unusual event. The trial at the upper court took place late in October: there was then a wait whilst the sentence brought before the Governor and the Council for consideration. In that period, Chan was allowed visits from family. Once ratified, the sentence was carried out by hanging within the prison compound on 28th November. It must indeed have been a sombre moment for all when the turnkeys arrived at the door of the Female Prison to conduct her to her fate.

The 1920s were troubled times in the gaol – there was frequent unrest amongst the male prisoners, reflecting the strikes and anti-foreign agitation in the colony and southern China. The inmates started food riots, went on strike, attacked staff and fought amongst themselves. However, each

198 See Chapter 7.

year a line in the superintendent's report notes that "the conduct of the female prisoners was uniformly good" or "the female prisoners took no part in the strike", etc. Part of the credit for the good behaviour of the inmates must go to the matron, Mary Bredenberg and the more stable staff team she built. In 1910 Helena Maria da Concieção joined, followed by Rosa Pereira four years later. Some pay increases over the years, and a graded pay scale saw the salary of these women rise to around $480 per year. They continued in their roles until 1922 and 1932 respectively. In 1922 the Prison engaged Laura Aquino, and she would replace Mrs Bredenberg as matron when the latter retired in 1926. Throughout these years the men's prison was staffed by about 75 Europeans and 180 Indians, together with a few Chinese in clerical or domestic posts. As in the Police Force, the Indian warders and guards came from regiments of the British Army. All, bar the few Chinese, had free quarters or a house allowance, and the Indians also had the benefit of a ration allowance. Most of the men had passed at least one examination in Cantonese or English, as appropriate, and received a few dollars extra in their monthly pay packet for that. Of the women's posts, only the matron had the benefit of quarters, and just one wardress received a house allowance. They had to have sufficient fluency in Chinese to be appointed, so none received the extra allowance. Yet their pay, meagre at it seems, was sufficient to keep them in their posts. There were many in the colony earning less than these women – including some of the Indians in the gaol, despite their additional benefits. Occasionally there were instances of unrest and petitions for better conditions from the male staff, but, aside from an isolated dismissal of a recently appointed wardress or two, these women gave the superintendent as little trouble as did their charges.

Victoria Gaol – straining at its fragile seams

Superintendent Franks had enough trouble to contend with in the conditions of the gaol buildings themselves. Now most were over sixty years old, and had been patched and altered, repaired and in-filled to the limit. In 1926 a survey condemned the roofs of F Hall and the Female

Prison,[199] with the comment in the annual report that these were to be renewed the following year. The Hall roof, on the opposite side of the site, was attended to as planned but there is no subsequent mention of that of over the Female Prison. A new prison was urgently needed, and in 1931 workmen began on a site adjacent to the men's prison at Lai Chi Kok.[200] It took longer than that one, since this was a new building. By the time of its completion, plans were being drawn up for a full scale removal of the entire department to a site at Stanley, on the south of the island. Thus Lai Chi Kok was built, or at any rate, finished, with the intention of it being only temporary. It provided accommodation for 120 women, with separate halls for long and short sentence prisoners, and for those awaiting trial or sentencing. As with the men's prison, there was little in the way of workshop space, although there was a laundry, a medical ward and a nursery of sorts. Reporting the forthcoming move, *The Hongkong Telegraph* told its readers of the division of prisoners into three groups, "for it is the opinion of the authorities that by mixing the good with the bad the latter are more likely to contaminate the former than the good are likely to have an uplifting influence on the lower types."[201]

However, it was not all cramped cells, monotonous meals and damp washing for the women by the late 1920s. With the agreement of the superintendent, Mr J. W. Franks, a group of concerned women had developed, in 1928, a plan to recruit a party of Chinese and British women to visit the Prison. These ladies would instruct the inmates in handicrafts, give them some basic education and teach them singing. The superintendent's wife became involved, but it was a Miss Atkins who was the main organising force. There was soon a committed and faithful group, who spent each Tuesday and Friday afternoon working primarily with prisoners whose sentences were three months or more (34 such that first year), teaching them sewing, embroidery, raffia work and basic writing and numeracy. Mr Franks recorded his thanks to them for their efforts, "under conditions at their best by no means ideal, and, in

199 Report of the Superintendent of Prisons for the Year 1926, 6th May 1927, *Administrative Reports, 1926.*

200 *Government Gazette, Supplementary Note 94,* 13th March 1931, call for tenders.

201 *Hongkong Telegraph,* 18th April 1932.

the summer season, hot, humid and depressing."[202] The 'lady visitors' received similar thanks in subsequent reports. In 1929 very good results were being achieved by the prisoners, except, perhaps, in the singing classes. These last, it appears, did not continue.

When the Prison moved to Lai Chi Kok, some from the original group of visitors continued and others, living nearer the Prison, were recruited. Their classes and sessions were popular with the inmates. The visitors bemoaned the situation that would see most of their pupils banished at the end of their sentences, but pragmatically expressed the hope that they would become useful members of society wherever they found themselves.[203] Mrs Bella Southorn had been an early supporter of this, as she was of many forms of social action that aided women and children. She was due to open the first 'Female Prisoners' Industrial Sale of Work', run by the visitors, at the Union Church in Kowloon in May 1933.[204] At the last moment she was unable to attend through illness, but sent her address, which the newspapers published in full. As well as thanking the women who had made the project possible, she told how engaged the prisoners were in the activities and how many showed an intense desire to learn, even though they had to first complete their normal prison labour. The women had even been able to grow some flowers in their small yard, and she thanked the head of the Botanical and Forestry Department for his help. The proceeds of the sale would buy fresh material for the sessions, with any surplus going to a fund administered by the superintendent for the support of discharged female prisoners. Church groups had sometimes interested themselves in the welfare of the women in prison, but seem to have been more involved with their lives after prison. In 1933, with the more spacious facilities at Lai Chi Kok, the superintendent authorised the regular visits of 'Lady Sisters from the Italian Convent' on Saturdays and 'Lady Visitors from the Church Missionary Society' on Sunday, the latter of whom gave religious addresses to the women.

---

202 Report of the Superintendent of Prisons for the Year 1928, 18th March 1929, *Administrative Reports, 1928*.

203 Report of the Superintendent of Prisons for the Year 1932, 8th March 1933, *Administrative Reports, 1932*.

204 *Hongkong Telegraph*, 24th May 1933.

Lai Chi Kok: fresh start but the same problem

The move from Victoria Gaol to Lai Chi Kok Female Prison in mid-April 1932, involved about 100 women and their wardresses. Two new members of staff were taken on in February, in advance of the move, including one who, with less than two month's experience, took the role of Acting Matron when Laura Aquino retired at the end of March. Lam Kit and Rosa Pereira had to 'show the ropes' to the extra staff which included a further four women recruited at the beginning of April. Once in the new building, the staffing increased dramatically, becoming a team of 32 the following year. But the recruits, many of them still in their teens, had signed up with little idea of what the job involved, and about a quarter resigned or were 'let go' within months. There does not seem to have been time or facilities for much training. Wardress Lam left in July, whilst 51-year-old Rosa Pereira took her pension of $226.99 per year the following year, after 19 years' service. She was the longest-serving female gaol employee to that date. Thereafter, none of the staff had experience of the former prison. This great expansion, although they had to cover a bigger physical space, was not driven by any immediate increase in prisoner numbers (although that was soon to come). It therefore raises the question that if such a large team was now required for 100-120 prisoners, how had the matron and her three wardresses ever coped before? Alongside the new prison, accommodation had been built for the staff. Each woman had her own room and there were bathrooms, a kitchen and a mess in the bungalow complex. Perhaps receiving some instruction and support from the senior staff of the men's prison, they had to build themselves into a functional team at very short order.

Superintendent Franks might have expected the new prison to be full, but could not have anticipated that within months it would often hold 200 and more on any day. Staff even had problems finding enough bed-space in the wards for all the arrivals. Meals had to be staggered and overseeing this fully stretched the staff. The idea that there would be plenty of space to keep all the prisoners occupied proved illusory. With the day-room space in wards turned over to sleeping accommodation, the work the women could do was severely curtailed. Some could make envelopes or weave in the wards, while the bookbinding machinery that had already been set up occupied a few. Other prisoners were responsible for the cooking and serving the meals, and the laundry. The buildings required constant maintenance and the whitewashing of the internal walls each year to help prevent mould was done by prisoners. But the reports suggest that many of the short sentence prisoners had to spend their days in idleness and boredom. Such would be the case for some years to come – from 1933 onwards the daily average was never less than 160 and often as high as 250 prisoners. But while plans and building work for the new Hong Kong Prison at Stanley was ongoing, the women must bide their time.

Hong Kong Prison, as the gaol in Stanley on the southern shore of the island was called, was three years in the building. Over a period of some months in 1937, the men moved out of Lai Chi Kok Prison and Victoria Gaol into the new prison. There they had 1,598 individual cells, which included six each of condemned and observation cells and two padded cells. And yet it was overcrowded from the outset, with some cells having to hold three men. Part of the old city-centre gaol had to be converted into a Remand Centre to hold prisoners awaiting trial, although these should, in theory, all have been at Stanley. The idea of building a permanent female prison close by was still on the cards, but the administration recognised that the international situation meant that further expenditure in the colony was unlikely to receive permission from London. Thus plans were drawn up in 1939 to extend their existing prison in Lai Chi Kok, a less costly option. Initially, the intention was to build an extra storey on the halls and this was put out to tender, but then the Public Works Dept. changed course, deciding instead to create further wings off the main corridor. A proper hospital ward was added with a purpose-built labour room and a wardress-nurse appointed, and the authorities took the opportunity to include adequate workshop space. Thereafter, the tailoring shop employed 35-40 women each day and a large laundry was busy with washing from the hospitals as well as that of the prison itself. On a usual day it employed about 100 women, and whilst the work was still classified as hard labour, electric washing machines and irons made it a lot less taxing than it had been fifty years earlier.

The women were in a new building but some things did not change. Food remained bland and monotonous. Women still received the same quantity as the male prisoners, and for the Chinese this was divided almost equally between breakfast and supper, with a pint of weak congee made from 2 ounces of rice and a small amount of beans at lunchtime. The main meals still consisted of rice: 9 ounces (250 grams) each time with either fresh or pickled vegetable or a small portion of fish added. Allowances of chutney, salt and oil were used in the manufacture of the meals, and their pint of tea was brewed with just one-quarter of an ounce of leaf. Women on hard labour received a couple ounces more rice at each meal, and long-sentence prisoners (over two years) a little meat on occasions. The European and Indian diets were similarly bland, the former based largely on bread and soup made with a few ounces of meat, while the protein source for the Indian prisoners was a daily few ounces of dhal with their rice. Not only dull to eat, its preparation must have been very tedious labour for those in the kitchens.

The congestion in the prison was a direct result of the great influx of refugees, and the strain this put on all aspects of Hong Kong's life. As already mentioned, with little ability to stem the tide or to provide relief to those arriving, it was no surprise to the colony that its courts filled with crimes of every description. In 1933, 1,609 women were given terms of imprisonment, three times as many as in 1930. Of the 1933 figure, 92% were for terms of less than three months. Five years later the number entering prison had increased by about 200, with the same proportion of short sentence convicts. Magistrates gave many the option of a fine, but this was often beyond their means. In that year, the bulk of convicted and sentenced offences for which women stood trial were for hawking without a licence. The courts heard over 8,000 such cases. Obstruction offences were also very frequent, punished by a very small fine. Of the crimes that would usually attract a custodial sentence, the possession of stolen goods or unlawful possession accounted for about 800 cases with female defendants, whilst liquor and opium offences provided another 250. Still, as throughout the whole century, few women appeared at the Criminal Sessions. Of those that did in 1938, four were charged in connection with heroin, and one for forgery. One woman received a two-year sentence for the kidnap of a small boy – the Chief Justice agreeing to lighten her sentence as she had given the police a lot of help in recovering the child from a Chinese village. Then on 23rd May 1940, prisoner Kwan Lai-chun arrived at the prison. Charged with the brutal murder of her husband's concubine, and suspected of killing two others, she had been in the Government Civil Hospital since the night of the crime, two weeks earlier.[205] Now, in this larger building, few of the prisoners would have been aware of her presence, even when she returned from the Supreme Court sentenced to death. Whether she was transferred to Hong Kong Prison a few days before her execution, or just the night before is unclear. Her last night, though, would have been spent in one of that prison's condemned cells, and the Matron, Mrs Pearson may well have been obliged to stay on site. The execution of Kwan took place in the purpose-designed chamber early in the morning of 31st July 1940.

Six months after the long-serving J. W. Franks' retirement as superintendent in January 1938, the Colonial Office gave the management of the prisons the same status as that of the Police Force by creating the post of Commissioner of Prisons. The first occupant of the role was Major J. L. Willcocks, who arrived in the colony in July of that year. One of his first actions was to enquire into the working of the Female Prison, and he was aghast to find that the remuneration given to the women managing it had scarcely changed from the days of Victoria Gaol. The matron, Mrs Jennie Pearson, had taken up the post in 1934 at a salary of $1,260. With annual increments, by the time Major Willcocks was enquiring, this had become $1,500, and could increase to a maximum of $1,560. But this equated to just £97 10s. per year – an amount even the Under-Secretary in London described as 'absurdly low'.[206] The new Commissioner wrote, "The Matron (Mrs Pearson) is, in fact, doing the duties of Matron Superintendent. She is in entire charge, under my supervision on periodical visits, and holds a position of considerable responsibility. For this she can reach a maximum salary of slightly less

---

205 See Chapter 9.

206 CO129/578/8 Correspondence between Colonial Secretary, Norman Lockhart Smith and Secretary of State for the Colonies, 6th September 1938 - 2nd May 1939.

than £98 a year. I feel ashamed to hold her responsible for the proper conduct of the prison at such a rate of pay." The Colonial Secretary (in the Governor's absence) also considered the salary "grossly inadequate for her responsibilities", and concurred with Major Willcocks that the same applied, although in slightly less degree, to her immediate assistants. The Commissioner advocated a thorough-going increase in salaries: the Colonial Secretary and the Councils did not assent to this. With their better knowledge of Hong Kong conditions, they considered that the pay for wardresses (between $540-$720 per year) was in line with salaries for women's roles not requiring particular qualifications. Government decision-making not being that much speedier than sixty years earlier, it was May 1939 before Malcolm MacDonald, Secretary of State for the Colonies, gave his assent. He accepted the figures Major Willcocks had proposed for the Matron, Assistant Matron and Principal Wardress roles, and allowed the increase to be backdated from 1st January. Jennie Pearson now received $2,400 each year, with would rise by yearly increments of $200 up to $3,600. The lower roles also received substantial increases. This magnanimity brought the Matron's pay up to something just under two-thirds of the lowest European warder's salary. However, although women still had (and have still) a distance to travel to achieve economic parity with men in Hong Kong, at least posts in the Women's Prison were not defined by the ethnicity of the holder. The staff included Portuguese, Chinese, Indian and British women, all on the same (small) salary scale.

This was the still the situation of the Women's Prison towards the end of 1941, when an invasion by the Japanese looked inevitable. Any British nationals on the staff (aside from the matron) might have already been given the option of evacuation to Australia. Hong Kong had resigned itself to having to undertake its own defence, with no hope of Britain diverting much needed fire-power from its European mission to protect the far distant outpost. Before looking at the fate of the prisoners and staff in that momentous month, it is possible to travel forward just a few years, for greater detail about the prison and women's lives there than any pre-war record provides.

After the overthrow and surrender of the Japanese, on 30th August 1945, there was quite a swift resumption of all government buildings, either for their original purposes or for use by the interim British military administration. There was little money, in the immediate post-war period, to do anything other than basic repairs and the eradication of signs of Japanese presence, yet Lai Chi Kok Female Prison was back in operation in January 1947. The building seen by "Eleven women newspaper correspondents from the local Press" on 16th July 1948, during a two-hour tour with the head of the Prison Service, was thus substantially the same as that vacated in December 1941.[207] It was built off a single wide corridor, with five wings on each side. Two such wings housed the large dormitories, which could accommodate 150 each. Another pair held the 24 cells, each 6 feet by 9 feet, and 14 feet high, the passage leading to these being gated at the corridor end. The women journalists had entered through the reception and office wing, and then went along the passage to see the weaving room, which was opposite the kitchen. Wash rooms and the laundry were at the far end, the visitors reporting that the former seemed to be "adequate in number for the inmates". Another wing contained the hospital ward and labour room. The tour also took in the wardresses' quarters, close by but separate from the prison, with individual rooms for 28 and communal space. This, the journalists were told, had been used as stabling by the occupying army.

The 1948 matron told the reporters she had worked in this prison since it opened, when she joined as a 16-year-old wardress. Miss Griselda dos Remedios became the Principal Wardress and had been the third beneficiary of the new senior salary scale in 1938. Now still only 32, she recalled that before the war the prison held two 'lifers', but now the longest sentence any woman was serving was for six years. Pang Yiu-mui, convicted in 1939 for the murder of young Wan Hang-cheung was one such (see Chapter 9). Sir Atholl MacGregor, the Chief Justice, had promised her that, though sentenced to life imprisonment, she would not serve many years of it. In the event, she was there for just over two. What happened to the prisoners when the invasion was imminent? The author has seen no documentary evidence of any plan or action, but has been told by a most reliable source of the testimony of a senior member of the prison staff, given after the war. The New Territories and most

---

207 *China Mail*, 17th July 1948.

of Kowloon were evacuated of British nationals, except military and police by early in December 1941. Before the Japanese invaded Hong Kong territory on 8th December, the men in the prison in Stanley, all bar those considered dangerous political prisoners, were formally discharged, ferried to Kowloon and then released. It would seem reasonable to assume, therefore, that the women in Lai Chi Kok were similarly released. Their matron, Jennie (Jane) Giralda Pearson, was interned by the Japanese in Stanley Civilian Camp. The Chinese among both prisoners and staff might return to their homes and survive the next three-and-a-half years as best they could. Any other British or American national on the staff would also have been interned, whilst the Portuguese and any third nationals might slip over to Macao and wait out the war there. It is unclear whether Miss dos Remedios was alone in returning to her post following the liberation.

CHAPTER 7

GETTING RID OF THE MAN

The luckless George Perkins, who had sailed out from Hawaii to take up a post with an American trading firm in Macao in 1854, only made it as far as Hong Kong waters.[208] Perhaps he had been advised to charter a boat to take him the remaining journey, rather than rely on the public service. He settled on a fare of seven dollars with a boatman, and they were soon under way. When out of sight of other craft, the boatman stabbed Perkins, relieved him of his valuables and then, with the help of his wife, tipped his body overboard. It was only when his firm raised the alarm about his non-arrival, several days later, that enquiries commenced.

The boat concerned was traced and soon the crew and the woman were in custody. Enquiries amongst the fishing-folk led police to the boat owner a few days later. The testimony of the crew pointed to the married couple only as involved in the murder, and the trial proceeded against them alone. The hearing, however, occasioned grave concerns amongst the public due to its shoddy conduct. Not least of the failings was that Chun Cheong-tsai and Chun Cheong-she had no defence counsel, although lawyers were present in court and unoccupied whilst the hearing was in session. Chun said that the boat had been pursued by pirates and that Perkins had jumped overboard and drowned. At the time of the attack his wife had been down below, since she was pregnant and sick, so she knew nothing of it. The prosecution case rested on the evidence of the crew, who told of the stabbing and robbery. In *Anglo-China,* Munn recounts the story of the trial and its limitations.[209] He demonstrates how

208 *China Mail,* 22nd June 1854.
209 Christopher Munn, *Anglo-China* pp. 194-6.

the Attorney General, Mr Bridges, had rushed the case to court, perhaps without allowing time for the proper collection of evidence. Then in court this man had even bullied and heckled the Chief Justice.

The couple were both sentenced to death. However, doctors soon confirmed that Chun Cheong-she was with child and the Governor commuted her sentence to one of transportation for life.[210] The man had admitted the crime before his execution. Chun had her child in the small Women's Prison and even in those early days, Chun would have had the attention of the Colonial Surgeon, had there been difficulties with her labour. Like her husband, she had already confessed her role in the disposal of Perkins' body. But public feeling was still on her side, and she was counselled to apply for a pardon, citing that she was acting on her husband's orders. Along with five Europeans and ten Chinese, Chun Cheong-she received a Royal Pardon on 24th May 1855, on the occasion of Queen Victoria's 36th birthday.[211]

Wong Po and the Wanchai murder

Wong Po enjoyed her pleasant life in Macao.[212] The foreign gentleman whose mistress she had become a few years earlier was good to her, not stinting on money when she needed it. So when he became ill and his chances of recovery declined, she was both sad for him and anxious for her own future. She had no wish to return to her old profession – she was too old for that now and, anyway, there were always other people attempting to control you and claim your earnings. Perhaps she knew that her gentleman would provide for her but she had still been pleasantly surprised when the man's executor handed her some $500 after the funeral. This was the equivalent of about five years' wages for most working Chinese men in 1900, and far more than she might have earned as a prostitute in that time. Soon she moved back to Hong Kong where

---

210 Government Proclamation, 22nd June 1854, *Hongkong Government Gazette*, 24th June 1854.

211 Government Proclamation, 24th May 1855, *Hongkong Government Gazette*, 26th May 1855.

212 This case is reported in *The China Mail,* 6th February 1901, *Hongkong Daily Press,* 22nd & 23rd February 1901, 22nd, 23rd & 26th March 1901 and in the other newspapers.

she had friends. Who knows, she might meet another man – there was less competition in the British colony where there were fewer women than in Macao.

It was not long before she found out the whereabouts of an old flame, Kwong Cheung. She had been his concubine years ago, but had left him when the rows with his wife became too much. He had a stable job as a messenger at the Supreme Court, where he had worked for many years, enjoying regular hours, light duties and a steady income. Although at 51 he was now getting on in years, he was still an attractive man, tall and now even stouter than she remembered – this latter attribute speaking of enough money to satisfy life's necessities and more. He lived in Queen's Road East and now rented the whole of the first floor of No. 143, subletting bed-spaces and cubicles out to respectable working men. He shared the front of the apartment with his wife of eighteen years and their twelve-year-old son. His good financial position suited Wong, and she made quite a play for him. By April 1900 she had moved in as his concubine and Kwong gave her a cubicle to herself, at the back of the front room of the property.

Such proximity to Kwong's wife proved as difficult as it had years earlier, each woman resenting the other. Although a Chinese wife could not expect to dictate whether her husband might take a concubine, in marriages of considerable duration it frequently happened that he would leave the choice of woman to her, knowing that harmony between these two was desirable. But in this case, even though the woman had already caused problems between them, Mrs Kwong was given no say. Soon, though, there were other matters, and serious ones too, to concern the family. When Wong moved in she had brought with her some locked boxes containing her clothes and household effects, but also her jewellery and the money left to her. There was insufficient room for them in the apartment, so they were stored on the floor above, in the apartment of a trusted neighbour. That summer saw another outbreak of bubonic plague in the city and in the cubicle next to the neighbour's, a man succumbed to the disease.

Hong Kong's suffering during the 1894 plague epidemic had been profound, leaving over 2,500 dead there, while throughout the wider region many thousands perished. Most years since it had returned during the summer months without the same virulence, but in 1900 it seemed as though it might attack with a vengeance. However, Hong Kong now had a procedure that could snap into action whenever and wherever so required. During the original emergency, entire streets of houses had to be white-limed with every fixed object coated with the rough disinfectant, a process to which the occupants, of course, strongly objected. Now fumigation was a targeted and less drastic way of cleansing an individual property, but movable items still had to be removed. Kwong had Wong's boxes taken to the Supreme Court for safekeeping – perhaps she had insisted that there was too much of value in these for them to take their chance with the rest of the furniture, stacked out on the pavement while the fumigation was under way.

The disinfection seems to have been effective: there were no more reports of death through this disease in the area. The house returned to normal, but when Wong's boxes came back, she was sure that some money was missing – there had been $240 hidden in there, and now some of that was gone. Here was a new subject for arguments with Kwong, and one which Wong raised afresh, whenever she believed that the man was helping himself to her money. Towards the end of the year, Kwong retired from his post at the Supreme Court and with a gratuity of $100 in lieu of pension. This, rather more than his annual wage, seems to have encouraged him in his rather 'loose' habits, drinking and gambling with his friends, only returning home in the early hours. With his ostentatious style of living and a concubine who had money of her own, the family might well have been a target for the many thieves who lurked in the area, but the man did not seem to have qualms about leaving his son and women-folk unprotected by night.

The tensions in the house had not eased and at the start of 1901 there was a big argument between Kwong and Wong over a gold-mounted rattan bangle, a watch and some paper money. He claimed that Wong had stolen it from him, but the concubine considered that she had taken it in recompense for money he had taken from her, although she agreed to return his watch. The bickering between the two women also continued. One source of discontent was that Mrs Kwong considered

Wong lazy – she herself earned her living by taking in mending and spent most of the day sewing. It also appears that Kwong slept more often in Wong's cubicle than in that of his wife, which did not encourage friendly relations between the women. Often the rows involved all three. Finally, Wong decided that she had had enough. When Kwong arrived back from a late-night session with his friends on 3rd February she told him that she did not want to stay with him, in fact she did not want him any more. If he gave her $100 she would leave them and go elsewhere. The man became enraged at this and there was a battle of heated words, during which Mrs Kwong later claimed to have heard Wong threaten to kill her husband.

Woman sewing in the street, from the collection of Roy Delbyck,
with kind permission.

On the morning of 5th February, with nothing resolved between them, another row erupted over a woollen jacket that Mrs Kwong had taken in to mend. She accused Wong of having stolen it, whilst Kwong scolded his wife for having lost it. After that Wong did not join them for their morning meal of rice, but went to her cubicle. At around 9 a.m. Mrs

Kwong took her mending and went down to sit in front of the house to do it. She thought that her husband had gone into Wong's cubicle, but would not distress herself, since she had her work to do.

No. 143 Queen's Road East was then a regular Chinese 'shop-house' style building, but the shop on the ground floor was vacant and its front boarded up. Entrance to the upper storeys was from the staircase at the side. This gave no access to the shop, nor was there any rear door. The verandah of the first floor overhung the pavement, and it was beneath this that Mrs Kwong sat sewing. The road, still the primary east-west thoroughfare for the city, one block in from the Praya (waterfront), was busy and noisy. Her young son played with friends on the pavement whilst she was greeted by customers, neighbours and friends passing by. Still determined to have a few minutes' respite from domestic troubles, she heard but did not react to shouts and cries from above. A neighbour approached her and asked her why there was so much noise coming from her house, but she disclaimed any interest.

Close to 11 a.m. Wong suddenly emerged onto the verandah, screaming, 'Thieves! Robbers! *Gau meng!* (save life!)'. Soon a crowd of onlookers gathered under the verandah, calling up to Wong and asking what the matter was. A Chinese constable, P.C. U Yeung, pushed his way through the throng and hurried up the stairs and knocked at the door of the flat. Moments later he was joined by Sanitary Inspector George Hogarth.[213] In Cantonese this man demanded that Wong open the door. "Thieves, six of them, have broken in to steal my money and they have killed my man," she told Insp. Hogarth. "Killed your man?" he repeated, "where is he?" She pointed to the second cubicle. He pulled back the mosquito curtain that hung over the bed. Kwong was lying slant-wise across Wong's bed, on his back, but turned towards his left side. His legs were hanging over one side of the bed. P.C. U believed that he was just alive when they first saw him, but the inspector could find no pulse at all in his right wrist. Wong clutched at the officer and wailed "Official police, take care of me." He thought her very frightened, pale and rather wild in

---

213 As a uniformed member of the Sanitary Dept., who as part of the Public Works Dept. would be seen as 'official' by the general public, he had authority to enter buildings and to make arrests where necessary, which perhaps explains his readiness to enquire into this situation.

appearance, but she did not seem upset about the dead man. Meanwhile, Mrs Kwong had come upstairs and into the front of the flat, where she started arguing with Wong. "You have stopped Kwong from going to work," she exclaimed, whereupon Wong told her about the robbers and how they had come in to steal from her. They had smothered her with a blanket and thrown her to the ground and then murdered Kwong. At this point Mrs Kwong realised that more than a quarrel had happened. Upon seeing the dead body of her husband she dissolved into loud, wailing sobs. Suddenly, she remembered the mending, still on the chair below and dashed down the stairs to retrieve it, lest it be stolen. Returning, she started screaming at Wong. The latter turned to Insp. Hogarth and said, "Don't take any notice of her: she is a bad woman. She has a black heart and has threatened to do me injury."

Trying to understand what had happened, Insp. Hogarth asked Wong again. "Kwong was in his cubicle in the front of the house when the robbers came and attacked me. He came in to help me when I cried out and then when they threw me on the floor I could hear them attacking Kwong." The inspector was still puzzled, since he could see no particular signs of a struggle or a fight in the cubicle, nor could he see why Kwong had died. That he had been hit on the forehead was evident, but was that really sufficient a blow to kill such a robust-looking man?

P.C. U soon summoned more police help, and it was at 11.10 a.m. that Inspector Ford, in charge of the Eastern district, arrived on the scene and took command. He pointed out wounds to the chest – stab wounds, which in the gloom of the cubicle, Sanitary Insp. Hogarth had missed. Insp. Ford instructed his men to lift the dead man and take him into the front portion of the flat, where he removed first his vest and singlet. These were soaked in blood from two wounds, each about one-and-a-half inches wide. The inspector had noticed the knife and screwdriver which lay beside the body. It would appear that the former was the murder weapon. Holes in the garments showed where the knife had been driven into the right-hand side of the chest. Ford then removed the man's blue trousers, held up with a girdle (belt) to which he had attached his wallet. These were undamaged, but there was a deep gash in the man's abdomen. He reckoned that the contusion resulted from a blow to knock Kwong out, although the doctor would be able to confirm that. There were other smaller scrapes and abrasions on his hands and face, but nothing very significant. Ford then quizzed Wong about the robbers. When had they come in? Did she recognise them? "I didn't hear the men come in. The blanket was over me so quickly, I saw nothing." But she was sure that there were six men, and that they had stolen her money.

In the days following the attack, the police kept their own counsel as they tried to unravel the sequence of events and ascertain who were the perpetrators of the crime. The newspapers reported the fact of the murder but had no more information than they could garner from the neighbours and on-lookers. Many unanswered questions remained. Mrs Kwong had recognised the knife and screwdriver – one of her former tenants had left these as security on rent he owed the couple. Were any of the lodgers suspects? The question must have been asked in the locality, since any of them might know the circumstances, both financial and domestic, of the house. Or did the gang come from outside? Had anyone hired them for this job? And why, if they intended to steal Wong's money, had they murderously attacked Kwong?

This crime happened just a few months too early to benefit from the latest addition to police crime-solving armoury, fingerprint identification. Forces worldwide realised the benefits to be had from the system developed mainly by police in India, and Hong Kong was one of the first places to permit the use of prints in legal evidence. The colony initially used them to identify 'returned banishees' – those expelled from Hong Kong who had returned before the time stated had expired, and thus liable to a (further) term in gaol. The technology to make print impressions from objects was developed and first used by Scotland Yard towards the end of 1901.

All went quiet for two weeks whilst the police prepared their case. Then, without warning, on Tuesday evening, 19th February, officers visited No. 143 Queen's Road East and informed Wong Po that she was under arrest on suspicion of the murder of Kwong Cheung on 5th February. After a day's remand, she faced the magistrate on Thursday morning. The public gallery was crowded with neighbours and people from that part of Wanchai eager to learn what had happened to old Kwong. First to give evidence was Mrs Kwong, who was not identified by any name of her own in any of the English newspaper reports. She told of the situation in the flat; the tensions leading up to the fateful morning and of the discovery of her murdered husband. Her young son then corroborated her story. He answered the magistrate's questions in a very clear manner and earned a compliment for this. The next morning Wong gave her side of the story and told of the sudden attack on her by the six men and their murder of her paramour. With evidence presented Mr Hazeland committed her to stand trial at the next Criminal Sessions, a month hence, and she returned to gaol to await that.

On 21st March Wong faced the Chief Justice, Sir John Carrington, with the acting Attorney General, Mr H. E. Pollock, prosecuting and barrister Mr E. Sharp appearing for her. It had been early established in Hong Kong that the public purse stood the cost of a counsel for the defence in all capital cases, assigned by the court itself. The seven-man jury were all, bar one, Europeans. At the turn of the century there were just a handful or two of Chinese and non-Europeans on the list of men eligible for jury service, for which the qualifications were being a householder and having sufficient grasp of English.[214] It is likely that fewer than half the men on the panel spoke or understood Cantonese with any ease.

The Attorney General, as usual, opened the proceedings with an outline of events, as established and agreed by the parties. Giving the impression that he did not expect Chinese wives to grieve for their husband, he told the jury that Mrs Kwong had been very much upset by the events and was likely to be a less useful witness than otherwise. The case was not, he explained, one where the lesser charge of manslaughter might pertain: it would be the jury's task to ascertain whether Wong Po had wilfully murdered Kwong Cheung. Insps. Hogarth and Ford, with other police officers, recounted the story as they had experienced it. To the defence counsel they confirmed that Wong Po had been quite clear and consistent in what she said about the robbers, which they had accepted.

---

214 Compare this to cases in the 1930s and 40s, e.g. that of Kwan Lai-chun in 1940 (Chapter 9) where the jury comprised three each Chinese and European, and one Indian man.

Dr Thomson, who conducted the autopsy, detailed the position and extent of the injuries. The three stab wounds were each about one-and-a-half inches wide, and between three and four inches deep. The highest had punctured the right lung, the second, some inches lower, travelled through that lung into the liver. The wound in the lower right-hand side of the abdomen had damaged no vital organs. He recorded other marks on the man's right-hand side, on the knuckles and face and a bruise made by a blunt instrument on the forehead, confirming that this was of sufficient force to have stunned him. No mention was made of the lack of a hole in the trousers corresponding to that in the vest and singlet. Had these and the trousers parted company when the man raised his right arm to ward off the initial blow to his head?

It might seem that when Mr Sharp opened the case for the defence after the weekend there was little material evidence he could offer. But Wong Po had been fortunate in whom the Courts had assigned to her. Ernest Hamilton Sharp was an experienced and able barrister, well-respected in the colony and he argued forcefully for her.[215] Acknowledging that a "particularly dastardly" murder had been committed, he agreed that there were circumstances of suspicion against his client. "But," he continued, "there is nothing more dangerous in dealing with cases of this character than to rely upon what is called circumstantial or presumptive evidence… Circumstantial or presumptive evidence is evidence which does not purport to prove directly, as the evidence of an eyewitness does, but purports to raise the presumption or inference of a greater or lesser probability that the person charged did commit the crime."

"More 'miscarriages of justice'," he told the jury, "have been due to reliance upon circumstantial evidence than from any other cause." This had happened even when such evidence had been stronger than in this case. "The principle always to be applied in cases of circumstantial evidence is this: Were the facts proved inconsistent with the story told by the prisoner? I contend that here they are wholly consistent with the innocence of my client. My client's story, as told to the police and others, has been the same from beginning to end. I submit that if her story

215 Two years later E. H. Sharp was appointed King's Counsel, *Hongkong Government Gazette*, 18th July 1902.

had been fabricated upon the instant, discrepancies and inconsistencies would have crept in."

The alternative that Mr Sharp put forward, without making specific allegations, was that the robbery might have been instigated by someone else, the wife, perhaps. He reminded the jury of the ample evidence they had heard that spoke of Mrs Kwong's jealousy of both Wong and Kwong. Or, if not her, the crime could have been organised by another person, with a knowledge of the disposition of affairs in this family. He made it clear that he was not suggesting that Mrs Kwong had arranged for the murder of her husband. "I merely suggest that these men were instigated to robbery only and that this robbery accidentally led to the murder." He reminded the jury that Wong Po had told them how she had called out for help the moment she saw the first man and that Kwong had rushed to her aid. The stabbing had been the work of their panic and, alarmed by the noise and commotion caused, and at what they had done and its possible consequences, the thieves had fled.

The defence case had taken all the morning and into the afternoon before reaching its conclusion. Finally, Mr Sharp faced the jury and said "Gentlemen of the Jury, the question for you is, 'Has the prosecution proved this charge against the prisoner beyond all reasonable doubt and shown that the facts proved are not only consistent with possible guilt but inconsistent with her innocence?' I submit that the learned counsel for the prosecution has not done this. My client's story explains practically all the facts and is a reasonable one whilst the case for the prosecution is beset with difficulties and doubts from beginning to end."

Yet doubts do remain. The lack of court transcripts of the period mean that we cannot know for sure all that was enquired into by the police investigation, but there are several questions that appear not to have been addressed. If the prosecution case was correct, was Kwong standing or sitting when attacked? How would Wong Po have managed to strike a tall man a blow on the forehead sufficient to stun him if he was standing? If he had been lying on the bed, how came he to be found slant-wise across it? What was the instrument that struck this blow and was it found? How likely is it that a single attacker, i.e. Wong, would first use one weapon to concuss then pick up a knife to stab? Would it not be more probable that she would continue to attack with the first weapon? What motive did she have for murdering the man? Although she appears to have lost money through the liaison, she did still have resources of her own. And if she had fabricated the whole story, why did she choose to have <u>six</u> robbers – surely a lone attacker would make for a more plausible story?

On the other hand, if the robbers had invaded the flat, how, unless with Mrs Kwong's knowledge, did they enter and then leave without, apparently, being seen? Were neighbours around questioned as to what they had seen? Then was the blanket used to smother Wong to hand? Surely there would have been some disturbance of things in her cubicle as a result of the invasion, yet such is not mentioned.

As was to be expected, in his response the Attorney General dismissed the possibility of Wong's story having any truth, after which the judge, Sir Justice Carrington, spent a considerable time in summing up. At half past five he sent the jury out to consider their verdict. They took just ten minutes to find unanimously that Wong Po was guilty of the wilful murder of Kwong Cheung. The judge asked her if she had anything to say as to why the sentence of death should not be passed upon her. In what must have been a remarkably controlled and rather moving response, the woman, for the final time, reiterated her account of the events of that morning and asserted her innocence. But the Chief Justice concurred with the verdict: he told her that he believed it to be the correct one and, donning the black cap, sentenced her to death by hanging.[216]

Wong Po was then taken from the Court building and returned to the Women's Prison, where she occupied one of their six individual cells, with the matron, Mrs Lewis, keeping watch on her state of mind. Within a few days three doctors examined her, and confirmed that she was pregnant. This was information which urgently had to be communicated both to Sir John Carrington and the Governor, Sir Henry Blake. British law did not permit the execution of a pregnant woman since that would involve the denial of life to an innocent child. Even in Britain, where the death penalty had been passed on many women, once the execution was

---

216 This would appear to be the first time that a woman had been sentenced to death since that passed on Chun Cheong-she in 1854.

postponed until the birth, the sentence was usually commuted to life imprisonment.

Both the Attorney General and the Chief Justice were aware, though, that there was no direct evidence linking Wong to the killing, and the defence Mr Sharp had made had at least some right on its side. The matter was brought to the Executive Council at a meeting on 9th April, to which the Governor invited the Chief Justice. Here the latter man reasserted that he believed the verdict to be correct and could not, on the facts proven, reduce it to a conviction for manslaughter, but he stressed that the evidence was entirely circumstantial. For this reason and because of the possibility that the crime had been committed under provocation and in the course of a quarrel, he did not advocate the sentence being carried out. The judge then departed, leaving the Governor and the Council members – five officials of the Government including the acting Attorney General and the head of the Police, with two 'unofficial' or appointed members – to decide Wong's fate. When a vote was taken on whether the sentence should be carried out, all the official members voted in favour. The unofficial members – and the Governor – disagreed. Sir Henry Blake then informed them of Wong Po's pregnancy, which would necessitate a reprieve until delivery. Having made his views known, it was almost incumbent on the other members to agree with Sir Henry that carrying out a death sentence after such a reprieve was certainly not customary. The decision of the Council – that Wong Po's sentence would be commuted to imprisonment for life – was communicated to the Colonial Office in London. In due course, the Secretary of State for the Colonies, the Right Honourable Joseph Chamberlain M.P., signalled his assent.

But Wong Po was not destined to serve her time in gaol.[217] Hong Kong had suffered from malaria since the coming of the British and before, but at the turn of the century there was an increase in the numbers suffering and in those dying from malarial fever and malarial coma. In his report of 1901, Dr J. M. Atkinson, Principal Civil Medical Officer, noted that a female prisoner, some eight months pregnant, suddenly had a fit on 1st June. Just over two months into her sentence, Wong was taken to

217 *Report of the Principal Civil Medical Officer for 1901,* 15th April 1902.

the Maternity Hospital, already unconscious. At first a renal condition associated with pregnancy was suspected but tests ruled that out, yet her temperature continued to rise and she remained semi-conscious. The following day her baby was born naturally, but was already dead. Further treatment was tried, including ice-packing to bring her temperature down, while blood samples taken the next day showed the real problem, large amounts of malarial parasites in her system. She died on 7th June without regaining consciousness. Wong Po is not named in the report, but that it does relate to her is shown by the statement by the Captain Superintendent. Noting that Keung (*sic*) Cheung had been murdered by his paramour, whose death sentence was commuted, he adds, "She died shortly after admission to gaol."[218]

The West Point poisoning

Wong Po had been rather an exception in that she had engineered her (re-)entrance into Kwong's family. But concubinage was so much a regular part of Chinese life in this period that the English-language press adopted the local custom and referred to a woman in this relationship as a 'wife' or 'widow'. It was not the usual habit of the press to remark on the origin of these women, but there are just sufficient references to confirm that most had been selected according to customary Chinese practice, from or nearby the man's home village and introduced to him by third parties, often at festival time. Easy and cheap travel to and from Hong Kong and Guangdong made regular home visits a usual part of life for all but the poorest, thus arriving as a new wife alongside the *kit fat* wife was a common experience for many. However, there were also great numbers of young women who were trafficked into the colony or came with varying levels of willingness to enter one of the brothels. For some of them, moving on to concubinage provided a more settled and domestic, and perhaps more comfortable, life.

How young Lam Kui, sometimes known as Mo Ho, came to be the concubine of the foreman stonecutter was not told when she came to

---

218 *Report of the Captain Superintendent of Police for 1901,* 17th February 1902.

public notice.[219] Designated 'wife' by the press, she had ousted Cheung Fo's *kit fat* wife, who now lived with her son on the opposite side of High Street, West Point. According to Lam's statement, recounted at the trial, Cheung had been suffering for some days with severe stomach pains.[220] To give him some relief, Lam had managed to get some leaves of the Ho-mun-ting bush from friends who lived in the New Territories. When she returned from collecting them on the afternoon of 17th November 1907, she brewed them up in a tea, according to the instructions they had given her. It was a Sunday and her husband was at home, so he drank some straight away. But rather than improve, the aches turned into agony and had the man rolling around in his bed. It was in this condition that his nephew found him, and while the younger man was there, his pains became so severe that he could not talk and at one point rolled off the bed. Lifting him back onto the bed, the nephew asked his uncle what was the matter. Cheung feebly pointed to Lam, then to a bowl on the table and then to his mouth. Lam first went to rush from the house but the nephew stopped her. He went to get the *kit fat* wife and while Lam sat with the man, Cheung died. Lam took a draught of the tea and soon felt unwell herself.

But Lam's story was not quite the whole one. When the nephew returned with Cheung's first wife and son, they found the man dead and the bowl nowhere to be found. He already had his suspicions. When he had stopped Lam leaving, she had been carrying a box of his uncle's and on his return now he had again intercepted her flight. That box, he knew, contained his uncle's money, so he rushed out to find a constable. With Western Police Station just two hundred yards down the hill, it was not long before officers were in the house and questioning all concerned. Meanwhile, Lam had become seriously ill and had to be sent to the Government Civil Hospital – but not before the police had arrested her on suspicion of intentionally causing Cheung's death.

---

219 *Hongkong Telegraph*, 23rd November 1907, *Hongkong Daily Press*, 21st January 1908, *Hongkong Telegraph*, 24th January 1908.

220 In Chinese customary marriages the "*kit fat*" wife was the principal wife, but other wives or concubines were permitted. Regulations restricting such arrangements under "Chinese custom" were not introduced in Hong Kong until 1971.

Lam Kui soon recovered: she had taken only a small portion of the 'medicine' and was given a strong emetic at the hospital. But she had been fortunate in receiving prompt attention, for the Ho-mun-ting bush from which the leaves came was the flowering shrub *gelsemium* and although occasionally used medicinally in tiny doses it was a recognised lethal poison. Once recovered, though, Lam took matters into her own hands. Although a constable was stationed at the door of the small ward where she lay and an amah was continually on duty, when the latter's back was turned Lam climbed out of the window and made her escape. But she did not get far. The hospital immediately raised the alarm, and the police soon had her in custody.

On Wednesday 20th November she appeared at the Magistracy before Mr Hazeland, to be remanded to prison. After further adjournments Lam was committed to stand trial at the next Criminal Sessions for the wilful murder of Cheung Ho. On Monday, 20th January she stood in the dock before the Chief Justice, Sir Francis Piggott and the usual seven-man jury. Then the fuller story unfolded.

Lam had for some months been entertaining a lover, Ng Nin, who visited her when Cheung was out at work. The latter knew of the liaison and was angry with Lam about it. On 15th November, two days before his death, he had arrived home earlier than expected, accompanied by his nephew. Perhaps hearing noises below, Ng Nin emerged from Lam's cubicle and encountered the men on the stairs, whereupon he fled. Furious, Cheung had a heated argument with Lam and hit her with an umbrella that was to hand. The situation was apparently at stalemate. Cheung's box, that the nephew had twice taken from Lam when she attempted to abscond, proved to contain $30. The next day the police found the bowl in which Lam had brewed the tea, hidden under some wood. Lam's little daughter told first the police, and then the court, that she had seen her mother put the leaves in a pot, boil them up and give them to Cheung.

In her defence, Lam claimed that she had not known it was a poison. Ng had told her to give this to her husband. The Attorney General asked her why, in that case, had she drunk it herself? If it was not poisonous, why should it have anything to do with her husband's death? For the

Crown this was a clear case of premeditated murder. He instructed the jury that, should they find her not guilty of murder, there was no other offence (manslaughter etc.) of which she might be guilty. The newspaper reports give no further indication of her defence, just recording that the jury returned with a verdict of guilty, followed by the bald statement that "His Lordship passed sentence of death."

There the story as it appears in the newspapers of the year seems to end. The press was not squeamish about reporting on actual executions, and sometimes they were invited to witness the hangings, yet there is no notice of this happening. Nor is there apparently any notice in the extant records of the commutation of her sentence. However, it is through a chance remark in a later case, in 1923, that we learn that the woman convicted of murder 'some sixteen years ago' and whose sentence was commuted to a life term had just been released.[221] There being no other capital case involving a woman in those years, it appears that we do know Lam's fate. She, like Wong, had been pregnant, and it was her unborn child that saved Lam Kui from the gallows.

The would-be adulterer on Lantau Island

At the beginning of the 20th century Hong Kong was coming to terms with its tenfold expansion following the acquisition of the New Territories on the mainland and the surrounding islands. Within the first few years, police stations had been hurriedly established, land surveys made, government rents set and already roads and the railway to Canton were under construction. Once more, a people with strong family and clan traditions and practices found themselves living under Western concepts of law and justice, based on alien values. For many, the distance from either Hong Kong Island or even the 'local' police station meant that there was little reason for these new laws to interfere with the well-tried methods that communities had for sorting out quarrels and problems. But some offences would attract the attention of Colonial authorities and, not infrequently, villagers took disputes to their resident representatives of that authority, the police constable or sergeant, especially when such external involvement might be advantageous to them.

---

221 *Hongkong Telegraph*, 24th October 1923.

Lantau Island was such a place. Although the largest of the newly acquired islands, its population – estimated as 5,420 in 1911, was very thinly spread around the shoreline. The police station was positioned at Tai O, on the far west and where the greatest number of villagers lived. However, there were no roads connecting the village to the rest of the island, and boats were the only means of reaching other areas other than a long hike in rugged country. The eastern side of the land mass was more easily accessed from neighbouring Cheung Chau. A tiny, dumb-bell shaped island, the location of a former Chinese Maritime Customs house, Cheung Chau was home to about 4,500 fisherfolk and warranted its own police station. That customs house had become the Station and in 1907 Sergeant Angus, assisted by a Chinese interpreter and three or four Indian constables kept watch over the mainly peaceful place and collected the government rents from here and neighbouring east Lantau.

It was on a Monday morning late in August 1907 that Sgt Angus received the first intimation that a serious event had occurred on his patch.[222] Fisherman To Hing-chau moored up near the Cheung Chau Police Station to report that a robbery had taken place the previous night. Several men had rushed into his house and one lunged at him with a dagger, but he defended himself with a bed-board, he told the police. His wife had helped him capture this man and together they tied his legs, but four other men got away, taking with them a fifty dollar note and three ten dollar notes. They lived in Pak Ngan, a compact village in the fishing area of Mui Wo, about six nautical miles from Cheung Chau. While the sergeant listened to this, another man from that village came in. He was accompanied by his brother's wife and the Station interpreter. Fan Muk-yau had told the policeman of the murder of his brother, Fan Muk-fat. Catching sight of To Hing-chau with Sgt Angus, he cried out, "There's the murderer! That's him!"

Now it was Fan's turn to tell Sgt Angus what had happened the previous evening. He had been roused from sleep and, when stepping out of his house, had seen To holding his brother, Muk-fat, by his queue. While he was thus captured, To's wife, Ho Yung, was attacking him with a chopper,

---

222 *China Mail*, 31st August 1907, *Hongkong Weekly Press,* 16th September 1907, *Hongkong Telegraph,* 20th September 1907.

striking blows to his head and legs. Muk-fat collapsed to the ground and his brother ran to him and asked him what it was all about. The stricken man, hardly able to speak, told him that had lent To two or three dollars and when he saw the couple return from their day's fishing, he had asked for repayment. He then groaned and seemed to be in intense agony. The next minute his body relaxed, his anguish over. Muk-yau looked round to where the attackers had been, and was just in time to see Ho throw away the chopper and disappear into the hills.

With To's story now being recognised for the fabrication it undoubtedly was, Angus arrested him on suspicion of being involved in the murder of Muk-fat and locked him in the station's single cell. But had To really been murdered for a few dollars? Along with his constables, he followed Fan and the widow back to Pak Ngan. In To's house they found three choppers and an eighteen-inch bladed knife, but no sign of Ho. They also discovered a piece of queue about 24 inches long and a blood-soaked jacket. Muk-fat's body, though, was not where his brother had last seen it. They eventually found it, hidden beneath grass. His queue had been cut, with just a few inches of hair remaining. His legs showed signs of having been bound tightly together and there were wounds from a blade on his head and smaller ones on his right knee.

By the end of the week, the police were ready to bring the case to the magistrate, since they had begun to have an idea of the motive behind the attack. Ho Yung had not evaded capture for long: a couple of days after the murder she had sneaked back to her house to collect rice, but found that a constable was there, waiting for her. Arrested, she was taken over to Hong Kong Island and to the gaol, where her husband had already been transferred. On Saturday 31st August they appeared before Mr Melbourne, with Sgt Angus prosecuting. The Medical Officer at the Government Civil Hospital, who had conducted the postmortem examination on Fan Muk-fat, was the first to give evidence. The cause of death, he stated, was a rupture of the spleen. On examination, this organ proved to be three times its normal size and therefore, with the membrane holding it stretched very thin, would rupture either spontaneously or at the slightest violence to the region.[223] Dr Heanley agreed that any of the choppers found might be responsible for the wounds on the body. He would not say for sure that the piece of queue discovered had belonged to the deceased. At this, To cried out, "It is his queue!". After the evidence of the brother and the sergeant's account of the arrests, the case was remanded for more investigations to be made. However, little more had been uncovered by the time of the second hearing, so the couple were committed to stand trial at the Sessions, on 19th September 1907.

Before the Acting Chief Justice, Mr A. G. Wise, the couple were defended by Hon. Dr Ho Kai.[224] Dr Ho had, he explained, only received the deposition papers the previous day but since the jury had already been empanelled and he was the only barrister present in the colony, the judge prevailed on him to continue. "Dr Ho Kai, I am sure you will do justice to the defence," he remarked. The couple had pleaded not guilty to the charge of murder, although, at the time of his arrest, To had claimed that had he not killed Muk-fat, the latter surely would have killed him. When she was arrested, Ho told the police that she had attacked him because he was assaulting her husband. The Attorney General stated that, because of these claims, but primarily since the death had not been caused by the chopper blows themselves, the Crown would be satisfied if the jury, exercising its discretion, returned a verdict of manslaughter. This course was further strengthened when the doctor agreed that there were no marks of violence around the spleen and its rupture could have been the result of the man's fall. Then a Chinese constable was asked whether having the queue cut had any particular meaning. He told the Court that it happened when a man was caught attempting adultery. At this To stated that on that night, as he lay in bed, he had heard Fat enter

---

223 Enlargement of the spleen was a frequent result of the repeated bouts of malaria suffered by many people in the region. In fights or attacks, death, caused by the rupture of this organ, often followed a fall or blow to the chest.

224 Hon. Dr Ho Kai (1859-1914) was the first Hong Kong-born man to qualify as a doctor in western medicine, and one of the earliest Chinese to qualify for the Bar. A teacher of Sun Yat-sen, he both campaigned for reform and worked to further the cause of the Chinese in the colony through his position on the Legislative Council.

the house and go to his wife. When he saw that she resisted him, he went to help.

The jury had little problem agreeing the verdict of manslaughter against both prisoners. To Hing-chau received a sentence of three years with hard labour and Ho Yung, despite it having been she who had been seen to wield the chopper, eighteen months' imprisonment.

The Aberdeen boat murder

Perhaps one of the most troubling cases, and the most unsatisfactory in terms of its reporting, is that of the murder of an Aberdeen boatman in 1923.[225] In the course of the hundred years of newspaper reporting in the colony there is a slow but perceptible shift in journalistic attitudes. Gradually the western men writing the reports of court cases – especially those at the magistrates' courts – became less likely to use what they saw as descriptive, but pejorative terms (native, heathen etc.) about the Chinese defendants and plaintiffs, and became better acquainted with Chinese customs which they now saw as familiar part of the Hong Kong landscape. Chinese names and transliterations became less of a mystery to the writers and standardised spellings were adopted. Nevertheless, whilst from the beginning newspaper reports had always given the names of Europeans appearing in court, even by the 1930s there was often a laziness in according the same treatment to Chinese. Admittedly, the difficult acoustics of the courts could cause problems for all but the most experienced 'China hand'. But cases were now (usually) better reported, a move that was also occurring in Britain, where the concerns and crimes of the poorest began to receive the attention previously reserved for their 'betters'.

In the light of this, the reporting of the incidents of this murder and the subsequent trials would appear more typical of a time fifty or even seventy years earlier. There was no concern for detail, a very limited investigation and little attention to the defence case. It has not even been possible to find an account of the appearance of the accused at the Magistracy, and it is only in the Chinese-language *The China Mail* that

---

225 *Hongkong Daily Press,* 28th August 1923, *Hongkong Telegraph,* 22nd & 24th October 1923.

the names of the parties were given.[226] Moreover, an examination across the four English language and one Chinese paper suggests that this was not only lazy reporting, but reflected the whole conduct of the case.

On the morning of 27th August 1923, the typhoon signals hurriedly hoisted surprised all those whose business took them onto the waters or shoreline around Hong Kong. There had been little warning of the storm, but now the Observatory expected it to make land less than 100 miles north of the colony. By mid-morning, signal 5 was raised, and in the harbour small craft and sampans on both sides of the harbour were hurrying to the shelters. On the south side of the island there was perhaps less urgency, but the water was still choppy and not favourable for any fishing vessel setting out. The papers of that day and the next gave less than a column inch to the news that, "A boatman, a boatwoman and the latter's daughter were charged at the Magistracy with the murder of an aged fisherman in Aberdeen Channel. The prisoners were formally remanded."

The previous morning a little boy had rowed the "aged fisherman", Wong Tai-hei, from the sampan on which he lived to the shore. The child, who was his son or adopted son shared his home. Later the man went, with two women, to a boatyard in Aberdeen. Outside a boatbuilder's shed they were overheard arguing about who should pay the last instalment on a boat for the women. The older woman, Chan Pak, was the fisherman's wife, although the two women lived on a separate sampan. The relationship of the younger woman to the couple is not clear. Also present, but not involved in the argument, was another man. The boatbuilder was unable to identify him later, but the police assumed this to be Wong Yuk, whom they arrested with the women. He later claimed to be the prospective husband of the young woman. Later that day the group went to Aberdeen police station, with the expectation that the constables there would be able to sort out their dispute. Instead, they received short shrift, and the police told them to stop their quarrelling and be on their way. The constables could identify the three arrested and

---

226 I am indebted to Dr Kwong Chi-man of the Baptist University, Hong Kong for these and for the translation that appears towards the end of this section.

thought the fourth was the murdered man, whose body was not recovered. They did not record the incident or the names of those involved.

The next morning at about 11 a.m. a gardener, outside his mat-shed by the shore, heard cries of *"Gau meng!"* – "Save life!" Looking out across the channel towards the island of Ap Lei Chau, he saw a man struggling in the water. A rowing boat was pulling away from him, as if heading towards Deep Water Bay. The gardener pushed his boat out into the water and rowed towards the man. Before he had got far, he saw the other boat return to the man in the water. To his astonishment, rather than help him, he saw two of the three in the boat push the man further down with an oar and a pole, before rowing off again. The gardener, realising that the man in the water must by now be dead, started off in pursuit of the group, hailing another boatman to help him. He swiftly told this second man, a fish-dealer, what he had seen and together they caught up with the rowing boat and held on to it and its occupants until the police could arrest the group. The papers do not record whether it was the Water Police, who routinely patrolled Aberdeen harbour, or the local force who took charge.

At the police station statements were taken from all involved. Chan said that she had lived with the fisherman for some years and that she had no life. Wong explained that the old woman had told him she had been hit by her husband and that he once had nearly killed her. She had asked him to help her get rid of him, and, believing what she said and being in love with her daughter, he had agreed. But he had not pushed the man overboard, as the gardener had later stated, nor had he pushed the man down into the water. He had fought with the old man, who had lost his balance and fallen accidentally into the water. He had no part in his drowning: that had been the action of Chan alone, pushing him down and holding him under the water with an oar.

The magistrate heard evidence the next month, then sent the case straight to the next Criminal Sessions. When the case was heard at the October sitting, the Attorney General, Mr Joseph Kemp, prosecuting, told the jury, "One cannot help but suspect that there might have been, in those arguments, something which to the more or less simple minds of these boat people, seemed to be a sufficient reason for the violence they did to the old man." But, he warned, the jury's responsibility lay not in trying to understand and allow for that simplicity, but to judge the case on the evidence alone. What sounds to contemporary ears both patronising and down-right rude reflected the attitude, not only of privileged westerners, but of established Hong Kong, Chinese and western, towards a group on the margins of society. With some similarity of situation and treatment to the Travellers and Roma people of Europe, the boat people of Hong Kong were frequently moving around, and only tangentially dependent on the land population. But they were seen as an integral section of the people of the colony and appeared, albeit approximately, right from the earliest population estimates, in the official count.

The Attorney General's introduction to the case proceeded upon much the same line, with many repetitions of the phrases "appears to be" and "seemingly" when discussing the relationships between and actions of the accused. The papers make reference to, but do not detail, evidence brought forward by the Crown. This may be the witness' testimony of the gardener and the fish-dealer, since the case seems to rest entirely on what that first man said he saw.

With such slim pickings, the counsel for the defence, Mr T. N. Chau, could only try to mitigate the offence and made a robust case for it being one of manslaughter rather than murder. He was representing all the three and first attempted to show that, had Wong Yuk wanted to murder Wong Tai-hei, he would have chosen a better time and place and brought the means to do so with him. Southern China was awash with weapons and, "a dagger or a pistol is, as you all know, very easy to obtain nowadays". He reminded the jury that the gardener was also an old man – implying, perhaps, that his sight was impaired or that he was rather fanciful in reporting what he claimed to see. He had, Mr Chau said, made up the story about the boat's return and the actions of the occupants. There was no truth in this and no case against either of the women.

The Attorney General rebutted this, especially the idea that the case should be one of manslaughter. The young man had made no reference to there being a quarrel on the boat at his arrest: indeed, his words were "She told me to kill him." Why was he on the sea with the group and away from his workplace, if not for a very specific reason? The Chief Justice,

Sir William Rees-Davies, struck another nail in the coffin for the defence when he corrected Mr Chau's assertion that a charge of murder required premeditation. This was not the case in English law, he explained, and the absence of it here did not alter the offence to one of manslaughter.

The jury retired for about fifteen minutes, after which they returned with guilty verdicts for the Chan and Wong, and a not guilty one for the younger woman, who they believed had not left the tiller throughout the affair. Sir William promptly acquitted her. He then asked the older woman first, if she had anything to say as to why he should not pass the sentence as required by law. She gave a vigorous denial of the entire case, "I had (*sic*) never done such an unvirtuous act as to murder my husband. We lived in perfect amity for many years." She denied that she had asked the other man to kill him, claiming that it was he who had both struck him with the oar and then pushed him under. Wong had even pushed her aside when she had tried to go to her husband's aid. Sobbing, she repeated over and over, "Let me go so I may bring up my young children."

Wong Yuk, who the papers report with approval, "made a clean breast of the affair", again told how Chan had asked him to go out in the boat and help him murder her husband. "I am young and inexperienced, so I did what she asked. I would never got into the boat but that the girl is my sweetheart. I hit the man and accidentally killed him." The Chief Justice then sentenced both to death, adding that it did not matter whether the old woman had struck any of the blows: she had instigated the murder and was thus similarly guilty. Chan wailed, "Be kind, be kind, do not let me go!" as the pair were taken down. But four people had left Aberdeen in a boat that morning and only three returned. Even if the old man's falling into the sea had been an accident following on from a dispute, there had apparently been no attempt to rescue him.

The Hongkong Telegraph gave a front-page column to the fact that a woman had been sentenced to death. It recalled that it was sixteen years since any female had "stood in the dock before a black-capped judge in the Colony and heard the dreaded words". It noted, however, that the woman then – Lam Kui, in the poisoning case at West Point – had been pregnant at the time and so escaped the scaffold. In fact, she had just been released from prison six months earlier. The journalist had enquired of an 'old hand' of the court – perhaps one of the bailiffs, whether a woman had ever been hanged in Hong Kong? This man said that he could not recollect such, and that a previous Chief Justice had spoken strongly against such a penalty being carried out on a member of the weaker sex.

But Chan Pak was destined to be the first.[227] There is no record of any appeal, either on behalf of her or the man. On 28th November a working party of prisoners erected the scaffold within Victoria Gaol and the condemned pair were executed side by side. Executions had long been carried out away from the public gaze, but there were occasions, such as this, when the court permitted the press to witness the event. Those officially required to be present were the Superintendent of the gaol, the Colonial Surgeon, the Chaplain, a warder-executioner and two warders. The newspaper considered it worthy of record that the woman showed no fear and went to the scaffold singing a Chinese song. Wong Yuk also seemed calm and said nothing, until near the very end, when he rebuked the old woman for singing.

To return to the remarks made at the opening of this section, this case raises more questions than the scant newspaper reports answer. By this point in Hong Kong's legal history, the judges conducted capital trials cautiously, with the presumption of innocence to the fore. But in this case, certainly as recorded, there seems to be an acceptance of a lesser standard of evidence. It is difficult not to conclude that this has much to do with the status of the defendants. They are not the usual defendants, not from the colony's resident hard-working poor. Poverty does not seem to be a factor here, except, in as much as the Attorney General's 'simple minds' might equate to 'without education.' These people remain literally anonymous and 'other' – outsiders and yet subject to the legal code of the place. The journalists display none of the little hints of sympathy or even puzzlement that slip into other reports of women on capital charges. What do we really learn about these people? Not till the very end do we hear this woman's voice. Were the couple really old? The younger woman is perhaps in her late teens. Are the girl and the young boy actually their natural children? Who are the other children the 'old' woman has to raise? Is she a grandmother, or is this the cultural blindness that cannot see past the toll that a hard life, with constant exposure to the sun and rain, wreaks on the frame and face?

Turning to the conduct of the case, it is difficult to imagine a land-based murder proceeding thus. We hear nothing of any evidence the girl could give. Was she not called, or not understood? The defence counsel appears not to have challenged the paucity of the material with which he had to work. Even though the whole trial depends on the evidence of the gardener, the defendants do not challenge him, or raise questions about his motivation in giving it. Did they even know they had that right?

Whilst it might be imagined that the journalist on the Chinese paper had a better understanding of the people involved, the absence of trial reports suggest that he had only gathered his material at the execution itself. In the event, the account only adds to the confusion.

Death Penalty for a Treacherous Man and a Promiscuous Wife

Chan Pak, a woman who lives on a boat off Aberdeen, and Wong Yuk, a boatman, killed an old man Wong Tai-hei by drowning off Aberdeen. After trial, it was found that Chan Pak was the wife of the deceased, but Chan and her lover plotted to kill the deceased because Chan thought the man was old and poor and wanted to remarry. The judge decided the two to suffer the penalty of death by hanging. The penalty was carried out yesterday morning in the gaol by the warden.[228]

A village solution – the Au Tau killing

Pun Chiu-ling tried to be a dutiful daughter-in-law. Her husband's mother was fine, she got on well with 63-year-old Tang Yung. It was the father-in-law who made life miserable. Cheung Pak-yau had such a vicious temper, he was always shouting at everyone. He had an old dagger that he kept sharpened and used to threaten anyone who displeased him. The village of Sheung Tse was not big: just twenty houses or so and the ancestral hall, and everybody there was scared of Cheung. At 7 a.m. that Monday morning, she carried a bowl of rice to her father-in-law. Tang

---

228 香港華字日報, 29th November 1923.

was already out in the fields, but would be back for her meal soon. Pun had just put the bowl down when the old man pulled her trousers down and dragged her onto his lap and started fondling her.[229]

Pun struggled and fought against him, but Cheung was strong and held her fast. Her relief was great when Tang came in just at that moment and hit her husband on the head with the stick she was carrying. Sobbing, Pun pulled her clothes back on and rushed out. She could hear Tang screaming at the man and he cursing and hitting her. A short time later, Tang came to find her daughter-in-law, and bustled her out of the house, and along to the house of her brother-in-law (i.e. Cheung Pak-yau's brother), Cheung Lau-yuk, where they sat talking about the incident. It wasn't the first time that the 63-year-old man had done this to her. "I will tell Yuk-shun when he comes back," said Tang, "He will sort his father out." But Pun was not so sure. She doubted that her brother-in-law could do much: he was as afraid of his father as she was. Pun had been living with the old couple for seven years now, ever since her husband went abroad to make some money. She wished that he would return.

As far as most of the 1930s English reading public in Victoria or Kowloon knew, the Au Tau district, let alone the little village of Sheung Tse, in the Pat Heung Valley, might have been in the deepest recesses of China.[230] If they were drivers, they might have passed the police station that stood on a ridge at Au Tau, guarding the road that encircled the New Territories. The 1931 census showed that the area had just shy of 13,000 inhabitants, and, indicative of how different this was from urban Hong Kong, there were equal numbers of males and females. But those inhabitants were thinly spread. The area reached midway to Ping Shan in the west, Tai Po in the east and Lok Ma Chau going north. Yuen Long was then just another small village in the district.

Cheung Yuk-shun had left Sheung Tse early that morning to sell firewood in a neighbouring village. When he arrived back home at midday, Tang wasted no time in putting him abreast of that morning's

229 The case is best documented in the *South China Morning Post*, where it appears on 30th September, 2nd October & 19th-21st November 1930.

230 Sheung Tse, probably the village now called Sheung Che and one of a group of 30 in present-day Pat Heung.

events. Reluctantly, he agreed to tackle his father, and remonstrate with him. "You are a man of sixty years old and more, why should you behave indecently towards your daughter-in-law?" Cheung Pak-yau rounded on him, "Get away from me! Go on, get out! Never mind my affairs, keep your nose out of them!" Getting nowhere, Yuk-shun returned to his uncle's house to tell him and his mother what had happened. But soon the irate man roared in. "I told you not to interfere in my affairs! Why are you talking to other people about it?" and swinging his dagger, he lurched at the younger man. But Yuk-shun was quick on his feet and avoided the blows, so Cheung turned on his wife. She had nothing with which to defend herself this time, and it was just by chance that none of the frenzied slashes fell on her. It was only when Lau-yuk stepped behind Cheung and overpowered him, taking the dagger from his hands, that the scene ended. Lau-yuk pushed the old man (his brother) out of the house.

During the afternoon, Yuk-shun went to the Ancestral Hall to talk over the situation with other villagers. This was getting out of hand, but what could they do? They dared not banish the old man for fear of the reprisals he might take. The initiative had to come from Tang. That would be the proper course. The old lady's thoughts had been running along similar lines and she, too, went to the Hall. Soon about 100 people had gathered around them. "The problem is that we're not part of China here," said one man. They all agreed – there was no need to spell it out – in China justice would have been swift and sure.

Tang detached herself from the crowd, and stole back into her house, passing Cheung, who was sitting on a stool in the doorway. She had already thought things out. A strong bamboo pole that they used in the fields stood by the door. Grasping it in both hands, Tang brought it down as hard as she could on Cheung. She was aiming for his head, but the pole was long and unwieldy, and instead she caught him a blow on the shoulder, but it was enough to knock him off the stool. Full of rage, now, she smashed it down on the cowering form again and again. Pun had followed her in and stood watching her for a moment, then found a thick piece of planking and started battering her former assailant. At first Cheung cried out, but abruptly his screams stopped. The women stood back. Was he dead? Pun thought so, but Tang did not trust the old villain. "You must help me strangle him," she ordered the younger woman. "Go, get some rope, quickly!" As Pun left, the wife called in the men: they had crowded round the door of the house, anyway. "Bring him outside." They lifted the unconscious form and set him down a few feet away. Pun had made a noose of the cord and slipped it over the man's head. The women did not need to say anything. Each took an end and pulled hard. Pun could see it cutting through the skin of Cheung's neck. "Again," ordered Tang, and then, job done, sat back.

Looking up, she addressed the men. "You must bury him. You know how, don't you?" Of course they knew how, all the village would know the proper, customary, way of disposing of such a man. They attached ropes round his shoulders and feet and slung the body between two poles. A procession carried the lifeless form up the hill, behind the village. They had come prepared and already agreed on the place. Not too close to the village – some rough land, where no-one ever went, was where they were heading. Shovels broke the damp ground easily: no need to dig deep, about three hand-spans should do it. There was no covering for the corpse: he was just in his singlet and shorts. Untied from the pole, they rolled the body over so it lay face down in the grave, then covered it with earth. No marker, either. This was a man they intended to forget. They could return to some peace.

As the rural farming communities of the north were unknown to the office-bound city dwellers, so too, in return, was the British colony a rather irrelevant closed book to them. Except when it came to paying their quarterly rates, they saw little of these officials. It would never have occurred to them to take their dispute with old Cheung Pak-yau to the official policemen. But even here news had a way of travelling, and it was not long before the Chinese constables at Au Tau Station picked up on gossip that was circulating. It was rumoured that a village had got rid of one of its elders, and that it was the man's wife who had done the deed.

But did Tang, a woman with more experience of the world than her daughter-in-law, start then to consider what might happen if some inkling of events reached official ears? Did she decide to take the brunt of the blame, if it should come to that, and shield the girl, so that her son would have a wife to come home to? If the police came, the village would be likely to take its cue from her. Or had she really been the sole actor in the drama, with Pun's part perhaps limited to hitting the man when instructed and fetching the rope when told to?

Two days after the events, Sgt Charles Baysting arrived in the village with a team of Chinese and Indian constables, including a detective. The clam-like attitude of the villagers was no surprise, but eventually they confirmed that a man named Cheung Pak-yau had died two days earlier. After more fruitless questioning, a man who gave his name as Cheung Shiu-hing stepped forward and volunteered to show the police the grave. They photographed it and then the constables set about the grisly exhumation. There were aspects that surprised the sergeant, even with his experience of policing this region. Aside from the position of the corpse and the cords still round its neck, the flesh had decomposed so much that there were few features remaining on the face and the arms and back looked as if they had been already eaten away by decay. Officers took the body away to Kowloon Mortuary, while Sgt Baysting and his detectives returned to the village.

Still the villagers were not forthcoming. "This was a village matter, and we settled it in the Chinese way," was all they initially said. Eventually he learnt that Cheung was a bad man, who had tried to kill his wife and son before this. The British had banished him once before, and he had been in prison for kidnap, but he had returned unreformed. There was such general agreement about this that Sgt Baysting understood why they had all closed ranks. Then, as he was speaking to his colleagues, the wife of the deceased man separated herself from the group and stood in front of the officer. "When I came back from the fields, I saw him trying to embrace my daughter-in-law, so I hit him with a stick. But he tried to hit me with a dagger. He did not succeed, he missed. When I hit him he was not dead, he could still speak, so I told my daughter-in-law to help me strangle him. My clans-people came, and I told them to tie up Cheung and take him outside. Then I took some rope and put it round his neck and pulled it tight. I did that twice. After that, I told my people to take him away and bury him."

At the mention of Pun Chiu-ling, had the police considered what part she played in the murder? Did they see her as not responsible for her actions, or so terrified of Tang she had no option but to follow orders? Did they question her then? There is no report of it in the story the newspapers told of the arrest. If so, what was her account of her share in the events? After Sgt Baysting had obtained warrants from the inspector at Tai Po Station, it was Tang and four of the clansmen, including Cheung Yuk-shun and Cheung Shiu-hing, whom they arrested. The former was charged with murder, the men with aiding and abetting her. But there was one village member keen to be a witness, the 13-year-old son of Lau-yuk, and thus Tang's nephew, who claimed to be in the room when the old man was lashing out with his dagger. But his story was very confused, and he seemed to make some of it up on the spot.

Kowloon was still waiting for a new Magistracy and the stop-gap, in the old Yaumatei Police Station, could not cope with all the cases the area produced. The trials of offences committed in the New Territories were sent to a makeshift court in the Police Headquarters for the region at Tai Po. The story of the events of the day come, in the main, from the first two days of the hearing there. But Tai Po was a long way from the centre of things, and the coverage of this whole case was very scrappy, with none of the English papers reporting it in full. There is no account of the initial hearing, nor weekly adjournments, so it was almost a month after the events before the public heard of the murder, when the case commenced at Tai Po Police Court.

On 29th September before Mr Wynne-Jones, the prosecution of Tang and the four men was opened by Assistant Crown Solicitor, Mr L. R. Andrewes. He recounted events but referred to the statements taken from Tang and her son Cheung Yuk-shun at the time for the fuller story. Then Dr Utley, who had performed the postmortem, gave medical evidence. He was puzzled by the swiftness of decomposition, which prevented him for saying with any certainty if the cords had been place round the neck before or after death. Had the man been hit? He could not say for sure, it was impossible to see if there had been any bruising. But no bones were broken. Later, at the hearing at the Criminal Sessions he would confirm that multiple blows would have broken down the skin and tissues so much that decay could set in fast. However, no single blow that he might have received had been sufficient to kill the man. Then Mr Andrewes called Pun Chiu-ling as a witness. That day she only told about her situation in the family and how Cheung had pulled her onto his knee, something he had done before, about a year earlier. The prosecutor then showed her the dagger with which Cheung was alleged to have threatened Tang and Yuk-shun. She knew it but had not seen it that day. At that rather inconclusive moment, the case was adjourned.

But the next day, soon after Pun had continued her evidence, Mr Andrewes asked for permission to treat her as a hostile witness, since her evidence did not tally with the statements she had made to police. What points had prompted the request, and at this stage is not clear. He then pushed the young woman into admitting that her father-in-law had pulled her trousers down, not just 'embraced her', as both she and Tang had maintained until this point. She then gave a brief but clear account of the attack that she and Tang had made on him. It had been led by Tang, but in the story she now told, she had taken a full share. Why, before she had progressed too far with this, did the magistrate, Mr Wynne-Jones, not stop her and read the caution? Had the police already offered her, or did they intend to offer, some immunity from prosecution if she gave evidence against Tang? The accounts of the magistrate's hearing breaks off here, noting that it was again adjourned, but there are no accounts of any subsequent hearings at this level. Tang had (apparently) not yet been called, neither had anything been heard about the case against the four men.

What becomes apparent by the opening of the case at the Criminal Sessions is that the story – not of the killing, but of its investigation – heard at the magistrate's court was not the full one. On 4th September, the day after the police had arrived at Sheung Tse, Pun had been taken to Au Tau Police Station. From there they went to Kowloon Mortuary. Presumably she was there to identify the body, and perhaps the police questioned her about the state of it, or about the cords around the neck. They then returned to the Police Station, where she stayed for some time with the 13-year-old boy. On 5th September, she was questioned by Inspector Dorling, who began the interview with the customary caution.

He would later explain that the statement she made to him was markedly different from that which she subsequently gave to the magistrate. The implication is, that in the first statement she did not portray herself as having any share, or any significant share, in the killing of Cheung. Then, at some date that Pun could not recall, she was interviewed by a Chinese Detective Constable at the police station. The boy was with her – so this may, or may not, have been on 4th September. At that interview, the constable said to her "You must tell me the truth, otherwise it will be hard on the police. A police constable, like everybody else, has to support his family." He also said, either on this occasion or later, that she must repeat exactly what she had said to him to the magistrate, otherwise she would be put in prison for many years. Pun had thought he was quite kind to her – he didn't hurt her. Called later to comment on this, Insp. Dorling said that he was unaware that any other officer had interviewed Pun.

The third factor absent from mention, at any rate, before Mr Wynne-Jones, was that Mr Andrewes had interviewed Pun on 24th September. The substance of this interview was never revealed – that it had happened only came to light just before the closure of the case at the Supreme Court. Had Pun reverted then to her original statement? If it instead resembled that which she (presumably) gave to the detective, why did her change of evidence come as a surprise to him on the second day at the trial? On 16th or 18th October (dates vary even within the same account), they finally charged Pun with the murder of her father-in-law. Tang's hearing had been scheduled for the October Sessions, due to start on 20th, but on that day its postponement was announced, quoting "developments in the case since the woman was committed for trial which require investigation."[231] It was not made public at this point that Pun was under arrest.

When the "Sensational Au Tau Murder Case" did finally come to the Supreme Court, on 18th November, both Pun and Tang were accused of murder, but it was the younger woman's case that was heard. She had been assigned the young but very able Leo d'Almada to defend her. Before the Acting Chief Justice (Mr Justice Wood), Mr Somerset Fitzroy had to admit how many blank spaces there were in the prosecution's knowledge

---

231 *Hongkong Daily Press,* 21st October 1930.

of what had occurred on the day. The gaping holes in the procedural story also became apparent. The trial started with the story told as Pun had recounted it at the Tai Po court hearing. Medical evidence followed, with further discussion and speculation about the death. Pun's brother-in-law, Yuk-shun, was brought as a witness for the prosecution, but he explained that he was satisfied that his father's killing was justified. Had they been in China, he told the court, the Chinese government would have shot the man. He then spoke not about Pun's involvement, but told the jury how he had learnt from his mother that she, Tang, had killed Cheung.

When Mr Fitzroy began to recount the statement Pun had made against Tang when first questioned, Mr d'Almada objected to this as inadmissible, since she was then a prosecution witness, not a defendant. But it was the interview that the detective had with Pun that really gave the defence counsel the grist wherewith to break the prosecution's case. This confession, he maintained, had been obtained by third degree methods. By threatening her with prison, any statement extracted from her had to be regarded as unsafe. He stressed how negligent the police had been in taking evidence from her – how she had fared worse than even an arrested prisoner and that they should, in fact, have taken more care over her. "The accused is of a highly ignorant type, of a low mentality, and that if anyone merited and deserved assistance she did." Laying aside the rather unpleasant language in which the barrister framed this criticism, it would appear that the young woman had very little understanding of her circumstances. She had changed her statement, admitting greater guilt, perhaps, as she said, because the policeman was kind to her, and then, threatened with prison, had to stick to the story. It would appear that Pun did not appreciate the difference between telling a story and presenting a factual account, and with no experience of the latter, had walked into a capital charge.

Mr Justice Wood was reluctant to accept Mr d'Almada's charge of third degree methods, but the Crown, in the person of Mr Somerset Fitzroy, was more troubled. When the Chief Justice enquired of prosecuting counsel whether his case was concluded, to the surprise of the court, he asked for an adjournment. He would consult the Attorney General whether the Crown should not issue a *nolle prosequi*, in favour of both

Pun and Tang. The court reassembled on the next day, 20th November, but without Pun Chiu-ling. Addressing the jury, the Acting Chief Justice said that they would note her absence. They had heard Pun's confession, but the Mr Justice Wood thought it would be very unsafe to proceed any further relying on that. The Attorney General had already issued a *nolle prosequi*. Perhaps earlier that morning or even the previous evening, Pun had been told that all charges against her had been dropped. The same message had been given to Tang. Both were now free, and their rather bizarre twelve weeks at the hands of British justice was over.

CHAPTER 8

CHILDREN, CRIME AND THE COURTS

Before Mr J. R. Wood this morning a wee mite of a Chinese lad named Ah Fung pleaded guilty to the charge of hawking without a licence in Jubilee Street.

"Do you know that you ought to be whipped?" inquired His Worship.

"Yes, Sir," meekly replied the boy.

"Well, then, don't do it again," said the magistrate, and discharged the diminutive offender.

The China Mail, 23rd May 1917

Everyone needed to make a living somehow. In the first decades of the 20th century around 86% of the children in the colony received no schooling, and most were expected to contribute to the family purse almost as soon as they could walk and talk.[232] Hawking wares in the street – carrying around a little basket of potatoes or a handful of peanuts – was the easiest way to make a few cents, and to ensure a meal that day. But hawking was strictly regulated by the government, through the limited issue of licences. At the turn of the century these cost $2 per year, payable in quarterly instalments. In 1903, this increased to $4, and half-yearly payments, making the scheme more manageable for its administrators, the Registrar General's Office. Without such, the streets would quickly become impassable, it was believed, with thousands touting their wares.

---

232 No official figure for the percentage of children in education exists at the time, but from the 1911 census and the 1911 Education figures, there are c. 70,000 school age children in the colony and appear to be around 10,000 school places. It was not until 1978 that nine years of education was made compulsory.

A Hong Kong nuisance – the little vagabonds …

Few of the myriad of children tugging at the sleeve of each passer-by to attract his attention to their tray of bits knew, cared or understood about such things as licences. They just knew that they had to avoid policemen. The Magistrates' Courts had a stream of these young offenders each day. Sometimes fines, between $1 and $5, were imposed, but since most had no means of paying, and were rarely accompanied by any adults, this was often fruitless. Adults were sent to gaol for a week or two for the offence of hawking without a licence, but, since the latter part of the 19th century, there had been an understanding that this was not appropriate for young lads. So the boys would be birched, usually receiving six strokes, unless they were 'repeat offenders'. But corporal punishment was regulated, and the boys were first taken to the prison doctor, who assessed their physique and state of health. Not infrequently he vetoed the punishment, when the boy was too puny or ill, and then the police dismissed him with a telling-off.

These children had been on the streets since their earliest days and were very wise as to the best answers to give. In a debate conducted between 'Adversaria' of The China Mail in June 1920 and 'Policeman', the former had lamented the 'persecution' of the poor, especially the young, by the police and magistrates, and suggested that all juvenile hawkers be offered a ten-cent licence. Policeman, who claimed a quarter-century of service in the colony, pointed out that "the poor of Hongkong are the poor of China", that no provision would ever be adequate and such a licence would see the roads clogged with young street-sellers. From personal experience he told how enquiries into the hardship claimed by the little 'orphans' often revealed homes and parents, and "the greater number of these same little boys are accomplished thieves and liars and incorrigible rogues". Yet the miserable lives of which the newspaper reporters spoke were the daily reality, as Policeman admitted. The very survival of these urchins depended on their ability to make those few cents, which required them to be as slippery as any little character from Oliver Twist.

An altogether nastier crime was that of snatching of earrings from small girls or babies. While it was an offence committed by males of all ages, the culprits were predominantly boys just tall enough to reach up to the baby on the back of its mother and nimble enough to make off in quick time. The magistrates dealt severely with the culprits, and they often found themselves in gaol for a week or two, with a birching at the beginning and end of that time. Of course, many crimes committed by children were directed and arranged for them by adults. An example, that features the youngest defendant the author has found in court comes as late as 1928.[233] A detective charged the boy with stealing a silver jug, two silver cups and a clock from a Mrs Black of King's Terrace, Kowloon. She had reported the theft almost immediately and the items were soon found in a pawn-broker's shop. Meanwhile, the six-year-old boy was seen scrambling up the verandah of the King's Terrace property, on his way back for more. He was taken to the police station, where he admitted stealing the silver. That afternoon, his aunt arrived to ask why her nephew was being held by the police. The following morning police charged her with accepting the items without ascertaining their origin and then pawning them. At court, the magistrate gaoled her for three months and reprimanded the pawn-broker for accepting silver items from a woman who obviously would not have such possessions. The little boy, who had been charged with larceny, was, "having regard to his age… discharged with a warning". But did the lad have other relatives to look after him? It is unlikely that the woman would have been allowed to take him into the prison with her.

Not all the western boys in Hong Kong were beyond reproach either. Reports of the cruel treatment of dogs and other animals by 'European boys who ought to know better' occur a few times in the early 20th century papers, while the firing of 'caps' and catapults and such nuisances are the subject of various 'Letters to the Editor'. One boy, John Adams, appeared before Mr Melbourne at the Kowloon Magistrates' Court, accused of stealing $36 from the second engineer of one of the steamship companies.[234] Henry Thomas had found the thirteen-year-old prowling round the *S.S. Yat Shing,* early one morning, just after Easter in 1917. The boy had seemed curious about the ship and Thomas had shown him round then invited him to have breakfast. Later he had seen Adams

233 *Hongkong Telegraph,* 20th March 1928.
234 *Hongkong Telegraph,* 11th April 1917.

come out of his room. After the child left the ship, he went to a drawer and found that his money had gone. Thomas gave the police a good description of the boy, and Det. Sgt Tim Murphy tracked him down and arrested him that evening. Adams had not let the money burn a hole in his pocket – he had already bought a new briefcase, several toy pistols, tennis shoes, swimming trunks and an electric torch amongst other things, and still had $3.40 left of his haul. Det. Sgt Murphy reminded the magistrate that, just the previous month, he had sentenced the boy to 12 lashes of the birch for stealing. "It doesn't seem to have done him much good," remarked Mr Melbourne. "No, your Worship. The boy is incorrigible." Hoping that a short, sharp shock might shake the boy out of his ways, he sentenced him to a week in gaol, with another birching. All the newspapers reported this, and gave the boy's name and age, no doubt causing embarrassment to his parents, in the small European community.

...and their wayward sisters

Girls, of course, did get into trouble with the law, but to far less a degree, and less conspicuously, than their brothers. There are just a handful of examples from the 19th century which can be really attributed to a female child under 16 years of age. Until 1920 or so there are very few reports of girls arrested for the most frequent juvenile offence, hawking. Of those whose activities did come to police attention, approximately half would appear to have been directed by parents or other adults. Part of the problem, though, is of identification, since journalists tended to describe every young-looking woman as a 'girl'. Reporters also display a mix of chauvinism and understanding in their attitude to young Chinese girls, including brothel inmates, recognising the limitations they had on their freedom of action.

However, the magistrates did not always show the same degree of compassion. An Indian constable brought to court someone whom the *Hongkong Daily Press* reporter described as "a miserable little article of a girl, fifteen years old", for spitting into his face.[235] She was employed by

---

235 *Hongkong Daily Press,* 9th January 1868. The account erroneously records the policeman as being both a Sikh and a *Mahomedan.*

a brothel as a servant, and the constable had asked her to sweep in front of the house. The paper does not speculate, but, since it describes the policeman as "immense", the girl must have possessed considerable nerve and an excellent aim to achieve the feat. But Mr Charles May was not disposed to see the lighter side of the matter, especially as the constable had felt affronted, it being the eve of a special Muslim fast (almost certainly the beginning of Ramadan). Mr May concurred that the girl's behaviour had been outrageous, and fined her one dollar.

Girls, whether acting on their own volition or not, could be quite as cunning and opportunist as their brothers. Described as a little girl and a big liar by Revenue Officer Arthur Grimmitt, the child he found carrying 36 taels of prepared non-government opium in July 1929 had led the man on a merry dance to start with.[236] He realised that the girl was working for someone else but did not give very much credence to her tale that a man had given her the bundle to carry and then had gone back to China. She said that she had only just arrived in Hong Kong and when Insp. Grimmitt told her that if she led him to where she had been given the opium, he would help her, she started concocting fictitious addresses. After a couple of these, and perhaps because R.O. Grimmitt, a former policeman who had been in the colony for twenty years, became more severe with her, she took him to Chinese Street, a tiny lane between Pottinger Street and Queen Victoria Street and just a block further inland from Connaught Road, where he had found her. Here she pointed out her little brother who greeted her, then quickly abandoned the game he had been playing and ran away upon sight of the great 'foreign devil'. R.O. Grimmitt found nothing to suggest that the people in the house they had come to had anything to do with the opium. They were quite frank with him and explained that they thought the children were orphans: they had been around for some time and they let the girl and her brother have their meals with them. But both disappeared somewhere else at night, they knew not where. Nor did they know what the girl did all day, they only usually saw her at meal times. The little lad was soon caught, but told the Revenue Officer almost as many tales as his sister, so nothing could be learnt from him.

---

236 *China Mail,* 29th and 31st July, 1929.

At the Police Court later that morning, magistrate Mr Hamilton heard the tale from R.O. Grimmitt and another version from the child. He agreed with the inspector it was a case for the Secretariat for Chinese Affairs, who could better enquire whether the pair had relatives in the colony. The girl was put into police custody for 48 hours for those investigations, during which time she would stay at the Po Leung Kuk. Two days later, nothing further had been discovered, but the magistrate was sure that the girl was just being used by a smuggling ring. He discharged her and asked R.O. Grimmitt to arrange that she would return to the Po Leung Kuk, with a recommendation that she should not be released, as the gang would surely find her again. But before she was allowed to leave the court, Mr Hamilton had stern words for the child. After telling her what was going to happen, he said, "But whatever happens, remember, no more smuggling! If you are caught again, you will go to prison. Would you like to go to jail for six months?" A squeaked out "No!" was the frightened reply. "Then don't do it again!" "I won't dare to," she told the magistrate. So she was taken off to the S.C.A. in the first place, but what became of her little brother is not mentioned. Maybe the kind people in Chinese Street took him in.

The previous year Revenue Officer Tallon arrested a ten-year-old girl when he found her with 20 taels of prepared opium, which she said she had picked up in the streets.[237] At the Kowloon Magistracy she said that she lived with her aunt in Reclamation Street. Her mother was dead and her father away at sea. When her aunt was questioned, she claimed to know nothing about the matter. From her behaviour, the police had no reason to suspect her, so the magistrate was prepared to release the child, if the aunt could find someone to underwrite a bond, guaranteeing the girl's good behaviour. The woman went away to ask around her friends and the child went to the Po Leung Kuk. Some months later another young girl was in the dock before Mr Hamilton.[238] This child lived with her grandmother in Kowloon, but had met a woman who had designs on the older woman's property. The child had been persuaded to steal 36 pieces of jewellery, $30 in notes and some house bonds and then take them all

237 *Hongkong Telegraph,* 10th April 1928.
238 *Hongkong Daily Press,* 13th December 1928.

to the other woman. She had then returned home to her grandmother's house, but when the loss was noticed and suspicions raised, the woman came round to the grandmother's and took the child back to her flat. When the police uncovered the trail, the child admitted the theft. The pair were taken to court, where Mr Hamilton dealt first with the adult, hearing charges against her of receiving stolen property and harbouring a child without proper authority. Taking a particularly serious view of the woman's offences, because she had obviously both preyed on the child and led her into crime, he sentenced her to six months' hard labour for each charge but allowed that they might run concurrently. To the little girl he had stern words to say. "You are a very bad girl to steal these things and then to run away from your comfortable home. If you had been older, I would have sent you to prison," he told her. "I will discharge you, and let you go back to your grandmother, but you must obey her now!" he warned.

The thirteen-year-old daughter of Wong Mui was also 'put up' to a theft.[239] Mother and daughter had visited an acquaintance, Cheung Wai-lan, who afterwards found that her gold ring and chain, valued at about $200, were missing. Detective Constable Ho Sung investigated, following up leads amongst the claimant's friends until he arrested first the girl and then her mother, Wong. By 1940 Hong Kong's laws about juveniles and crime had changed to reflect the reforms in Britain, but space and manpower did not always allow for complete attention to the regulations. Thus the pair were placed in the same cell in the police station. While they were here, Wong was overheard to tell her daughter that the gold jewellery was in a salt jug. The day after their arrest, the girl appeared before the Juvenile Court, where she pleaded guilty to the theft in front of the magistrate, Mr Himsworth. He sentenced her to spend six months in the Salvation Army Home for Women and Girls, the maximum term he could impose under the *Juvenile Offenders' Ordinance*. Later that same day Mr Himsworth was sitting as magistrate in the police court in Kowloon and heard the mother's case. Whether she was told that her daughter had pleaded guilty, or that she had been sentenced before her appearance is not recorded. However, Wong Mui saw the opportunity to

---

239 *Hongkong Telegraph*, 11th July 1940.

lay the blame on her daughter and disclaimed all knowledge of the gold. She had not been at home when the girl came in with the jewellery, she said. Moreover, when the police had overheard them in the cell it was not her, but the girl who had been speaking. However, the previous day she had been taken back to her home by D.C. Ho and had shown him where the items were hidden. Neither the inspector in charge of the case nor Mr Himsworth believed her protestations. The magistrate commented that the theft had been a very cunning one. Wong Mui was found guilty of receiving stolen property and given the option of paying a $50 fine or going to prison for six weeks with hard labour.

Twenty years earlier there had been no such recourse as the Salvation Army home for young detainees, so sometimes gaol was the only option. In the cramped housing that many had to endure, keeping valuables safe, even from neighbours, was always a challenge. And when the neighbours were light-fingered little girls who slipped in and out of your cubicle almost before you had time to register their presence, it could become near-impossible. A young thief was charged before Mr Wood one Monday morning, having, on the Saturday, abstracted five gold rings, three bracelets and $30 from the room of a lady with whom she and her mother lodged. The child told the police and then repeated to the magistrate that her mother had told her to take them and then the woman had pawned them. With the money, she had purchased three different rings for herself and one for the girl, perhaps as a reward. But when detectives looked into the story, they found no evidence that the mother had ever had the jewellery, nor pawned it. Unfortunately, the papers do not record whether the items were recovered, but Mr Wood was satisfied that the mother had nothing to do with the theft. He convicted the girl "on her own confession" and sent her to do hard labour in the prison for one month.

But not all examples of personal enterprise ended so sternly. The story of the multiply-traded girl who used her initiative to help set up in the stationery business is told in *Policing Hong Kong – an Irish History*.[240] Sixteen-year-old Wong Kin-man impersonated the sister-in-law of one of

---

240 Patricia O'Sullivan, *Policing Hong Kong – An Irish History*, pp. 248-9, *China Mail*, 12th September 1918.

her former mistresses, apparently a cruel woman, and gradually acquired a good stock of inks, pencils, writing paper, inkstands and calling cards, amongst other things, all on supposed credit. The case, which was sympathetically investigated by the author's grandfather, Inspector Patrick O'Sullivan, came before Mr Wood, who expressed similar concern for the girl. All the stock was returned intact to its rightful owner. Wong is last heard of being placed in the care of the Po Leung Kuk, while the inspector tried to ascertain whether her claim of a husband in Macao had any basis in reality. This is an unusual tale, in part because although she claimed that she was accumulating the goods for her husband, there was no hint that he (if he even existed) had told her to do this.

Hong Kong was rather ambivalent about the age at which it considered a female to be an adult. Officially there was no difference between the definitions it used for males of 'juvenile – adult' and later 'child – young person – adult', but in practice magistrates were loath to consider a girl really as an adult until she was 18, or even 21. And yet boys and girls of 16 could be tried on a capital charge and face the death penalty. The next, confusing case, is one where the lawyers, despite their best efforts, seem to have failed to keep consideration of the girl's age and stature out of the jury's deliberations.

So small a girl, so brutal a murder

Ten-year-old Lin Heung was 'bought' by a woman on Cheung Chau. Whether the transaction had been between this person and Lin's parents, or her previous mistress is not known.[241] In 1920 the child had cost the new mistress $100, but she would be working for the woman's mother, who was then approaching 70 and lived alone, also on Cheung Chau. Her new home was a two-room hut in Sai Wan, a hamlet on the coast a few hundred yards south-west of the main streets of the island. As the years went on, the purchaser was happy to find that the child and her 'grandmother' got on well.

---

241 The accounts of the Criminal Sessions trial were in all the papers of the day, including *The China Mail*, 20th and 21st February 1928 and *Hongkong Daily Press*, 21st & 22nd February 1928. The initial report of the murder appears in *The China Mail*, 23rd December 1927.

But on the Wednesday evening before Christmas 1927 all that changed. Perhaps only two points are quite certain. On 21st December the old woman was savagely murdered by blows to the head by one or two choppers. Two days later a gold hair-ornament of hers was partially melted down on the instructions of a woman who had no direct involvement. But the components of this story were to shift as fluidly as the sands on the island's beaches, and despite a unanimous verdict by a jury two months later, what actually happened remains as much a mystery now as it must have been then.

News of the murder first appeared in the papers of 23rd December, under the headline "Woman killed, armed robbers paltry haul". A man and a woman had broken open the door of the hut and, as seventeen-year-old Lin told the police, the noise had woken her and her grandmother out of their sleep. The old woman had risen and left the back room, where they both slept, in order to investigate. Lin had lain awake a few moments more, but when she heard her grandmother calling out, she had rushed in to her. She found the old lady being half-throttled, trying to plead for her life between gasps. When the attackers relaxed their hold for a moment, she told them to take what they wanted but to spare her. The female attacker then went into the bedroom and ransacked it. At this, Lin saw her opportunity to get help and slipped out, running along the track that connected the scattering of huts until she reached a neighbour's home. This was where Yue Cho-chuen, a market gardener, lived with his family. She told them what was happening, and the gardener returned to the hut with her, summoning help from other neighbours as he went.

The woman's home was in darkness, but by the light of their lanterns they saw her lying face down in a pool of blood, great gashes all about her head. A chopper, covered with blood, lay beside her and a second, also blood-stained, was a few feet away. When the police arrived and asked Lin if she had recognised the pair, she explained that they had painted their faces black, so there was no way she could tell who they were.

In the days that followed, the police questioned Lin further. What had been stolen? All that she could say for sure was a hair clasp, only a few dollars in value, if that. She then told the police of her suspicions about two men who shared a hut nearby. They had not been on Cheung Chau long, and Lin was sure that they had something to do with it. On the strength of this, the police called Wong Tam Suen and Wong Tam Fook in for questioning. The District Officer took depositions from them, but these prompted rather different questions, since the pair had been part of the rescue party that evening, and witnesses attested to this.

By then Lin had remembered other things about that night and she now believed that Yip Choy, a local man, had been responsible. But now the police were inclined not to attribute her statements to random speculations due to shock, but to be attempts to mask her closer involvement. The official questioning broadened out to find whoever could shed more light on that dark night's events. A man who had been on the beach attending to his fishing nets that evening told them how he had heard the old woman cry out, "Lin Heung, do not strike me. I'll say no more about it, but do not strike me!" He had heard this not just once but several times. The fisherman had added that he had seen a man and a girl leave the hut a few minutes after the cries. He could not identify either, but the girl was about the same height as Lin, and was wearing a white jacket. Another man, living some little distance away, had also recognised the old woman's cries, although not what she said, round about 10 p.m.

There were questions to ask about the hair clasp, too. If it were not that Lin had told them of its absence, they would know nothing about it. No great disturbance in the rooms pointed to a robbery, and the old woman's daughter, who had gone to the hut in the following days, had not missed it. The account that the Wongs had given was certainly different from Lin's and had some curious features. From a hint picked up there, two detectives went to a goldsmith's in the main village. They were just in time – the smith was in the process of melting it down. The craftsman had been given instructions to turn it into a single piece of gold by the woman who brought it to him, and he was able to give the police her name. Wong Tam Suen had claimed that, before going to Yue's home, Lin had called at their hut and pushed him to accept the jewellery as a present. She had then told them, quite without emotion, how her mistress had been attacked, cut in the neck. When Lin had left, the old woman was bleeding freely, she said. This had surprised the man a great deal, and he was most reluctant to keep the hair clasp, but Lin had insisted. Not wanting to be found with it, he had given it to a woman friend, asking her to have it melted down, and then to sell the gold and buy him some clothes with the proceeds.

It started to appear that Lin had fabricated a robbery to provide a motive for the attack. If so, what, together with the reports of the cries heard, did this say of her part in the murder? Yet could the police trust Wong's evidence? When they found that both men had suddenly decamped, and were not on the island, further suspicions were aroused. Even more so when they searched their hut and discovered that one had left all his belongings whilst the second man had not even bothered to claim $40 wages owed him. Did these men in fact have a greater part to play in the story? Had Lin been correct to throw suspicion on them?

Meanwhile, evidence was still being amassed that implicated Lin. The two Wongs and Yue, the gardener, had all said how she did not appear distressed or upset at the time. She had been wearing a white jacket that night – and that jacket proved to have human bloodstains on it. But were the stains there before she returned to the hut with the men? The detectives were sure that most of her original tale was a fabrication, and that there was the basis of a case against her. But they were still interested in Yip Choy. Would he prove to be the man seen leaving the house with Lin? Certainly there were rumours around that Lin entertained Yip at home some nights, after the old woman had fallen asleep. Accordingly, both were arrested in connection with the murder and brought before the magistrate early in the new year. But here the newspapers appear to fail us. A systematic search in the publications for the weeks between the murder and Criminal Sessions trial has yielded no report of this hearing. It is only through references within the proceedings at the Session that more of the story can be filled in.

The police had no concrete evidence against Yip, only rumours, suppositions and Lin's accusation: no basis of a prosecution. The magistrate thus dismissed the case against him and sent Lin alone to await trial at the upper court. Meanwhile, under further questioning, and taxed with Wong Tam Suen's evidence, Lin admitted that she had given the man the hair-ornament. She had wanted to make it look like there were two people involved in this attack, she told the police. It had been at Yip's brother's insistence that she should shield her lover by doing all she could to throw suspicion away from him. Then what could explain there being two choppers at the scene? To this Lin responded that she had smeared the second one with blood, before going to get help. It had to look as if two people had been involved.

The case continued to puzzle both the police and the Assistant Crown Solicitor, Mr T. S. Whyte-Smith, so it was not until 20th February 1928 that Lin faced the charge of murder at the Criminal Sessions.[242] The judge that day was Mr Justice Wood, one of the oldest legal hands in the colony and, of course, a defence barrister, Mr Instone Brewer, had been provided for her. But perhaps her best defence was the very picture she made. A tiny girl, sobbing continuously, she looked thoroughly unkempt after her weeks in gaol. Her head did not even reach the rail in front of the dock and she could only peer out at the court through the iron bars. No one, it seemed, had thought to provide her with a box upon which to stand – or had her counsel cannily suggested that she did not avail herself of one, if provided?

Opening the case, the Crown Solicitor had to warn the jury not to let sentiment and a natural solicitude for the girl interfere with a dispassionate assessment of what they were to hear. "You may think", he said, "that there is something incongruous about so young a girl being charged with murder. But from the evidence you will hear, you will see that there is a clear duty on the Crown to pursue this prosecution". As he recounted the events and the subsequent investigations, he had to admit that there was no apparent motive for the crime. It might be assumed that two people had been involved in the murder, since two blood-stained choppers were found, but that there were inconsistencies throughout. Not least of these were the changing stories the prisoner gave to the police. Turning to the more suspicious elements of her behaviour, he noted that when running for help, she had not gone to the first hut, but passed quite a few homes before arriving at the market gardener's. The defence might claim that her

---

242 It was not until 1952 that the minimum age that a death penalty could be imposed in Hong Kong was raised from 16 to 18. Legislation for the same passed into English law in 1933.

white jacket became stained with blood when she was helping clean up, yet there were witnesses to say that she was then wearing black clothes. And to the idea that so small a girl would not be physically capable of inflicting such blows, he reminded the jury that a *mui tsai* was used to hard work, and thus had better-developed muscles than other girls of her age and build. The Medical Officer, Dr J. E. Dovey, admitted that he had not examined the girl, but the weight of the choppers used meant that little force would be needed to inflict such injury with them. The woman's back showed bruising and damage to the ribs, which would be caused if someone knelt on her back while she lay prostrate.

In her defence, Mr Instone Brewer responded to some of the prosecution's remarks. It was quite natural, he maintained, that she would seek help from a family house, not from the huts where "bachelors of the coolie class" lived. He refuted the testimony of the men who heard the old woman cry out. What victim would use her attacker's name like that? How much more natural that this was the old woman calling to Lin for help when being assaulted? He suggested that the crime had been committed by one of the men she had implicated, perhaps Yip Choy, and these were her attempts to shield him. This became all the more plausible since it had been found that one of the Wongs who had disappeared was Yip's brother. The story about strangers coming he disregarded and noted that the woman kept three dogs who always barked when unknown people came. There had been no mention of their barking that night.

The judge gave a lengthy summing up – necessary, given the often tortuous and conflicting evidence. Of Lin's various stories, he dismissed the first, which he thought had been designed to shield someone. The final one was also unsatisfactory and did not address all the circumstances of the case. He thought that the jury would have to disregard the evidence given by the two men (the Wongs) who had since disappeared. His remarks on the witnesses to the old woman's cries reveals a point not made clear earlier in this hearing. These two had apparently come forward when Yip was the accused, and partly for this reason, Mr Wood suggested that their evidence should also be disregarded by the jury. It was a brutal crime and their unpleasant duty to try it, but, he reminded the jury, they must not be influenced by the age of the prisoner. He felt that the only "sensible" conclusion was that both choppers had been used in the attack.

> It is difficult to avoid coming to the conclusion that between 8 p.m. and 10 p.m. that night the prisoner assisted a man in the house... that she went so far in her assistance that she used one of the choppers which she herself later hid.

Reminding them again that the case was now entirely in their hands, but should they find her guilty, the sentence of death would have to be passed, he sent the jury out for their deliberations.

Fourteen minutes later they returned. To the question whether they found the prisoner guilty or not guilty, the foreman replied "Not guilty, my Lord". Was that their unanimous verdict? It was. Lin Heung was immediately discharged and left the court. Two months after the events of that night, the girl walked free. What became of her then?

Towards a solution: remand homes – boys

Delinquent boys, whether individual urchins or gangs of near-feral youths, had been part of the town's underbelly from the outset. Viewed as so much detritus by most, both western and Chinese, many had been orphaned, or, in the words of Father Thomas F. Ryan, had been "left over from the tens of thousands who passed through the colony in the various waves of emigration" in the years of the gold rush and beyond.[243] The 'boy problem', although so very apparent, had not been addressed by the administration, but had caught the attention of the Catholic priests and brothers, who were working to establish schools throughout the island. During the 1840s and 50s, there were various schools, mostly short-lived, run by the religious orders. Early in the 1860s a more permanent school, St Saviour's, was planned in Pottinger Street. As this was being built in 1863, a house in Wellington Street became available, allowing the priests to open a small reformatory. From the outset, the object was to give boys the means by which they could earn their own livings, and thus not need to resort to crime. Twelve boys who had been previously detained by the

---

243 Thomas F. Ryan, S.J. *The Story of a Hundred Years*, p. 35.

police and another eighteen 'strays' were the first pupils, and were taught shoe-making, tailoring and carpentry, reading and writing. The place was a marked success and the following year had visits from the Acting Chief Justice, Mr J. D. Ball and the Governor, Sir Hercules Robinson. Both were impressed, and the latter gave the Fathers a larger piece of land out at West Point. Three years on, and the annual report of the West Point Reformatory, as it was now known, showed that 78 boys were on roll, with the government paying for twenty places.

The Reformatory continued to attract general approval, but only addressed the tip of the problem. Already, in 1867, editorials appear in the papers which lament the lack of a larger, government-run institution.

The want of a reformatory seems to be sadly felt in the colony just now. Of late there have been a number of lads from ten to fifteen years of age brought to the police court on various charges of petty larceny… the number of young vagabonds who pick up their living by pilfering appears to be very great. The only outlet for these outcasts is the Roman Catholic Reformatory at West Point, in which excellent institution the Government pays for the support of twenty boys annually, but this complement has long been filled up and is greatly inadequate to the want of the colony.[244]

Fifteen years later, the same sentiments were still being expressed. A fourteen-year-old boy, who had already been in gaol twice, was convicted of pick-pocketing twenty dollars, and sentenced to a year's hard labour with a beating. Both the Crown Solicitor and the judge in the case, Mr Justice Snowden, expressed regret that they did not have a more appropriate place to send the youth.[245]

In 1886, the *Reformatory Schools Ordinance* was passed.[246] Based on similar legislation in Britain, this sought to bring such institutions under the jurisdiction and oversight of the Superintendent of Prisons and the Justices of the Peace, yet preserving their autonomy in day-to-day functioning. It creates an impression of a full system of such institutions,

---

244 *Hongkong Daily Press,* 12th October 1867.

245 Norton-Kyshe, *The History of the Laws and Courts of Hong Kong vol. 2,* p. 351-2, 29th March 1882.

246 *Hongkong Government Gazette,* 1st May 1886, *The Reformatory Schools Ordinance,* Ordinance No. 19 of 1886.

but, of course, only then applied to the West Point home. It had been prompted by the discovery that the magistrates had no powers to detain young offenders there, and so had to send them to gaol.

Another ten years passed before the government adopted a more practical response by provision of a site in Causeway Bay on which businessman and philanthropist Emanuel Raphael Belilios offered to fund the building of a secular-run institution, specifically for young offenders. The magnificent Belilios Reformatory opened in 1900 and was staffed by the Education Department. Yet in the next two years it only had one pupil and then was used as an annex for Victoria Gaol, especially when the plague hit there in 1903 and more space was needed. For some years it appears not to have functioned in the way that Mr Belilios intended and even stood empty. Meanwhile, a change in the management of the West Point Reformatory, which was passed to the Maryknoll Fathers in 1921, saw its name change to the St Louis Industrial School. Five years later it was transferred to the care of the Salesian Fathers, who already ran a similar school in Macao.

As Hong Kong's population expanded during the late 1920s and 1930s, the provisions for young offenders again came to the fore. The Juvenile Remand Home was opened in Causeway Bay – presumably in the Belilios building. The report of the escape of two youngsters in 1934 mentions that there were 41 boys detained there. In line with changes to the law regarding young offenders in Britain, the administration passed the *Juvenile Offenders Ordinance*. This defined a child as a person under fourteen years of age, a young person as one of 14 or 15 years, and laid out, for the first time, the roles of guardian and probation officer.[247] It provided significantly more protection for the young than had existed earlier. Their cases were to be heard in a Juvenile Court, and unless a homicide was involved, could not be sent to any other court. The sentence passed on juveniles was to be completed within a place designated and regulated as a House of Detention, and they were to be protected from contact with adult criminals. In addition, it allowed for children and young people found begging, destitute, living in a brothel (if without

---

247 *Hongkong Government Gazette,* 12th March 1932, *Juvenile Offenders Ordinance,* No. 1 of 1932.

a responsible mother there) or associating with known criminals to be brought to the Juvenile Court and then taken to a House of Detention. Further legislation, the *Industrial and Reformatory Schools Ordinance* was then required to cover the new institutions, defining them as such.[248]

At the time the *Juvenile Offenders Ordinance* was passed, the St Louis School was the only such institution certified to receive pupils thus. The Juvenile Remand Home was then defined as a Place of Detention by the Inspector General of Police on 22nd August 1935, although its use by the magistrates predated this.[249] The Aberdeen Industrial School, another project instigated and built by philanthropic men, in this case Messrs Li Yau-tsen and Fung Ping-shan was built on a site given by the government and then entrusted to the Salesian Fathers to run.[250] Just the shell of the building cost its benefactors twenty times the $12,000 that the Belilios Reformatory had required, but this school was to house 300 boys. While some of its pupils would be sent by the courts, it was primarily a vocational school for the poor of Hong Kong.[251] Meanwhile, in 1941, some of the now empty buildings in Victoria Gaol were converted into the Victoria Gaol Juvenile Remand Home.[252]

Towards a solution: remand homes – girls

But for girls, who were now more regularly appearing on the charge sheets, there was only the Female Prison or the Po Leung Kuk. This latter had previously sought to repatriate kidnapped children: now this was rarely possible, and its resources were considerably stretched by the many cases brought to it. Although it was the best-placed organisation to locate the parents or relatives of any wayward girl, for most it could provide temporary shelter only, as in the case of R.O. Grimmitt's 'Little girl, big

248 *Hongkong Government Gazette,* 18th March 1932, *Industrial and Reformatory Schools Ordinance,* No. 6 of 1932, and its amendment, No. 21 of 1933.

249 *Hongkong Government Gazette,* 23rd August 1935.

250 *Hongkong Telegraph,* 18th September 1933, *Hongkong Daily Press,* 27th March 1935.

251 Reflecting this difference, it was certified on 6th April 1935 as 'fit for the reception of youthful offenders' by the Governor, Sir William Peel, under the *Industrial and Reformatory Schools Ordinance* (No. 6 of 1932). *Hongkong Government Gazette,* 14th June 1935.

252 *Hongkong Government Gazette,* 18th April 1941.

liar'. The Female Prison was severely overcrowded, and urgently in need of the replacement being built at Lai Chi Kok, but this would not open until 1932. Any separation of child and adult offenders was well-nigh impossible.

The Salvation Army, a protestant Christian organisation, originating in the East End slums of London in 1865 and dedicated to very practical charitable works with the poorest and most marginalised in the community, had been in Hong Kong at the turn of the century. The Army – which was and remains structured along military lines – had, from the outset, given equal status to women, and consequently had very able and experienced female leaders. On that first occasion they had been focussed on providing support, material and spiritual, for the soldiers and sailors. But in this they were entering an already crowded field, with a number of long-established charitable concerns. The first officers withdrew, disillusioned by their reception and severely afflicted by the diseases of the place, having lost a number of members. By the 1920s a mission was running in northern China, and in the spring of 1930 they sent envoys to assess whether there was scope for their work amongst the young of the colony. This was an auspicious time for such a project. In January 1930 the Society for the Protection of Children had been established at a long and very well-attended meeting in City Hall.[253] The first patrons were the then Governor and his wife (Sir Cecil and Lady Clementi), and the officers and committees included many prominent residents, both Chinese and European. The Salvation Army representatives were well-received and given enthusiastic assistance, particularly from Bella Southorn, the socially engaged wife of the Colonial Secretary, Mr (later Sir) Thomas Southorn. She arranged a meeting at Government House where representatives of the Army met with, amongst others, Sir Robert Kotewall and Mrs Frederick Mow Fung, to discuss the direction their work could best take in the colony. In April Major J. E. Sansom of the Salvation Army arrived and acquired the lease on a property close to Prince Edward Road, Kowloon, for the reception of 20 young Chinese women wishing to escape brothel life. He was shown the work of Mrs Mow Fung, the wife of a prominent businessman, who was running a day

---

253 *China Mail,* 22nd January 1930.

school for such girls. Her enterprise was highly regarded and supported, but could not go the further step and provide a refuge, so the women had to return to their 'unhelpful' situations in the evening.[254] It was anticipated that some of her 'girls' would avail themselves of the new home, as well as others sent from the S.C.A. and the Po Leung Kuk.

Later that month, the matron, Ensign (Miss) Rains arrived. She had been working in northern China and was State Registered both as a general and a maternity nurse. The Salvation Army Women's Industrial Home started rather sooner than they intended, as the first women in need of protection arrived on their doorstep on 2nd May 1930, before preparations had been made. In the first years the residents, rather than being former prostitutes, were mostly former *mui tsai* sent there by the S.C.A., although, since one of the prominent supporters was the Inspector General of Police, they also received some girls directly from the courts. In 1934, negotiations were begun between the government and the Salvation Army to provide an official home for girls sent by the Juvenile Court. Larger premises were urgently required, allowing these girls to be separated from the 'home' residents. A house in Embankment Road, off Boundary Street in Kowloon seemed ideal, as the area was surrounded by park land and woods, far removed in atmosphere from the squalor of the poorer areas of Hong Kong that would have been the only home most of the girls knew. A change in leadership saw the resourceful Major Dorothy Brazier take charge of the home, now renamed the Salvation Army Home for Women and Girls. The Home was certified by the Inspector General of Police on 14th September 1934 and appointed a House of Detention. On the same day Miss D. B. Brazier was appointed a Probation Officer.[255]

She oversaw the development of a tripartite home – the ground floor was for the Juvenile Remand Home girls, and the upper floor for the girls and women seeking refuge. Whilst sleeping, bathing and laundry of the two categories was separate, all came together for education, meals, prayer and recreation. The third and smallest part of the home was the isolation unit, in little outbuildings, set up in 1938. Child ex-prostitutes, many only 12 or 13, infected with venereal diseases, were accommodated

---

254 *Hongkong Daily Press,* 16th April 1930.

255 *Hongkong Government Gazette,* 14th September 1934.

here and taken to hospital for daily treatment until fully recovered and able to enter the first floor home. Under Major Brazier's management, the home acquired a very good reputation and enjoyed the patronage and support of all the great and the good in Hong Kong, including Sir Paul Chater, Sir Robert Kotewall, the Governor, Sir William Peel, and the Chief Justice, Sir Atholl MacGregor. Practically, she fought hard to make the place as home-like for all the women and girls, realising that 'home' was itself a novel experience for many, and that the girls had to be helped to adapt to the idea. The Inspector General of Police, Mr E. D. C. Wolfe, insisted on a sturdy perimeter wall topped with barbed wire, having apparently heard that the first *mui tsai* had run away. In fact, these girls had returned just a few days later, having realised that they had left a better situation than any they could find for themselves. As much as Major Brazier resented the barbed wire, she came to be thankful for it when, as a remand home, relatives of some of the girls tried to abduct them.

Everyone acknowledged that the Home could only reach a fraction of the destitute of the colony. Nevertheless, priority was given to the girls, who, having served their six month sentence on the ground floor, asked to be moved 'upstairs' for a further period, acquiring more education and self-confidence. In terms of recidivism, its record was excellent. In the years 1934-9, only one girl was sentenced for a second time. The girls in the Remand Home followed a more rigorous timetable than those on the floor above, but it was designed to provide stability by routine, education and occupation, and was not punitive. The home tried as far as possible to follow up on the careers of those who left, from both parts of the home, keeping in touch personally and by letter. But in the years immediately before the occupation of Hong Kong by the Japanese (in December 1941), the number of girls sent there by the courts declined markedly, although the home was always full. In 1935, the police brought 563 girls to them to await their appearance at the Juvenile Court on charges of hawking without a licence. The vast majority of these were dismissed by the magistrate with a caution, while 50 served short sentences at the Home. In the next years, the policing of such cases came to marry up more nearly with the magisterial approach. Poverty was such that it was recognised that if these children were not hawking, they would be begging, stealing or worse. In 1937 less than 20% of the 263 arrested for hawking were convicted. However, criminality had not disappeared. Begging and forestry offences sent six girls each to the Remand Home that year, while three more were committed for soliciting and three for the possession of dangerous drugs. Many were sent to the Home for the full six-month term available to the magistrates.

Of course, the Home was part of the faith-based work of the Salvation Army in Hong Kong, just as were the schools, orphanages, hospitals, homes and reformatories of the Catholic religious orders and the Berlin Foundling home of the German Protestant Mission. Whilst there were occasional disagreements about the government's financial support of the religious-run schools, specifically those administered by the Catholic church, there were no qualms about help given to the reform and industrial schools. There seems rather to be relief that, given the scale of the problem, the responsibility was, with the exception of the Causeway Bay Home, being shouldered by others. The annual grants to such places, a fraction of the actual running cost, were therefore a small price to pay. There can be no doubting the sincerity of the efforts to help these children, yet the place of the various institutions in the religious mission of the organisations should not be overlooked. The boys' schools – and by extension the reformatories – were perhaps those with the lightest proselytising touch. Here the great number that passed through each institution mitigated against attempts to convert them to Christianity. Whilst there were school leavers who joined the orders and became brothers, sometimes training for the priesthood at the seminary in Aberdeen, the primary concern here was to instil the moral values of Christianity into the boys, and to create good, educated citizens in a multi-ethnic British colony.

The two convents took in hundreds, indeed thousands of abandoned infants, mostly baby girls. Many were born in Hong Kong and brought to the nuns by the police or other concerned citizens, but some were 'collected' from the mainland and brought over. The majority of these babies were almost moribund when they arrived. Each was carefully tended insofar as their overcrowded facilities and meagre resources would permit, but the majority could not survive. Part of the care, and for the sisters, the most important and precious thing they could do for the child, was baptism. It was for the saving of souls that the convents primarily existed. The children who did manage to thrive after their desperate beginning were housed and schooled in the convent orphanages. Girls there were brought up in the faith, but the sisters were realistic about the chances of that faith being maintained once they married and returned to a wholly Chinese environment.

The Salvation Army were perhaps the most overt in their efforts and hopes for the conversion of their charges. The annual reports from 1935 onwards, published in the newspapers, occasionally cited examples of the strength and comfort found by individual girls, especially those sent by the courts, when they were introduced to the Christian gospel. The case of Lau Shuk-hing, a young mother convicted of killing her small daughter as part of her own suicide attempt, was highlighted in their 1940 report.[256] While the sentiments sound anachronistic now in terms of offender management, their work met with approval from the Chinese and western community alike. The respect which the Salvation Army enjoyed in Britain and beyond, known for their tireless compassion for the poorest, was replicated here with justification.

In advance of the arrival of the invading Japanese troops, the women prisoners at Lai Chi Kok were released (see Chapter 6). However, the orders concerned with this release did not, it seems, address the fate of the girls detained in the Salvation Army home, even though, as a House of Detention, it was part of the prison system. By 13th December, when no British military presence remained in Kowloon, there was anxiety as to what would become of the home residents, its two British and three Chinese female staff. Extraordinarily, Dorothy Brazier and her assistant, Doris Lemmon, were not taken prisoners and were permitted to remain out of internment. Heroically, given the circumstances, they continued to care for their charges, as best they could, through to the liberation at the end of August 1945. The challenges, deprivations and degradations they faced in that time can scarcely be imagined. It may have been that

---

256 See Chapter 9 for the story of Lau Shuk-hing. *Hongkong Daily Press,* 27th March 1940, Salvation Army Home's annual report for 1939.

the presence of the isolation unit was enough to persuade the Japanese authorities that this was a hospital and contained women who might infect their troops if the home was shut down. If so, that surely would be one of the more ironic twists of fate of that traumatic period. Her obituary in her home town of Bromley, Kent, records that after her repatriation to Britain to recover her strength, Major Brazier wished to return to her work, but this, on account of her impaired health, was not permitted.

CHAPTER 9

TROUBLED FAMILIES

"I think it is the only possible decision the Jury could have reached on the evidence as a whole. The law provides only one punishment for the crime of murder and it is my duty to pass that sentence upon you. But I am glad to say that the Jury have coupled with their verdict the strongest possible recommendation to mercy. That recommendation I gladly accept.

"Indeed, had there been no such recommendation, I should still have made one on my own behalf as trial judge. I think you may rest assured that, although it is my duty to pass sentence of death upon you, that sentence will not be carried out."

The Chief Justice, Sir Atholl MacGregor, was visibly moved as he spoke these words this morning to a frail, deathly-pale, middle-aged woman standing in the dock of the Sessions Court. For two days Pang Yiu-mui had, without displaying the slightest emotion, listened first to the evidence against her and then to her counsel's strong efforts to prove that at the time when she killed Wan Hang-chung, her husband's young concubine, on July 14, she was insane.

Exactly as she had behaved throughout the trial, when the death sentence was pronounced, the feeble figure merely bowed and said: "I ask the pardon of the Court." Then she was led gently down the stairs into the cells.

Inside the Court, however, two women relatives collapsed while several others sobbed bitterly.

The Hongkong Telegraph, 31st October 1939

Pang Yiu-mui – a case of justice and mercy

The day had been the hottest that year – 93°F (about 34°C), and extremely humid. There was no sign of much relief and the flat in Des Voeux Road West must have been sticky and uncomfortable. Yet when the family retired to bed on Thursday 13th July 1939 there had been nothing to suggest that their world would change irrevocably before the next day had dawned. Kan Chung-sui's household was a most respectable and well-ordered one.[257] He was an assistant in a chemist's firm in Bonham Road West, up the hill and about six hundred yards from his home. Of late he frequently slept at the shop, likely to protect it from the increase in break-ins that were occurring along with the flood of people trying to enter Hong Kong to escape the Japanese violence further north. He came from Sheklung (Shilong) a town on the Hong Kong-Canton railway route and had there married Pang Yiu-mui 23 years earlier. They had five children, ranging in ages from nineteen to seven years old, although only the youngest two, a son and daughter, were currently living with them. In 1930, when still in China, at the suggestion of his mother, Tin Fat-ying, he had taken a young concubine, Wan Hang-cheung. Wan was then sixteen years old. She moved in with the couple for about year, but by mutual agreement, Kan then found her another place to live.

Like many others, he realised that there was better money to be made by working in nearby Hong Kong, but that it was too expensive a place to bring his entire family. The cheap fares on the railway made it easy for him to visit them regularly and continue to support them in Sheklung. In 1936, his concubine, Wan, followed him to Hong Kong. The next year, likely conscious of the increasing threat from Japanese forces who were now closing in on Shanghai, Kan brought his wife and children to the city. The flat he acquired in No. 9 Des Voeux Road West initially housed the seven of them, with Wan still in her rented cubicle elsewhere. In April 1939 his elderly mother, Ting, fleeing the Japanese bombardment of the southern towns, joined them. At Pang's suggestion, Wan also came to live with the family. The young woman got on well with Ting and would help look after her. Whilst the flat was now crowded, it was not untypical

---

of the homes of many trades-people. The family were not poor: money was tight, but rising prices, food shortages and the expensive nature of the colony meant that most people were 'feeling the pinch'. In fact, Kan was able to employ an amah to look after his womenfolk, and his eldest girl, Kan Tai-yung, had recently made a good marriage. Perhaps another reason Kan had brought the family to Hong Kong when he did was his wife's state of health. She had suffered from beriberi for the last three years, and this had left her with a shuffling gait and pains in her limbs.[258] Chronically neglected teeth had resulted in pyorrhoea, an advanced gum disease, which caused her to be very anaemic. She had, since 1936, been an invalid and more often confined to bed than not. Her mother-in-law described her as a very meek woman, but one who sometimes 'turned her head to the wall and muttered inaudibly', perhaps suggesting that Pang suffered bouts of depression.

The relationship between the two women, the wife and the concubine, does not appear to have been unduly troubled. In a culture where such marriages were the norm, the women were not coping with a 'wife/mistress' situation, but one for which their upbringings had fully prepared them. Equally it was no very unusual thing that Wan had spent a lot of her nine years marriage to Kan living away from the family. Now, with all the women under one roof, there were the natural aggravations and irritations of the situation. But Tin's firm assertion that her daughter-in-law was fond of Wan and the latter's pregnancy was a source of joy to her showed that there were better feelings, too. Pang, she said, had looked forward to having another baby in the home again. By the time of the magistrate's hearing, the police had found people who claimed to know the family and who told them that Pang had scolded and argued with Wan, and had even heard her threaten to kill the younger woman. The papers made much of the jealousy motive, but there seems little direct evidence of this prior to the event of that night, nor was it suggested at the Criminal Sessions hearing. The only definite event that could suggest this occurred during the tea-drinking ceremony, when Wan was received into the family home back in April that year. In accordance with custom, the concubine had presented the *kit fat* wife with a bowl of tea as a sign of her

---

258 Beriberi is most commonly caused by thiamine (Vitamin B$_1$) deficiency.

deference for the older woman. Some female relatives had claimed that Pang had thrown the bowl to the floor, rather than accept anything from Wan's hands. However, Pang's own explanation was that her hands were shaking and she could not hold it, which, given her medical problems, could be correct.

On that sweltering Thursday, the eldest daughter, Kan Tai-yung, had visited the family and, after talking to Pang, had approached her father on the subject of getting the doctor in to see her mother. He replied, "She should first finish taking the medicine that we got for her. Doctors are expensive." Tai-yung did not press the matter – as she would tell the court later, her father was very caring to Pang and had spent a great deal of money on her health problems. But Pang had overheard the conversation, and called out, "You prefer to spend all your money on Wan. You'll see all your family die first, for all you care!"

Shouts of "Save life!" coming from Wan's cubicle at 4 a.m. the next morning woke the whole family – Tin, the amah, Li Sam, and the two children. Tin hurried there and found Wan sitting up in bed, her face and arms covered in blood, one upper arm dreadfully chopped about. Pang then emerged from her cubicle clutching a piece of firewood and pushed past Tin to hit Wan with it. She had hit the poor woman twice on the head before Tin could snatch it from her and throw it aside. Pang then stumbled to her cubicle and collapsed on the floor. Li Sam had followed close behind Tin and now leant over Wan to ask her what had happened. Weakly, she replied, "Sam Siu-nai (the family name for Pang) has cut and struck me." She was bleeding copiously and the shocked amah hurried out to find the means of staunching the wounds. As she left the cubicle, she heard Pang say, "You have hidden my husband from me. You did not let me know even long after you have begun to live together."

They sent for the husband and daughter Tai-yung, who both hurried to the apartment. When Tai-yung asked her mother why she had done it, Pang replied, "I do not know. It cannot be helped now, I have wounded her." Meanwhile, the amah was trying to stop the bleeding by plastering the wounds with a mixture of tobacco and ash, and made a rough bandage to hold Wan's left arm together, which was almost severed. But the bleeding would not stop and Kan sent for the Chinese herbal medicine man. His ministrations proved no more successful, so at around 8.30 a.m. they called the local General Practitioner, Dr Cheung Wong-tai who immediately summonsed an ambulance to take Wan to Queen Mary Hospital. Dr Cheung had also alerted the police and realised that Pang, too, would need hospital attention. The police, headed by Detective Inspector Louis Whant, arrived about the same time as the ambulance. Wan went straight to the hospital, whilst the police started the investigation of the attack in the apartment. Underneath a camp bed in Pang's cubicle they found the blood-stained chopper responsible for the gashes and cuts Wan had sustained. Before they could allow an ambulance to take Pang to hospital, she had to change out of her bloodstained clothing. Her trousers had many splashes of blood over them, and these would be evidence of her involvement. Just before she left, she whispered to the police interpreter, Yuen Hing-yeung, "It was I who cut her. You can see the bloodstains on my trousers. She has hidden my husband for several years. Do you think she deserves the cutting?"

Dr W. P. Kho, who treated Wan at the hospital when she arrived at 9 a.m. found that although her upper arm was nearly cut through neither the bone nor the main artery were damaged. Nevertheless, the blow must have been made with considerable force to cut through the tissue and muscle to the extent it had. The many cuts around the face had been made with less force but still had caused a great deal of bleeding. Wan had lost a huge amount of blood and had a very weak pulse. He administered an injection to sustain the blood pressure but to no avail. Wan Hang-cheung died within the hour. She was seven months pregnant. Dr Kho gave it as his opinion that had Wan been treated appropriately within an hour or two, her chances of survival would have been very good, since the major blood vessels were intact. The postmortem conducted later that day confirmed that death was due to loss of blood and shock. Although the application of tobacco to the wounds had done no good, Wan had not died of tobacco poisoning.

Pang remained in hospital as the doctors tried to reverse the chronic anaemia and cure, or at least ameliorate, the pyorrhoea. On her admittance later on 14th July she had a fever, with a high temperature that persisted for about a week. Perhaps because of the rather obscure nature of the remarks she had made, or maybe because the attack was apparently so out of character for the woman, there was, from the outset, questions about her state of mind. She was referred to Dr Wilkinson, an expert on mental disorders from Hong Kong University, who observed her on a number of occasions during her ten week stay in hospital. Pang claimed that she had various blank spaces in her memory, and that such instances were not uncommon for her. When the police formally charged her on 18th September, before the doctors had discharged her, she made a statement.

> I myself have been sick for the past three years. My sickness has made my mind so unbalanced that when I cut her, I did not even know it. Furthermore, owing to the fact that there were too few people that could save her, therefore she died in that manner. When I recovered my senses, I knew I was wrong. She is married to my husband for ten years, and I did not murder her. If I wanted to murder her, I could have murdered her earlier. I have given birth to five children and is it probable that I would give up my children than murder her? I thought it would be better to kill myself than to kill her. Now she has been killed there is no one to look after affairs. Hence it is miserable. I beg to request that my offence be forgiven.

When her case was heard at the Criminal Sessions in front of Chief Justice Sir Atholl MacGregor, Mr D. J. N. Anderson defended Pang, with the Assistant Crown Solicitor, Mr T. J. Gould prosecuting. Mr Gould outlined the case but had no fresh light to shed, and in calling the family members as witnesses portrayed a home where there was no particular animosity amongst the parties, and one which seemed, in fact, very caring. He suggested to Pang that she was very jealous of Wan and wanted to be rid of her, which she denied strongly. Well, in that case what did she mean when she said "You did not let me know even long after you began to live together"? Pang said that she had no memory of having said this. But the prosecutor persisted. What might she have meant by it anyway? Pang said that she did not know, perhaps she was just speaking at random. Of course she knew that Wan was living with her husband, they had been married for nearly ten years. She knew that. Well, what about her daughter's visit on during the evening before the events? But Pang claimed to have no recollection of that, either. "The only thing I remember about that time is sitting on the floor in my cubicle and hearing cries in the passage. Apart from that, my mind is a blank." Mr Gould then called Dr Wilkinson to the witness box, where he explained that although he had examined and talked to the prisoner during her hospital stay, he had identified nothing to suggest to him that she was suffering from any gross mental abnormality or that she was mentally unsound.

In the absence of any real motive, the case for the defence had to fall back on an attempt to prove that Pang was insane at the moment she committed the attack. Mr Anderson's questioning of the doctor resulted in him agreeing that there might have been great conflict in Pang's mental state, although she showed no outward signs of derangement. When cross-examining Pang, he asked her if she had known about the attack before she found herself sitting on the floor and heard cries. No, that was the first she knew, when people started telling her what she had done to Wan. "Between going to bed the night before and hearing voices the next morning, have you any recollection of anything at all?" her counsel asked. "Yes." replied Pang, "I had a dream. In the dream I saw two women, they were my dead sisters. One of them was blind. They both had their hair loose, spread out about their shoulders, then the blind one spoke to me. She said, 'Very soon you will be taken by someone to somewhere in the realms below. If I give you this to hold you will not be taken there.'" What was it her dead sister was giving her, asked the barrister? But Pang did not know. When asked whether she often had dreams of this nature, Pang explained that she was frequently visited my ghosts when she was ill. When Mr Anderson asked her about the attack, she confirmed again that she had no recollection of it. "And I had no reason to attack her", she added.

Mr Anderson made a long and eloquent address to the jury, in which he explained that the defence was that at the time of the crime she was in a state of semi-consciousness and the victim of a sudden attack of insanity. What her state was before or after that night was immaterial, it was the case that in those moments she had not been of sound mind.

However, in his summing up, the Chief Justice explained to the jury the legal definition of insanity, as being the condition of a defect of reason caused by a disease of the mind, such that the sufferer was unable to know the nature and quality of the acts being done. He recalled that the medical history, insofar as it was known, pointed to physical conditions, and that Dr Wilkinson, an expert in mental diseases, had confirmed that after conducting all the usual tests, he had found nothing to indicate that Pang was not perfectly normal. The doctor had also confirmed that even in a state of semi-consciousness the person knew both the nature and the quality of any act they undertook. Having reviewed all the facts established, he concluded, "If death had been due to poisoning from tobacco the position would be different, but this is not the case. Gentlemen of the Jury, if you are satisfied that the accused struck the blows, then the delayed treatment does not minimise the guilt of the accused." The Jury retired for just seventeen minutes before returning with the guilty verdict, with their strong recommendation for mercy.

What really had prompted Pang Yiu-mui's ferocious attack on Wan Hang-cheung? Had she really been nurturing a hidden jealousy of the younger woman? Had the heat of the time brought on some temporary loss of reason? Admitted to hospital, she had a temperature of 103°F – was she actually delirious during those early morning hours? Did she perhaps suddenly imagine that her husband's absence from the home was due not to his work (which included acting as caretaker for the chemist's shop), but to the machinations of Wan? It appears that the statement made as little sense to the police then as it does to the contemporary reader. We can only speculate on what she intended to convey.

Governors of all British colonies were required to review all death penalties. The presiding judge had to submit a report, and this, together with any advice from members of his Legislative Council, formed the basis of his decision, whether to confirm the sentence or to commute it. Pang's sentence was commuted to life imprisonment. Given her medical condition, she may have spent much of her time in Lai Chi Kok's Prison Hospital. She was one of two 'lifers' in that prison at the time of the

Japanese invasion in December 1941and thus released. Presumably Pang Yiu-mui was then reunited with her family. Whether they survived the next four years is not known.

So many of the women encountered in this book had to do daily battle with hardship and adversity on a scale that few people know today. For some, as in the cases narrated in this chapter, there were serious consequences for their mental health. Nor had the upbringing of these women prepared them for dealing with the complexities of life in what was then one of the world's most densely inhabited cities. With minimal education, and almost none beyond the home, they had little training in thinking through situations beyond those normally encountered day to day. Unlike their menfolk, they were not expected to make decisions or be confronted with unfamiliar problems to solve. And they had been brought up with a moral code which diverged in significant ways from that of the colony's law makers, who did not appreciate their traditional outlook.

Nevertheless, the three stories in this chapter come not from the 1850s but from when those law-dispensers had almost a century of exposure to the culture of the land they had occupied. Whilst some of the values the women held did not find favour, there was greater understanding expressed, both in the courts and in the reporting of cases, of what lay behind these values, and what prompted their actions than in the earlier history of British Hong Kong.

Lau Shuk-hing – a young mother and her babies

It was the never-ending grind of poverty, the absence of hope for a better future and her own sense of powerlessness that drove twenty-two-year old Lau Shuk-hing to try to take her own life. In earlier years this crime had warranted a prison sentence, but from the fourth quarter of the previous century that had changed. So, now in 1938, although attempting to kill oneself was still illegal, Lau would not face prison, but a short appearance in the Magistrate's court, and an admonition from the bench. However, Lau's overwhelming tragedy was the action that followed her attempt, a momentary afterthought, that, to her sorrow, she acted upon. As she swallowed the opium dissolved in some hot water, her baby started crying.

She picked up her eighteen-month-old daughter – the child would only go to her, she wouldn't settle with anyone else. Lau suddenly realised that, after her death, the baby would have no-one who could care for her, so she fed her a spoonful or two of the liquid.[259]

In doing all this, she had to keep very quiet. Her husband of five years was not at home, but she shared her cubicle with his sister, Yuen Sui-yee, while his mother and two more sisters slept just outside, in a bed-space in the corridor. But by 5 a.m. Lau had been vomiting for some while and that now turned to retching, which woke Sui-yee. The baby, Yuen Mui-tau, was retching, too, but having been asleep when her mother fed her the fatal dose, had not ejected the poison with the alacrity her mother's body had achieved. When Sui-yee could get no response from Lau to her concerned enquiry, she called her mother, Yuen Sau. To the older woman, Lau cried, "I've taken something by mistake." When pressed further by her mother-in-law, she told her that she had given something to Mui, too. "Take Mui to hospital," begged the distraught mother, now fully realising what she had done, and desperate for her daughter to live. For herself, Lau said that she did not want help, not being aware that she had eliminated most of the poison and would not achieve her original purpose.

Lau Shuk-hing has been born in Hong Kong in 1917 to an impoverished family. Such education as she had received was rudimentary, with most of her childhood spent helping her mother. But, poor as they might be, her parents had scraped together enough to buy Yau a few pieces of jewellery, including bangles and rings, as a dowry for when she married Yuen Lung-chung. Young Lau might well have imagined a brighter future for herself, now allied to this gentle and hard-working man. When she became pregnant with her first child, she moved with her husband to his mother's home in Kongmoon (Jiangmen), a few hours' journey north of the city, on the Chinese mainland. Lau was a dutiful and thrifty wife, respectful and obedient to her mother-in-law, and met with general approval. But her little son had died in early infancy, and Lau had been heartbroken.

---

259 The case is most fully covered by *Hongkong Daily Press* and *South China Morning Post*, 6th & 7th, 25th & 26th January 1939.

To improve his prospects, Yuen had moved himself and his wife back to Hong Kong in May 1936. They took a cubicle in Square Street and Yuen found a job as a waiter in Ngan Loong Restaurant on nearby Des Voeux Road. It was one of the establishments that paid its waiting staff a purely nominal wage – in Yuen's case just $2 a month, on the understanding that they would work all the harder to get tips from the customers. Yuen might have hope for better, but the late 1930s were very hard times in Hong Kong, as elsewhere in the world. But here there was the added problem that the escalating aggression of Japan was pushing more and more people from southern China into the colony, seeking sanctuary, security and employment. Yuen was lucky to have a job at all, and by diligent attention to his clients, he could reckon on bringing home between $20 and $30 a month. This was about the salary of the lowest paid government coolie or messenger, but those men also received a rent allowance. And, of course, he was not supporting just himself and his wife. His mother and two of his sisters had joined them in late 1936, and although they went back to Kongmoon for a few months the next year, they soon had to return as life became too dangerous there. Thus the man had five adults to support on his wage, as well as his baby girl, Yuen Mui-tau, born in June 1937.

Money was so tight that in 1937 Yuen had to ask his wife for some of her jewellery, which he sold to pay off their debts. Lau knew that it was her duty as a good wife not to question her husband about this and willingly handed over what he asked for. But with too many mouths to feed, the situation was not improving and in the autumn of the following year, he had to pawn Lau's earrings for $5. In November 1938, to find cheaper accommodation, he moved the whole family across to Kowloon, where he rented the middle cubicle and some bed-space on the first floor of No. 5 Shantung Street. He was still working in Des Voeux Road, and the late hours there and the distance he now had to travel meant that it was often more convenient to sleep in the restaurant. He usually managed to return home first thing in the morning, at least a few times a week.[260]

---

260 Late-night ferry fares were higher than those of the Star Ferry service, which ended at about midnight.

His sister, Yuen Sui-yee had recently arrived, further increasing pressure on purse and space, and she had to share a bed with his wife.

As so often happened, the presence of her mother-in-law Sau changed the dynamics in the home for Lau, especially in terms of household management. When Sau was there, Yuen deferred to her, giving her the money for housekeeping, although he always paid the rent to the landlord himself. He tried to give his wife two or three dollars a month, but sometimes this couldn't be managed. If she really resented this, Lau had not shown it to the family. Certainly, Sau still held her in regard and showed real affection for the young woman. But Lau could not help feeling sore. She was only too aware of how poor they were, but being kept in ignorance of her husband's financial state, and knowing that he spoke about "money matters" with his mother was naturally trying for her. On 7th December he had given Sau $10 for food and necessities – he had about $20 at the time, but had not yet paid that month's rent. He did not give anything to his wife on that occasion. Mother and son both knew that Lau had heard them talking, but were not sure whether she had been able to hear what they said. However, they felt that even if not, she could have made a fair guess that Sau had received some money, since it was a frequent occurrence.

Two days later, Yuen paid another early morning visit to the family, when Lau asked him for five dollars to redeem her earrings. She had decided that she was going to get it from him if he had the money on him, and their conversation soon turned into bickering and then into a proper quarrel. "You refuse to give me money!" screamed Lau, trying to snatch at Yuen's purse. An indignant Sau came in and demanded to know why they were making all this noise and disturbing her sleep. In uncharacteristic fashion, Lau told her to mind her own business. She and Yuen were having an argument and it was nothing to do with her. But Sau replied that it did concern her, this was her son, after all, and that she would find somewhere else for herself and her daughters to live. Would Yuen give her maintenance for that? She would start looking that morning. Yuen offered his wife one dollar, but since that was not enough, Lau sulkily refused this. He told her that she wasn't getting any more, and to go away and stop bothering him.

After Yuen had left for work, Lau took her little daughter and went out to see her own mother. It can be imagined that the scene earlier in the day played itself over and over in her mind, probably reviving grievances which became distorted in the 'retelling'. Alongside her resentfulness there was a lot of anxiety and a level of depression, given the situation they were in. She hadn't heard about her mother-in-law moving out before. How would Yuen ever support two households? To make matters worse, Lau was fairly sure that she was pregnant again. She thought she had missed two periods now, but instead of feeling happy and excited, as she had on the previous occasions, the prospect of another baby just seem to herald more worry and expense. She had spent most of the day at her mother's apartment, but the visit had not eased her mind. By her return journey it appears that she had begun to see suicide as a way of solving the problems, but her thoughts were skirting around it, and she was not considering the consequences. When she was almost back in Shantung Street she bumped into a man she knew slightly, a labourer, but an honest man, and gave him a dollar she had kept by, with instructions to buy her some opium. She knew that it would arouse suspicions if she tried to purchase this herself. Much better to get this man to buy it for her.

The home was quiet when she let herself in at 6 p.m. Her sisters-in-law were already in bed or preparing for it, and Sau was out and would not be returning until midnight or thereabouts. As usual, her husband was at work on Hong Kong Island. Lau spent a fretful and largely sleepless night, until in the early hours she quietly got up, heated some water, poured it into a cup and mixed the opium with it.

It did not take the taxi long to get both mother and baby to Kowloon Hospital, although Lau was still reluctant to go in. On the journey she explained a little more to her relatives. They understood her to say, "I have been trying to get some money from Yuen to redeem my earrings, but he refuses me, so I had much better give up my life." They were both examined by Dr H. T. Bee, who recognised the symptoms of opium poisoning immediately. The doctor soon pronounced Lau to be out of danger, having been so violently sick, but there was nothing he could do for Mui – the little one had taken too much of the poison and was now far gone. She died two hours after arriving at the hospital.

Lau was kept under observation, but, as Dr Bee anticipated, she had fully recovered by the evening. Since she had volunteered the fact that she had given Yuen Mui the opium, the police had to be brought in. They examined the home later that same day, taking away with them the cup that had contained the drug, a bowl and spoon and the cloth that had been used to wipe up the vomit from the floor. When Lau was taken to Mongkok Police Station that evening, a search of her clothes produced a horn pot – the customary vessel for holding opium, and everything was sent to the Government Analyst. Whilst at the station she wanted to explain herself, so the police took a statement. She told them that her husband wanted to divorce her and so she was compelled to die with her daughter. She could not spare her – Mui was her own flesh and blood. Lau was held on remand at Lai Chi Kok Prison, while tests were conducted and enquiries made, until the police were ready to present their case fully to the magistrate. The sad affair had attracted only brief mention in the English press until this point, but had been the subject of much talk and speculation in the Chinese papers. There the balance of opinion had come down firmly in favour of sympathy rather than censure for the young mother.

The magistrate at Kowloon Police Court on 5th January 1939 was Mr Eric Himsworth, and he heard the story as put together from the police and medical evidence from the Crown Prosecutor John Whyatt. There was no doubt that Mui's death was due to opium poisoning, the fact corroborated by the 15 grains of the drug found on the cloth, seven in the opium pot and three in the child's stomach. Lau was duly committed for trial at the next Criminal Sessions.

The court was well aware of the public feeling regarding Lau's predicament. Both Mr Whyatt and the Chief Justice, Sir Atholl MacGregor, acknowledged the impossibility of not feeling sympathy for this young woman. Yet, both insisted, the jury must remember their responsibilities as "ministers of Justice," and not allow such sympathies to cloud their judgement of fact. At the outset of the trial Lau, consistent with her attitude all along, pleaded guilty, but at the request of her barrister, Mr T. F. Lo, the plea entered was one of not guilty. It was, Mr Whyatt clarified, on a charge of murder, not manslaughter, that the defendant was being tried. Did Lau or did Lau not wilfully take away the life of the child? In his closing address, he said that the question of premeditation did not enter into the discussion, since Lau's act was voluntary, intentional and unprovoked. The situation of the family was placed before the jury – and the reading public. Sympathy is uppermost in the language of this section of the court reports, with the terms "poignant" and "pitiful" frequently employed. Alongside their grief and anxiety, one can only wonder how family felt to have their problems so publicly aired. Presenting the prosecution case occupied the first day. From this, Mr Whyatt comes across as not without some sympathy for Lau. He occasionally seems to feel the need to build a case against her, as when he observes that there was direct evidence that the relationship between Yuen and Lau had broken down, but then does not pursue this. The reader now, and probably the jury then, are left with the impression of understandable squabbles, and rows between a couple under considerable external pressure. The two principal witnesses he called were Lau's sister-in-law, Sui-yee and mother-in-law Sau, and it was here that Sau spoke of the esteem in which she held her son's young wife.

On the following day, 25th January, Mr Lo questioned Lau closely. She repeatedly said how much sorrow she felt that her daughter had died. She had no intention of killing her. But since this conflicted with what she had said earlier, she was closely questioned by Mr Whyatt. What emerges is someone whose thought processes were as unclear to herself as to those in court. Lau's understanding of her own emotions and motivations was muddled both that night and when she stood in court. She did not *want* to kill the child, but neither could she face the idea of the baby not having her care. Lau gave her the opium with no idea whether the amount would kill her or not and was stricken when she realised that it might. She was frantic to get help for Mui and to have her taken to hospital, and yet still unable to bear the idea of being parted from her. During the questioning and at other times during the proceedings, Lau had collapsed and fainted.

In his closing address, Mr Lo told the jurymen that they had glimpsed into the awful reality of life for so many of Hong Kong's desperately poor. "You, Gentlemen of the Jury, are not trying a criminal but a most unfortunate woman who, by a cruel twist of fate, has taken the life of a child whom she loved and not her own as she wished....It is most important for you to remember that when the accused decided to commit suicide she did not think of her child at all. It was only after she had taken the opium that she realised her child's plight and under irresistible emotional impulse gave it the narcotic as well. Whatever might be unreal in this case, there is one thing that was real. It was her devotion to her child."

Sir Atholl had to remind the jury of their role once more. He was very aware of all the court would feel for Lau, but they must not let this overrule the performance of the duty. In a statement which almost contains a rebuke to the defence counsel, he criticised Mr Lo's suggestion that "his client was the slave of an over-powering idea. It is my duty to warn you explicitly that the doctrine of irresistible impulse is one which is unknown to the English law, and shall I devoutly hope, long remain unknown... in law every person is responsible for the consequences of his or her actions." It was the jury's duty to consider only the facts. They must keep sympathy in its proper place. There may, indeed, be such a proper place for that sympathy were their verdict adverse to the woman, but that would devolve onto the proper authorities.

The jury retired for eleven minutes. On their return, the foreman gave their verdict: that Lau Shuk-hing was guilty, but added that they wished, in the strongest terms, to recommend mercy. Sir Atholl told Lau that since she had declared herself to be pregnant, she must now be examined by two physicians to establish whether that was so. The two doctors who had been involved as witnesses in the case had been retained against this possibility, so the woman was immediately taken to a room beneath the court for the brief examination. They returned, and Dr Bee gave it as their opinion that Lau was about four months gone. After some discussion about the correct penalty to be imposed, Sir Atholl asked Lau if she had anything to say why he should not pass the mandatory life sentence upon her. Lau quietly said that she knew what she had done was wrong and asked for leniency. He then formally passed sentence that she should be confined to prison, with such labour as she was fit to perform for the term of her natural life. But then in words similar to those he had employed in Pang Yiu-mui's trial, told her that the sentence would be considerably shorter.

Lau Shuk-hing was removed back to Lai Chi Kok prison, but discussions between the Chief Justice, the Governor, Sir Geoffry Northcote, and members of the Executive Council soon commenced. It was felt that prison was not the appropriate place for such a fragile young woman, and she was quietly released, and transferred to the care of the Salvation Army Home for Women and Girls.[261] This was on the understanding that she would consent to stay there, and she would have her baby there, due in September. This was certainly an extraordinary turn of circumstances for Lau, and must have been very different to the best she could have hoped for, even after the Chief Justice's assurances. Then on 29th March came the news that the Governor had pardoned her.[262] She must stay at the Salvation Army home until October, but then she would be completely free. The newspaper article and the report of the Home give a little insight into her time there.[263] Had there been time and help to heal the wounds with her family, as well? What was the life to which she returned, ten months after that dreadful night?

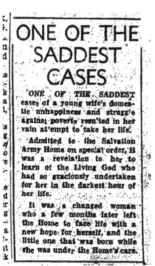

ONE OF THE SADDEST CASES

ONE OF THE SADDEST cases of a young wife's domestic unhappiness and struggle against poverty resulted in her vain attempt to take her life.

Admitted to the Salvation Army Home on special order, it was a revelation to her to learn of the Living God who had so graciously undertaken for her in the darkest hour of her life.

It was a changed woman who a few months later left the Home to face life with a new hope for herself, and the little one that was born while she was under the Home's care.

She chopped me, so I chopped her back – the case of Kwan Lai-chun

Late one warm Sunday evening in May 1940, Kan Wai, watchman responsible for Hee Wong Terrace, just off Sands Street in the West Point area, was doing his rounds.[264] Known to all as Uncle Wai, he was a

261 See Chapter 8, section on Remand Homes.

262 *Hongkong Telegraph,* 29th March 1939, *South China Morning Post,* 30th March 1939.

263 *Hongkong Daily Press,* 27th March 1940.

264 The initial report is in *The China Mail,* 13th May 1940, reports of the trials appear in all the papers of the day, including *The China Mail,* 24th & 25th June 1940 and *South China Morning Post,* 4th, 5th, 25th & 26th June 1940.

friendly and helpful man, who prided himself on knowing his area and its occupants well and being able to sort out troubles before they escalated into anything nasty. The road was quiet and dark – street lighting was rudimentary here – so when the door of No. 33 burst open and young Wong Miu-lin, old Chui's daughter-in-law rushed out screaming, he was momentarily taken off guard. "She's got the chopper, oh, Uncle Wai, she's murdering us!" Uncle Wai knew that the women in the second-floor flat were quarrelsome – the shrieks between the Chui Chuk's two wives could often be heard down at street level, but this sounded bad. Clutching her small son in her arms, the girl seemed terrified. He guided her back to the entrance to the flats, but by the hall light he saw that the young woman's dress had patches of what looked like blood on it. Taking charge, he told her to run towards the Police Station – she'd be sure to find a constable before she got far. "Tell him to call for some medical help, too," he instructed.

Alarmed now, Uncle Wai hurried straight up the stairs. He knew this family well, now, what could be so bad for Wong to be in this state? Half way up the second flight he found Lam Lin-kwai, Chui's concubine, slumped on the stairs. She was dressed only in her underwear, but that was soaked in blood. Stooping to see what he might do for her, he thought of the children in the flat. A sound made him glance up, and he saw Chui's wife, Kwan Lai-chun, leaning against the door frame, holding what, in the dim light of the stairwell, looked like a chopper. Leaving Lam for the moment, he carried on up and spoke to Kwan even before he had reached the flat. Keeping his voice very calm, he said, "What are you doing with that? Come on, give it to me. You don't have to make a family matter so serious. Let me take that." So saying, he took the chopper from Kwan, who did not resist and remained where she was, stunned. Uncle Wai put the chopper down on a little stool just inside the flat – it was covered in blood and seemed to have hairs and flesh attached to it. Turning again to Kwan, he realised that she must be bleeding – her clothes and hands seemed covered with blood. She mumbled something to him, but he didn't get it and had to ask her to repeat it. Even then he wasn't sure – was she really saying that?

The amount of blood around alarmed him further, and there was more on the floor so, cautiously, he went further into the flat. In the passage near the door Chui's 85-year-old mother, Au Sze, was lying in a crumpled heap on the floor – she wasn't moving or making any sound at all. Then he glanced across at the other cubicles – where were the children? Didn't Lam have a couple of kids? Checking to see that Kwan was still at the door – and the chopper was on the stool, he made his way further in. The first cubicle he tried was locked, the next empty, but as he made for the front one, he passed another bed-space in the passage. He had to hold the door frame opposite for support for a moment – the bed containing the two little bodies was a mass of blood.

At that moment he heard someone come up the stairs and went back towards the stairwell, relieved to find that P.C. Tsang Chung had arrived. Seeing the watchman – and perhaps registering the horror that must have been on his face – he confirmed that other help was on its way. "There's one of the fire service who'll be along in a moment – he'll be able to help the injured," the constable reassured Uncle Wai. "Well, take this out of here, will you?" the watchman whispered, handing him the chopper. The daughter-in-law, Wong, had done as the man had instructed and soon found Constable Tsang. He had called out to another watchman and the fireman who were down the road, but told the young woman to continue onto the police station and tell the officer on the desk there as much as she could.

P.C. Tsang turned his attention first to Kwan. Covered in blood though she might be, she did not seem to be in great pain. "Tell me what's happened here? Why is there all this blood around?" Her response, "On Tuesday, we are going to be separated at the S.C.A.", left him wondering whether she might be delirious. Uncle Wai directed the policeman's attention to the old woman on the floor. One hand was almost severed and blood was congealing round her head. He then pointed to the bed further down the passage, and could only nod his head to the policeman's "What, more!" Just as P.C. Tsang went along to investigate, there was a loud thump from the stairwell. Wai rushed down the stairs, slipping on the blood that was everywhere, and found that Lam had fallen to the first floor landing. She was lying face down, arms splayed out. He used her girdle to help him lift her and tried to support her against a door. He had no idea what to do for her, so was very relieved when a fireman ran up to the landing.[265] This man set to, trying to bandage up Lam's multiple wounds as best he could while Uncle Wai returned to the flat, leading another watchman who had just arrived. Kwan was now sitting on the bed in her cubicle.

It might be late in the evening, with most of the people in the vicinity already in their beds, but the news of some awful happening in No. 33 Hee Wong Terrace travelled fast. The many police vehicles that were drawing up augured ill. Before long, Chui Chuk had been found and told that he had better return to his home. He arrived, aghast to see Lam bleeding so profusely and found his flat had become a scene of carnage. Met at the door by Uncle Wai, the watchman led him through to Kwan, who by now was sitting on the side of her bed in the front cubicle. Looking up at her husband, she said, "Lam has taken revenge, she has chopped so many people to death." Uncle Wai looked sharply at Kwan, but her expression of stupefaction had not lifted. He recalled what she had mumbled to him when he had first arrived and was troubled, but said nothing to Chui.

Minutes later the building was full of police and ambulance men. The latter took the concubine Lam and the wife Kwan to Queen Mary Hospital. A doctor pronounced the old lady and Lam's son, Chui Yik-wah dead and had them sent to the mortuary at the Government Civil Hospital. Somewhat to the amazement of the ambulance attendants, when they started to move Lam's little girl, she sat up, bleary-eyed, but definitely alive. Although covered in her brother's blood, she proved to have no injuries and had slept through all the horrendous events.

The story of that dreadful evening had its beginnings years earlier. Like many men at the time, Chui Chuk had a home in a village near Canton but worked in Hong Kong. He and his wife of many years had not had any children, so the couple had adopted a son. At his mother's instigation he had taken a concubine, Lam Lin-kwai and had two children by her, the (now) eleven-year-old boy, Chui Yik-wah and a young daughter. But in 1929, two years after Lam came to live with them his *kit fat* wife had

---

265 Most of the Fire Brigade had St John Ambulance First-Aid training.

died.[266] The usual practice was for the established mistress to become the substitute, or *tin fong* wife, and be accorded the principal status even if another concubine joined the family.[267] Chui Chuk and his *kit fat* wife had lived most of the year in Hong Kong while Lam stayed in Canton with his elderly mother, Au Sze. So now, Lam was expecting to move to the colony with him and Chui was preparing to transfer the status of wife to her. But Au Sze was eager to have grandsons. She persuaded her son to find another wife, a young woman, who would be sure to provide the necessary male heirs and so the following year, in Hong Kong, he married twenty-one-year-old Kwan Lai-chun. Thus, instead of being presented with the red bridal chair that would show family and friends her elevation to the position of principal wife, Lam found herself still in Canton with her two children, although well provided-for and visited by Chui.

But the years went by and the longed-for sons did not arrive. It seems to have been assumed that the responsibility for this lay with Kwan. She may have felt quite isolated, living on Hong Kong Island with neither her own nor her husband's family around. Added to that, she knew that her childlessness meant she was out of favour with her mother-in-law, the real force in the family. About five years into her marriage Kwan started suffering from severe headaches and nerves and soon was going to the Chinese doctors for remedies, which gave her some relief. She felt anxious about her position, the more so as her husband, Chui, was talking about bringing Lam over to Hong Kong, as the situation in Canton was getting more unsettled. The two women had met at the infrequent family gatherings in that city, when they preserved a veneer of civility towards one another, keeping their animosity for each other concealed from their husband's relations.

In 1937 the political situation in Canton forced Chui to close the house there and bring Lam, her son Chui Yik-wah and daughter to live with them, Kwan's problems increased. Indeed, the whole family were under strain since Chui's business was not doing well and his recently married adopted son was frequently out of work. Recently the family had moved, perhaps for reasons of economy, and their second-floor flat on Hee

---

266 *kit fat* = 'tie up hair'.
267 *tin fong* = 'fill in room'.

Wong Terrace had few advantages. It enjoyed a view across the harbour entrance, but for all its recent construction, it had been built along the lines of earlier tenements, with flats divided into cubicles and a single kitchen and lavatory/bathroom on each floor. Their flat was crowded, accommodating the man, his two wives, two children and mother along with Chui's adopted son, wife and baby. Nevertheless, Chui decided that the rear part of it must be sub-let to make ends meet, so he erected a partition, about six foot in height, creating a small cubicle.

As money grew tighter, Au Sze, always inclined to scold Kwan, became even more critical of her daughter-in-law, accusing her of wasting money. Kwan suspected that she was trying to turn Chui against her. She had hoped that when Lam arrived from Canton, the latter's well-known animosity towards Au would deflect things away from her, Kwan. But perhaps the reverse was happening and the mother was now trying to conciliate the concubine.

Over the next three years tensions in the flat built with frequent arguments. The presence of the adopted daughter-in-law, Wong Miu-lin improved things for a time, for Kwan liked her and gained back some self respect through being able to help the girl. But then Lam accused Wong of stealing money from her and another source of acrimony opened up, with frequent vicious rows between Lam and Kwan. At other times Kwan would lapse into a sullen dejection, despairing of her childless state and feeling powerless to improve her lot. The Chinese medicine that had helped earlier could not cure her now and she sought help from the European doctors, who treated her for depression and deficiency of spirits.

By 1940, when Lam was 42 and Kwan 31, the moods of the latter were quite unpredictable. She believed that Chui was siding with his concubine, an opinion Wong, the daughter-in-law, would support at court later, saying she thought the man showed too much partiality to Lam. But he was concerned that his wife was increasingly irrational, and life had become so difficult for everyone in the flat. Thus on 10th May 1940, in an attempt to resolve the problem, he took both women to a teahouse to discuss the situation and arranged for his cousin, Chui Pak-kam to be there. Pak-kam urged both to live harmoniously, but, when it became apparent that no progress was being made, the husband suggested to his wife that she should go to the Secretary for Chinese Affairs to find out about separation and maintenance. This was not the first time that the S.C.A. had been mentioned to Kwan. This department, formerly the Registrar General's Department, acted in a semi-judicial fashion as arbitrators in such cases, standing between accepted Chinese customary law and the British legal system. It would seem that Lam had reminded Kwan of it several times, too. There is no suggestion that Chui was telling Kwan that he would divorce her, but that she would have to live apart from the family and that he would maintain her thus. Obviously, that this route should be proposed and in the presence of Chui's cousin, too, made Kwan feel very threatened. She would also know that this would be financially difficult for her husband and might have speculated about the sort of life she would then have. Kwan later claimed to have understood Chui to say that should she refuse to go to these authorities she would die. Pak-kam recalled that after the suggestion had been made she was very quiet.

It was two days after this teahouse meeting that events took such an irrevocable turn. At 7.45 p.m. on 12th May, when Chui left the flat, all was quiet. His daughter-in-law then went to bed and soon fell asleep. Her husband was out of the building while Chui's mother was sleeping on a camp bed near the door. Lam sorted clothes on the bed where her two children were sleeping. At the back, in the separate cubicle, Ng Shun and her daughter had already been in bed an hour. There had been little quarrelling that evening, only some squabble about a candle that the boy had broken. In fact, since the tearoom conversation, Kwan had been quiet, crying often. Kwan's account was that she had gone to bed at 7 p.m., but later got up to clean the spittoon. She had taken this back to her cubicle to finish. After a while she got up again, to turn out the light she had left on in the kitchen. On returning, she found her way blocked by Lam brandishing a chopper. Au Sze had got out of bed and tried to interpose herself and defend Kwan, but was struck by Lam, and fell to the floor. Kwan retreated to that where Lam's two children were asleep and fell backwards onto the bed. This woke the boy, who squatted behind her. Lam tried to attack her, but in the dark she chopped her own son.

Kwan thought Lam had not intended to strike the boy, for she was fond of him, giving him a bath every day and making sure that he always had clean clothes.

At this point Kwan snatched the chopper from Lam and turned it on her. Lam screamed "*Ai yah!*" (oh dear!), waking both Wong Miu-lin and the neighbour, Ng Shun.[268] Kwan hacked at Lam, chasing her back towards the cooking area, where Lam fell. At this, the younger woman stopped cutting her former assailant, asking her instead if she dared restart the fight. Lam, by now a mass of bleeding wounds, lurched to the door of the flat. Given the state that Lam was in, Kwan's question – which according to her testimony she put as a genuine query – seems extraordinary. Kwan later told the court that Lam "indicated that she did not want to continue".

In the close and crowded confines of a flat split into several cubicles, people learnt to sleep through any amount of noise their fellows might make. Thus it was only Lam's shrieks of "*Ai yah*" that roused Chui's daughter-in-law and their neighbour, Ng Shun. Ng had moved in, together with her young daughter just a few months earlier while her husband was in England. Alarmed, she got up on her bed and peered over the partition to find out what was happening. It was too dark to make out much, so she got down and turned the lights on, then went back to her vantage point. Then just the briefest glance sent her crouching down on the bed, shielding her daughter's head and covering the child's ears. In that moment she had seen Kwan slashing at Lam's head, three or four times, with the latter trying to protect herself. Soon after she heard something – or someone – fall heavily and a long sigh or groan from Lam. After that she heard no more until the watchman came into the flat. That was her cue to grab her daughter and get out of the flat as fast as they could.

Meanwhile, Wong had risen from her bed and gone into the passage where she found the frenzied Kwan cutting Lam, aiming at her head but slashing with fury wherever the chopper fell. Wong made an attempt to get the weapon from the woman, but was no match for Kwan in the full heat of her rage. Pausing only to pick up her baby, she made for the

---

268 Others reported hearing her call out "*gau meng!*" or "save life!"

door, almost stumbling over Au Sze. Aghast, she realised that the old lady was covered in blood, then looking down saw her own nightdress was splattered with Lam's blood. She needed to get help and flew down the stairs to look for Uncle Wai.

At the hospital it became apparent that Lam had a huge number of wounds all over her body, particularly to her head. Her blood loss was significant, and she soon became unconscious. Mercifully, she died at 4 a.m. the next morning. She had been treated by Dr T. K. Lien, who then performed the postmortem. He found that she had 71 cuts to her body and head, 24 of which went right to the bone. There was no doubt, he concluded, that Lam Lin-kwai had died through haemorrhage and the trauma of the multiple chops.

The situation in the flat after the police had completed their initial investigations has to be left to our imagination. It was recorded that Wong, still carrying her baby, of course, had crept back, but it was some hours before she and Chui, and perhaps Wong's husband, could start to take stock. Did Chui hurry to Queen Mary Hospital to enquire about his wives? Before they left, of course, the extent of Lam's injuries were all too apparent, but how badly chopped had Kwan been? Kwan had been taken to hospital in her blood-soaked clothes, as the ambulance crew believed her to have many injuries. She had been wearing her day clothes at the time of the rampage and her long silk dress was heavy with blood. But when the medical staff examined her, they found that she had just a cut at the base of her left thumb, a grazed knee and some scratches on her forehead. However, perhaps because of her somewhat strange responses and reactions, she remained in hospital, guarded and under observation for a full week. Whilst in the casualty room of of Queen Mary Hospital, Sgt McVey had told Kwan that she was under arrest in connection with the wounding of Lam and read the caution to her. Even though he was speaking in Cantonese to her, he suspected that she might not have really understood, so a Chinese constable repeated his words. It was at this point that Kwan began to give her account.

Early the next day, at the Victoria Mortuary, Professor Robertson undertook the grim examination of the bodies of Yik-wah and Au Sze. The child's head had suffered 16 lacerations, some of which had fractured the bone. Another chop had cut his throat. Astonishingly, when the first-aid trained fireman had seen him, perhaps some 30 minutes after the attack, Yik-wah had been alive – just – with a very weak pulse, but died a few minutes later, as the fireman was trying to treat him. Au had died of cerebral haemorrhage, with 12 gashes on the head, cutting to the skull and fracturing it in places. Her left hand was almost severed from her arm, held together only by skin and with the wrist bones visible.

Kwan Lai-chun was brought from hospital to the Magistracy on 20th May where Det. Insp. Whant attached to West Point Police Station charged her with the murder of Lam Lin-kwai on 12th May. Doctors at Queen Mary Hospital had discharged her into police custody on 23rd May without observing any evidence of insanity or mania. Week by week the case was remanded until her appearance on 3rd June, when the police investigations were complete. The English-language newspapers had initially given scant coverage to the tragedy since they had more or less given up reporting all but the most serious local news in favour of detailed coverage of the war in Europe and the Sino-Japanese conflict. Even the reports of the trials did not make the front pages, as they would a few years earlier. Not so the Chinese press, however, which had dedicated many column inches to reporting the case. However, they had been given little to go on by the police and thus resorted to repeating the various lurid rumours that were circulating, as if the truth was not frightful enough.

Police Magistrate Thomas Houston usually heard his cases in the smaller court of the Central Magistracy on Arbuthnot Road, but such were the numbers clamouring for access to the public gallery that the case against Kwan was moved to the larger court. The doors were shut to the public long before the hearing began and yet another 2,000 people and more swarmed around the building, blocking all the nearby roads. The Police Emergency Unit were called in to remove the public from the compound and 50 Special Police were deployed to control the crowds.

Crown Solicitor Mr J. P. Murphy presented the case for the Crown assisted by Det. Insp. Whant. Kwan was charged with the murder of Lam only, it not being possible to determine who had killed the boy or her mother-in-law, although it was the Crown's suggestion that she was responsible. After recounting events of the evening, the prosecutor called the medical evidence. He invited Kwan to question the doctors, whereupon she said that she had always suffered from "mental deficiency" and had been under the care of doctors who had prescribed medicine for this. The magistrate recommended that these doctors be called to testify for her. What she meant by this term was not examined. Throughout the hearing Kwan held to her understanding of events, even though it was often contradictory and muddled. Lam had accidentally killed both Au Sze and Chui Yik-wah. The mother-in-law had died trying to protect Kwan, then Lam had mistaken the boy for herself. During the course of the trial 14 witnesses were called, including two, Wong and Ng Shun who claimed that they had seen Kwan chop at Lam. Kan Wai gave his evidence and told the court what Kwan had said to him when he first arrived on the scene. "Uncle Wai, that *tan kee* has instigated [my] husband to divorce me and had a chopper to chop me. I snatched it away from her. I chopped all of them to death before I die." Asked by Mr Houston what he understood by *tan kee,* the watchman said that he did not understand it. The interpreter explained that it meant "a wife of a king or an emperor, used in reference to a wicked wife." Kwan protested that the man was lying, this was not what she had said. "I said, '*Wai Pak,* that *tan kee* has instigated my husband to divorce me on several occasions but did not succeed. She now got hold of a chopper trying to kill me. She has already killed the others.'"

The scenes around the Magistracy that morning had been similar to the previous day's melee, but in the courtroom itself Mr Houston did his best to ensure that Kwan received a fair trial. Her various interjections of the previous day had been confusing and Mr Houston counselled her not to say any more that day. "As this is a capital charge, you will, whether you can afford it or not, be provided with a defence solicitor and barrister. You need good advice and if you reserve your defence, you will be under their guidance and they will help you. This is just my personal advice to you, and I won't stop you if you want to make your defence now." Kwan had been listening carefully and replied "I will take Your Worship's advice". He thus committed her to appear at the next Criminal Sessions.

In Arbuthnot Road, hundreds of spectators waited for her to be led out and into the waiting prison van.

Three weeks later, on 24th June, Kwan appeared at the Supreme Court in front of Chief Justice Sir Atholl MacGregor. Once again the court and the streets around were thronged and there was some trouble ejecting all those who tried to gain access by using other passageways and corridors in the building. Kwan's legal team, solicitor P. Wynter-Blyth and barrister D. J. N. Anderson, must have had quite a challenge preparing a defence for her plea of 'not guilty' to the murder of Lam. Self defence, the only line that could be put forward, seemed rather thin when the injuries sustained by the two women were so dramatically different. No evidence of "mental deficiency" or even instability was mentioned. There were only small additions made to the accounts given at the lower court. To Kwan's claim that she had been in bed for most of the evening, the police produced photographs to show that her bed had not been disturbed, let alone slept in. And they also attested that there was ample light in the cubicles for Lam to have seen that she was hitting her son, not Kwan, if that had been the case. But beyond this, there were no revelations during the two-day trial.

In summing up Sir Atholl urged the jury to consider only what they had heard in those two days, not opinions and speculations they might have shared with family and friends before being called as jurors. He believed that there had been inequality of treatment of the two women which had led to the poisonous jealousies developing. "There is no question that there were bitterly strained relations between the two women, leading to hatred and enmity," he explained. Having reviewed the evidence for the jury, he asked them to give careful consideration to the prosecution's case as well as Kwan's story. He cautioned them to remember that, "to return a guilty verdict, you must be satisfied beyond reasonable doubt that the accused is guilty." The verdict must be unanimous.

It took the seven-man jury just ten minutes to reach this. Kwan displayed no emotion when the foreman responded "Guilty" when asked by the Clerk of the Court. She still did not believe that she was guilty. To the Chief Justice's question if she had anything to say why the capital sentence should not be passed, she replied, "I have not committed murder myself. Since Lam Lin-kwai tried to cut me with the chopper I tried to snatch the chopper form her and cut her back." Sir Atholl MacGregor formally sentenced her to death, after which she walked calmly to the cell below the courtroom.

Kwan Lai-chun was then returned to Lai Chi Kok Prison, where she had been held since her discharge from hospital. Here she was confined in an individual cell for four weeks, while the formal process of authorisation for her execution, which included communication with the Colonial Office in London, took place. There is no record of an appeal for clemency. On 30th July she was transferred to Stanley Prison on the south of Hong Kong Island, where she passed her last night.[269] Kwan Lai-chun was executed by hanging at 5.02 a.m. on 31st July 1940 at Stanley Prison. Unlike those who died two months earlier in No. 33 Hee Wong Terrace, West Point, her death was instantaneous.

On that day *The China Mail* published what they claimed to be part of Kwan's last letter to her husband, asking that they should be reconciled and that he would visit her, bringing some of her new clothes. She concluded by begging him to give her a proper burial, then send her ashes back to her village. Her execution was just the second time that judicial capital punishment was enacted on a woman in the colony. It was also the last while Hong Kong was under British administration.

---

269 *China Mail,* 31st July 1940, *South China Morning Post,* 1st August 1940.

CHAPTER 10

THAT WOMAN AGAIN!

The action in most of the cases so far seen took place behind closed doors and often within the privacy of the home. Women 'making a show of themselves' are the exception – such as the brawling women by the West Point water hydrants in Chapter 3. It has been earlier noted that the lives of Chinese women were less visible than that of their menfolk, but in this chapter we meet women who, for the most part, were used to living in both the private and public spheres. Some of them, indeed, were of the type that kept the female prisons full back in England, but the women in the central section of the chapter were trying to preserve or increase their advantage in an unfamiliar setting. Yet there are also striking similarities between these western women and their Chinese neighbours, even if some display a grating sense of superiority. Their offences are (perhaps with the singular exception of Miriam Monteith) borne largely out of the situation in which they involuntarily find themselves. Frequently it is a lack of comprehension of that situation which exacerbates the offence and for many, especially those at the beginning and end of the chapter, a constant struggle to provide for themselves overrides everything else.

Through the 19th century the courts regularly saw western men, out of work and out of luck getting on the wrong side of the law, in brawls and assaults on Chinese, or just making a drunken nuisance of themselves. European women, too, could easily find themselves living on the margins of society. The commonest cause of this was their husband's death or desertion. If a second marriage did not swiftly follow, making their own way in the world was fraught with difficulty. Add to these challenges a combative nature and newspapers eager for any gossip and a woman could quickly become notorious. And for the English-reading population, there

Queen's Road West, Charles Wirgmann, 1857.

was nothing quite so scandalous – and therefore irresistible – as the story of one of their own slipping up.

Such was the fate of Mary Ann Gard, alias Mrs Welsh, in the late 1860s.[270] She first came to public notice when she and her Portuguese landlady took their disagreement over rent first to the magistrate then to the Court of Summary Jurisdiction (the civil court). They had lived in Mosque Street, then moved to Aberdeen Street where they disagreed and came to blows about whether Gard had board as well as lodging. The cockney Gard provided great copy for the reporters, although they seem to regret that they did not understand what was at least the equal verbal vitriol coming from the landlady. Then, in August, she was engaged by one J. H. Brown as a barmaid in the grog-shop, Hotel des Colonies, which he had just acquired. Brown already had a conviction against him for keeping a disorderly house, and the police were soon watching this one. It was a rowdy place, full of seamen and it was known that 'women of objectionable notoriety' were harboured there. The suggestion was, of course, that more than beer and spirits were on sale. Dr Murray, the

270 *Hongkong Daily Press,* 1st & 8th April 1868.

Colonial Surgeon, in his capacity as Justice of the Peace, had seen women in the place. All of this came out at the hearing of the J.P.s on 29th October, when Brown was applying for a renewal of his liquor licence. The feeling of the meeting was already against him and hardened conclusively when he admitted that 'his female' lived upstairs and that he had a barmaid on the premises, although she did not live there. In the minds of the Justices, this was tantamount to promoting immoral behaviour. Brown claimed not to know anything about Gard, telling the meeting that he thought she was probably 'a soldier's wife or something'. His application was refused.[271] Next she was heard of bringing two men, Simmons and Lyle, employees of the Hongkong Gas Works, before Mr May for smashing up her furniture late in November 1868.[272] The case became a wrangle about ownership of the furniture, but Inspector Horspool and Magistrate May thought she had right on her side, to some extent. Simmons, who was most involved in the assault, received a $10 fine and had to pay compensation to Gard. Lyle, who had paid the woman's debts in the previous case, was fined just $1. But Simmons asked if the magistrate would make an order for Gard to stay away from him. To this Mr May readily agreed, requiring the woman to find a security of £5 to be of peaceful behaviour towards Simmons, but the man had to find a £10 bond to leave Gard alone. "If you come up before me again, on a similar charge, I will send you both to gaol, and without the option of a fine," warned the magistrate.[273]

Mrs Mary Moor, described as 'a woman of ill-fame', i.e. a prostitute, living at the corner of Shelley Street and Hollywood Road, had a stone-throwing fight with Josephine de la Ville, who lived next door.[274] The case was settled by the magistrate binding both over with security of $25 for one month. But when they left the court, Moor continued the fight in

---

271 *China Mail*, 29th October 1868, *Hongkong Daily Press*, 30th October 1868

272 *Hongkong Daily Press*, 1st December 1868.

273 The sentencing in this case again illustrates the fact that the Government and the non-Chinese community used both dollars and sterling, the former perhaps for immediate local transactions, and the latter more for longer-term commitments and transactions with an international element.

274 *Hongkong Daily Press*, 24th May 1876.

the Magistracy office. She grabbed de la Ville by the arm and spat into her face, screaming obscenities all the while. Taken back into court, she then went to gaol for three days. A house of ill-repute in Peel Street, run by Pauline Gordon, was causing distress to the neighbours in 1879.[275] This establishment attracted a very much rowdier crowd of European men than did the Chinese brothels reserved for the use of westerners nearby.

The area around Hollywood Road still had its share of western demi-monde forty years later. Myrtle Nicholas lived at No. 33 Wyndham Street, but plied her trade by going aboard the Canton steamers before they departed.[276] Passengers often complained about her and the officers of these vessels frequently had trouble getting her off the boats, since she had neither ticket nor pass to go to Canton. One evening in November 1915, she had become very drunk, and when one of the ship's crew had escorted her off, she had nearly fallen off the gangplank. Detective Constable Vincent was on duty at the wharf and, much to her chagrin, took her into custody 'for her own safety.' When he asked her for her name, she decided to be Hettie Ellis, and told him in colourful language what she thought of him. When brought before Mr Lindsell the next morning, charged with being drunk and disorderly, she admitted her real name, which, anyhow, was well known to the police, but vehemently disclaimed that she had been disorderly. Nevertheless, she was fined $10. Her fellow occupant of the Wyndham Street house, Jeanette Gilbert, had, a few months earlier, also received a $10 fine.[277] Her offence was to throw a bottle over her verandah into the street at 4 a.m. Someone might have been severely hurt, remonstrated P.C. Swan, when he went up to her room. However, since he received a torrent of abuse, he arrested her. The magistrate was prepared to be fair to her. Gilbert had said that she had pushed the bottle with her foot and it rolled off into the street below, but Mr Lindsell went to inspect the place in his lunch hour and found the verandah boarded in on all sides.

---

275 *China Mail,* 22nd April 1879.
276 *China Mail,* 22nd November 1915.
277 *Hongkong Telegraph,* 13th August 1915.

As has already been seen in the stories of Miss Nellie Moore and others, some European women had a great sense of superiority over their Chinese servants and tradespeople so that these, often long-suffering, people were driven to resort to the courts. There the women's objectionable attitudes and behaviour were exhibited for the world to judge. From the mid-1860s onwards, the magistrates were generally sympathetic to the claims of the injured parties, and although rarely imprisoning the 'lady' for her assault, they imposed fines and often required them to pay compensation to their victims. Two such cases, just small reports in the papers, but indicative of this, are given here. The journalist in this case from 1907 obviously had some fun writing his report, and it is reproduced in full. Thereafter, Amy Gillan's story tells of a troubled woman, equally unpleasant to her Chinese employees as she is to her western neighbours.

Strange behaviour in a leather artist's 'parlour'[278]

If Pan Shing only knew what was going to happen he would surely have fixed on a rubber heel to the boots Mrs Parson used on his forehead. But as he did not do so he now bears a very tell-tale plaster on that portion of his cranium.

Pan Shing is a shoemaker of 17 Wellington Street. Mrs Parson gave her address as 1 Beaconsfield Arcade. This morning, in the Police Court, before Mr J. R. Wood, she prosecuted the shoemaker for alleged assault, and he brought a counter-charge for a similar offence.

A pair of boots were the cause of all the trouble. According to Mrs Parson's story she took a pair of boots to the shoemakers shop on the 15th instant to get them repaired. There were revolving rubber heels attached to them. A few days later she sent her 'boy' to fetch them back, but he returned empty-handed, saying that they could not be got until the money was paid. At about five o'clock that afternoon she went herself to interview the shoemaker. She examined the boots and discovered that the rubber heels had been removed. She questioned him about them and the only reply she could get from him was they had been

---

278 *Hongkong Telegraph,* 20th October 1908.

thrown into the 'rubbish basket.' She demanded that the heels should be replaced, but her wish was refused, and as she was leaving the shop she alleged that the shoemaker seized her by the arm. This angered her and she struck him.

His Worship – You struck him on the forehead where that plaster is? – Yes.

The shoemaker's story was to the effect that in the afternoon in question Mrs Parson gave him two pairs of boots to be half-soled. One pair had no rubber heels; and the other had only one heel fixed. He had the boots repaired and a few days later she called for them. "She examined the boots carefully and demanded two rubber heels. I refused to do so seeing that there were none on the boots when they were brought to me. She was going to take the boots away without paying for them, and I stopped her. She then created a disturbance. I told her that I was a business man and would not allow such behaviour in my shop. She persisted, and threatened to take me to the police station. Just then she picked up a boot and struck me on the forehead." The shoemaker bled a great deal. A policeman was called and the party adjourned to headquarters.

His Worship found that Mrs Parson was to blame and imposed a fine of $4. The shoemaker was discharged.

Thirty years later, Hong Kong was a much more crowded place. Hawkers, already a common sight, had proliferated since the 1920s. The police prosecuted most of those without licences, but it seemed a never-ending task. Aside from causing inconvenience to everyone by congesting the footpaths, their continuous calling out of their wares was a source of annoyance to residents. Mrs B. Pears of Austin Road, Kowloon, took the law into her own hands and borrowed her neighbour's air-pistol to shoot at one unfortunate knife-grinder who had the temerity to get on her nerves.[279] She fired several times and hit him on the forehead. As the magistrate told Pears, had her aim been just three inches lower, she would have shot him in the eye and now be facing what he described

---

279 *Hongkong Daily Press*, 2nd September 1939.

as a "very, very, very serious charge". Inspector Cunningham had called at her flat when the message about the injured man came through, and at first Pears had denied all knowledge. But then her neighbour handed over his unlicensed air-pistol and she admitted shooting at the man, who had already been taken to hospital. She escaped with a fine of $50 and a warning that she should go through the proper channels if she was again bothered by hawkers.

The 'hymn' singing poison pen

Detective Sergeant Edmund O'Sullivan had, for once, something a little less serious to investigate. He had experienced his share and more of violent crime in his twelve years as a Hong Kong detective, including a political murder, murder-suicide shootings and chopper attacks. Now this wasn't even a poisoning, just poison pen letters.[280] That Saturday afternoon a note had arrived on his desk, asking him to visit a European woman in Carlton House. The boarding hotel, in Ice House Street, was a few minutes walk from Central Police Station, so, having finished his tiffin, he collected his hat and cane and strolled down the hill.[281] That June day in 1907 was so hot and humid, no one would willingly rush around. The doorman directed him to the right room, and the lady welcomed him in. She produced the unsigned letter on a rather distinctive paper. It was vicious, accusing her of immorality in coarse language. It had come that morning, and had shocked and upset her, she said. "Do you have any idea of who might have written this?" he asked. "Is there anyone who holds a grudge against you, or might want to hurt you?" She had no enemies and couldn't think who it could have come from. But the sergeant thought she was being a little evasive, so spoke reassuringly in his soft Irish brogue, until she told him more.

"There's a woman who used to live in a room on this floor. Her husband is an officer in one of the coastal lines. She's a very loud woman and was always rather rude. She would use terrible language if anyone was in the bathroom when she wanted to use it. We were all happy when she left."

---

280 *Hongkong Telegraph*, 3rd July 1907.
281 Tiffin was a term imported from British India to describe a light midday meal.

She admitted that she had seen her in the street recently and had crossed the road to avoid meeting her. Sgt O'Sullivan did not believe this would lead anywhere, but then the woman added, "She left me notes a couple of times, oh, nothing bad, just ordinary ones about taking in a parcel and the like. But that's why I think this is her writing. Its rather unusual, isn't it, the way she forms some of the letters?" The woman, Mrs Gillan, had not moved far, just round the corner to Duddell Street, although his informant did not which house she lived in. "May I ask, have you mentioned this letter to anyone else?" She hadn't told her husband yet, she did not want to disturb him at work, but she had mentioned it to her neighbour. "And you haven't heard if anyone else has received a letter like this?" he continued. "Oh no, but it's not the type of thing you want to talk about, is it?" She'd told her friend, because she was so upset that she had to tell someone, but she was sure that lady wouldn't gossip about it.

Promising that he would be in touch, the sergeant took his leave and was about to go downstairs when one of the Chinese floor-servants approached him. The man wanted to talk to him, so Sgt O'Sullivan ushered him to the end of the corridor. Fluent in Cantonese, he knew that they could speak with no fear of the western occupants of the floor understanding them. "The lady told you about the bad letter she got?" Chan Kwai asked. So much for friends who don't gossip, thought the officer, if the servants had already got to hear about it. "We think it was Mrs Gillan who sent it. She's a very nasty woman – I know, I used to be her boy. I'm very glad she moved. Do you know what she did to me once? She had called me to her room in the morning – she was still in bed. I was late because I had jobs to do for someone else, and when I came in, she leapt out of bed and pointed a gun at me. 'I give you kill' you, she screamed at me." Well, thought the sergeant, this was a turn of events, but he had to be clear. "What did she mean by 'I give you kill'?", he asked. The man looked at him – what hadn't this policeman understood? "She give me kill, she fire gun, I die!" he clarified. Right, well, no need to put words into the man's mouth. Enough time for the magistrate to do that if it went that far. He questioned the man further about the gun, a revolver, obviously, and whether he had seen it before. The man had, and not only that, but he knew that there were more bullets somewhere about, too. The policeman cautioned him sternly about not telling the other servants about any of this. "If I find all this is true, you will have to come to court to give evidence. You must say nothing about it to anyone else, other wise you will be in big trouble with the magistrate." Suitably cowed, he agreed that he would be silent. It was important to get some time frame for this, so Sgt O'Sullivan asked Chan to recollect what day this had been. Before the (Chinese) New Year, after the new moon… with the help of the sergeant's pocket diary they fixed the day to Friday 18th January.

The sergeant was rather more concerned about this woman's possible possession of a revolver than the letters she was allegedly sending. Maybe she had a licence for the gun, but it would be as well to check. He returned to the Central Station to obtain a warrant and soon was examining the door charts of the houses in Duddell Street, just off Queen's Road. He did not have far to look, the name he was seeking appeared on the chart for No. 3, and in a top floor room he found Mrs Amy Gillan. "I've come to search for arms, madam, guns, ammunition…" "Well, there's certainly nothing like that here. Do you think I've got a gun? You won't find any here, I can assure you." Had her husband a gun?, he suggested. Was she quite sure? Gillan was adamant. "Come, now, Mrs Gillan, it's no use you saying that. I know you've got a gun. I am going to search for it. You had better hand it over to me." At this, she capitulated. How did he know? She couldn't be sure, but people in Carlton House had probably seen it, she suspected. Gillan opened the wardrobe door. "You'll find it in there, on the bottom shelf," she told him. Sgt O'Sullivan extracted a small revolver, and seeing that it was fully loaded, swiftly removed the bullets. "It's not mine, it doesn't belong to me, it's my husband's," she claimed. "And would you know if your husband has a licence for this?" Gillan did not reply. "So," the officer continued, "Are there any more bullets lying around, Mrs Gillan?" Once more, this was firmly denied. He looked round the room, making as if to search. On the writing desk he picked up a sheet of notepaper, which he reckoned was the same colour and size as the 'poison pen letter' he had in his pocketbook. All the while the woman was still wrangling with him about the ammunition until, again, she gave way and took what proved to be 61 rounds from a drawer in the desk. From the press reports it would appear that the policeman made no mention of the letters, but put the sheet of paper away, along with the revolver and the ammunition. Amy Gillan would surely have known that having a gun without a licence was a serious offence, but was probably still shocked when told that she was under arrest, and would have to go to the police station. What would happen then, she wanted to know? She would appear before the magistrate on the Monday morning. But she could come home later this evening, surely? The sergeant did not seem to think it likely.

Her appearance at the Magistracy on Monday morning was brief since the police had more investigations to make. Gillan, who was not given the option of bail, found herself back in the confines of the Women's Prison, where she had unexpectedly spent that weekend. She was without access to sufficient funds to engage a solicitor. Perhaps she could not contact her husband, whose work on the steamers of the China coast took him away from Hong Kong for weeks at a time. But the investigations continued, and week by week she came before the magistrate just to hear another request from Detective Inspector Hanson, who was now in charge of the case, for a further remand. More letters were coming to light, as another lady from Carlton House came forward. This unsigned, offensive missive was clearly by the same hand, and on the same distinctive paper as the sergeant had removed from Gillan's writing desk. It dated from about a month earlier, and made reference to a popular new tiffin room (luncheon room) and bakery, Weismann's, at No. 34 Queen's Road. On enquiry, Sgt O'Sullivan found that Mr Hans Weismann had also received an anonymous letter, warning him off serving that particular lady, making nasty allegations about her moral standing.

When the case finally came to court on 3rd July, Amy Gillan was facing charges in connection with illegal possession of a weapon and ammunition and disorderly conduct calculated to provoke a breach of the peace. Det. Insp. Hanson asked that the gun case be taken first. She claimed that the gun was her husband's and denied ever pointing it at Chan Kwai. She also denied ever writing the letters. The magistrate, Mr Hazeland, made short shrift of the whole case, and would only consider the first three letters the police produced. The lady who had first made the complaint had decided not to press charges. While she might have thought that Gillan, having been in prison now for almost three weeks, had been sufficiently punished, she would also be aware that soon enough, this woman would again be a close neighbour. On that basis, Mr Hazeland was not minded to impose further penalties, aside from requiring her to produce a bond for $100 that she would keep the peace for one year. Naturally, the revolver and ammunition were confiscated.

But Amy Gillan was not a peaceful woman. It is unlikely that her near neighbours in Duddell Street welcomed her return after her sojourn in Victoria Gaol, and doubtless she had unfriendliness or even animosity to endure. However, she does seem to have contributed her share to the trouble in the apartment block. Scarcely eight weeks had passed before the police were receiving complaints about her again.[282] This time it was from Mr and Mrs William Wolfe, who lived on the same floor of the building. When they had taken their room Gillan was in prison on remand, and the house had seemed a nice quiet place to live. That changed, though, after 3rd July: Gillan straight away took against Mrs Wolfe, sticking her tongue out at her and making faces whenever they passed in the corridor. Described as 'religious-minded', Gillan was fond of repeatedly singing a small selection of hymns, at all hours of the day, and accompanying herself, not very expertly, on her rather out-of-tune piano. 'Human nature could stand it no longer', the Wolfes' solicitor explained in court, especially as the woman liked to change the words into bawdy parodies that scurrilously recounted what she thought Mrs Wolfe had been up to. The persecuted woman had to escape to friends' houses, and the couple were making enquiries to move out. Gillan also alleged – in song – that her neighbour had improper relations with her husband's brother, who was employed by the Public Works Dept. Matters came to a head on 28th August when, after repeated requests that she should desist from the 'hymn' singing, Mrs Wolfe asked her husband to go to talk to her. As he knocked on her door and called out, she rushed to the verandah, blowing a police whistle and screaming, "Help! Murder!" Needless to say, a crowd soon formed and three officers hurried up to the third floor. In amongst all this, Gillan tried to throw a bowl of water onto Mrs Wolfe's head.

282 *Hongkong Telegraph*, 3rd, 9th & 20th September 1907.

When the case first came to the magistrate's court, Gillan, who now had Mr F. X. d'Almada e Castro representing her, had instituted a counter-claim, for the Wolfe's disorderly conduct towards her.

The magistrate adjourned the case for two days, during which the rumour that the Wolfes had heard, that the landlords had given Gillan notice to quit her room, was confirmed. He threw out her claim and simply bound her over for a year, since she would soon be gone from Duddell Street. Yet, on 20th September, before the week was out, she was again at the Magistracy, to press a summons against two women for assaulting her and using indecent language towards her. One of the woman had brought a counter-claim, for disorderly conduct towards her eighteen-month-old son. Proceedings did not get very far that day, since one claim had been incorrectly submitted. But the press reporter said that, from the details given, it sounded as if the police would soon have another case against Gillan. Then there was also the matter of the binding-over that had been made on her back in July. Inspector Hanson raised it with the magistrate and arranged that a summons would be issued to her for breach of that order.

Here the story of Mrs Amy Gillan fades away. It had been followed, with some relish, by a reporter on *The Hongkong Telegraph,* but the other papers had given it scant room. Now even that paper could find no place for it, since the big news story of the day, "The Hongkong Tragedy", as the press called it, pushed such domestic trivia out.[283] Early in August there had been noxious smell in the baggage room of a steamer moored in the harbour, and the steward in charge had noticed a suspicious oozing fluid coming from the joints of one trunk. When opened, it proved to contain the decomposing body of a woman, who went by the name of Gertrude Dayton. A *chanteuse* from Singapore, she had recently being keeping company with a fellow American, ex-marine William Hall Adsetts. The man led the Hong Kong police on an extended merry dance, getting into fights with the Force's best boxers, before being caught. He had to be extradited from Singapore to Hong Kong and had vowed to kill the policemen who were sent to take him there. Det. Sgt Edmund O'Sullivan's life reverted to its accustomed blood, gore and danger. He

283 Patricia O'Sullivan, *Policing Hong Kong – an Irish History,* pp. 220-222.

had been involved with the case from its outset and had volunteered, with a colleague, to bring the murderer back to stand trial. At the dockside, he told the waiting journalists how they had not dared sleep during the 72-hour voyage from Singapore. Locked in a cabin with the violent Adsetts, they had to always be on their guard since the shackled man made frequent attempts to break loose and attack them.

Glamour at the Gaol Gates

At dawn this morning Miss Monteith arrived from Shanghai by the *S.S. Linan*, in the custody of Detective Murphy. In the detective's office I saw her smilingly and good-humouredly detailing the list of her property to Detective Murphy. Her elbows on the desk, and her white teeth flashing as she smiled upon the scribbling officer, she appeared more like a woman making a complaint against some disobedient amah or dishonest coolie than a woman about to say goodbye to liberty for nine months.

She looked rather pale and her white blouse heightened the pallor of her cheeks, but her eyes seemed so merry that one could barely conceive that she was under sentence and was shortly to answer to a number. She wore a panama hat with a black band, a soft collar and black tie, black skirt and silk shoes of the same sombre colour, relieved by silk bows. Her cabin trunks and travelling-rug were lying near.

…After the entry had been made in the police books, and the customary formalities had been concluded, she was led by the detective, who had her in charge. …As she passed down the gangway she smiled at an officer leaning against the rails. He wished her "good bye" and she smiled in reply.

That smile was the only indication of sadness I could perceive, and it was sufficient. Till then I had felt that she was treating the affair as though it was a great joke. …She endeavoured to carry the whole thing through to the end with a lightheartedness … She did not walk, but strolled into the gaol as though it were the reception hall of a hotel. But the momentary thought of a hotel was dispelled by the clang of the iron gates that shut her from the world and freedom.

The Hong Kong Telegraph, 28th June 1912

In the days before passports were compulsory for travel, and when people were not expected to have a copy of their birth certificate, proving one's identity could be troublesome. Conversely, slipping in and out of different personas was easier than it would later be. Cultivate the right acquaintance or two, then letters of introduction, a little money to have a respectable address for a while and then some spare to deposit, and one might have a bank account in a new country. Such <u>may</u> have been how Miriam Monteith, perhaps *alias* M. MacNaughton, operated. But her case is curious. It had occupied the courts in Shanghai and Hong Kong and fascinated Europeans and Chinese alike, as this apparently affluent society woman was accused of committing fraud in Peking. Just as the trial was set to begin, this case had to be withdrawn, only to be supplanted by a second indictment, instituted by the Hongkong and Shanghai Bank in Shanghai. After hearings that involved many twists and turns, the jury found her guilty, having retired for only ten minutes.[284]

The lack of passports does not mean that we cannot know something of this woman, although such information would not have been available to the authorities then. Yet even here, we are beset by Monteith's apparent determination to create confusion. She was in London when the 1911 census was taken, living in grand style with a fashionable American society hostess. She told the enumerator she was then 34, British and born in Edinburgh. A few weeks later, having crossed the Atlantic in a first-class cabin on the *R.M.S. Mauritania*, the American immigration records show her as 5 feet 4 inches (1.62 m.) tall with brown hair and eyes. But she displayed a great reticence about who she was, who her parents were, or how and why she came to be in China and Japan. The trouble was that a Miss M. MacNaughton had also visited Kobe, Shanghai, Peking, etc, and was equally evasive about her history. She may have been a writer or a journalist, as she sometimes claimed, she may have been friends with Monteith – or she may have been Monteith. MacNaughton left a trail of

284 *Hongkong Telegraph,* 9th, 21st, 24th & 27th May, 21st June 1912.

cheques drawn on bank accounts in several countries, and Monteith had cheque books from Simla, Rome, Beirut, London and New York. And some of these seemed to link up to accounts in MacNaughton's name.

MacNaughton's *modus operandi* seems to involve persuading a gullible gentleman to advance her a sum of money, for which she gave him a cheque, drawn on an account in another country. International banking being well developed by this time, such a request would not be so very strange or difficult to transact. Needless to say, the respectable-looking lady's cheque would not be honoured, but MacNaughton/Monteith seems sure enough of her victim's discomfiture that she even stays in touch with some, knowing that they will be too embarrassed to come chasing. Fritz Materna, in Peking, was the exception, and started the case against her. But soon he had cold feet and would not submit himself to the shame of being duped by a woman.

The Hongkong and Shanghai Bank had no such sensibilities, and it was for the recovery of $250 that they pursued her at the Shanghai court. Her arrest had been made in Hong Kong by Det. Lance-Sgt Tim Murphy in April 1912, whilst she was staying at the Peak Hotel. After an initial hearing at the Magistracy, Murphy took her north to stand trial and there the Chief Justice sentenced her to nine months' hard labour. With no suitable prison for a British woman in the international settlement, she returned to Hong Kong to serve her time. But as the eye witness who reported to *The Hongkong Telegraph* suspected, life in prison was a stark contrast to the Peak Hotel. As a western woman she may have been afforded the privacy of a cell, but, rather unusually, the prison at the time had six long-term inmates, of whom three had sentences of more than five years. Such were often held in the cells, rather than the association wards, so Monteith might have had to shift with the roughly 20 Chinese women in the convict ward. For the first three months, breakfast and supper comprised 6 ounces of bread and a pint of watery gruel. The midday meal was a similar amount of bread and potatoes, with a rotation of suet pudding, a few ounces of cooked meat or a pint of vegetable and meat soup added. After three months of this, water-based cocoa was substituted for the gruel on some days, and a little more meat added, with 8 ounces of curried fish as a special Sunday treat. Women's hard labour that year was laundry work for a few, but oakum picking for most.[285] At the end of her sentence both Monteith's complexion and hands must have been in a sorry state.

But as uncomfortable as the summer was in the prison, it was during the dank, colder winter months that the Gaol saw most illness. The cells and wards were unheated and prisoners had no way of getting dry after their compulsory 'exercise', outdoors in all weathers. Constitutions that were unused to such conditions suffered most. In December Monteith's health broke down, sufficiently for telegrams to be exchanged between Hong Kong, Shanghai and London over Christmas itself. Prisoner Monteith was ill and needed to be removed.[286] Would the Chief Justice in Shanghai who had sentenced her consent to this, asked the Governor? Certainly. He suggested that she was sent back to London straight away. The Colonial Office agreed, and the confirmatory letters start the predictable discussion about who would pay for this. But perhaps her health improved, as she did not return at this time. The discussion recommenced early in March, when she had just three weeks of her sentence to serve. It was debated whether the Governor should exercise his prerogative and pardon her for that portion of her sentence. No reason for this early release was given. By the time her sentence was due to end, the Superintendent of the Gaol had to disabuse London of the idea that the woman had funds of her own. Her last jewellery, he told them, had been given to creditors against a debt. She would leave Hong Kong with only her clothes and a few pounds he had collected for her from a charitable fund and some concerned gentlemen in the colony.

Hong Kong reported to the Colonial Office that Monteith had left on the *S.S. Delta*, on 15th March, a few days early, since there was no passage to London closer to the proper end of her sentence. They had furnished Scotland Yard with a description of her. Understandably, her name does not appear in the *Passengers Departed* lists in the newspapers. However, neither does she arrive in London on any of the steamers that connected

285 Gaols and Prisoners for 1912, *Blue Book* CO133/69.

286 Multiple despatches from Governor F. H. May to Lewis Harcourt, Secretary of State for the Colonies and from Foreign Office to Hong Kong and Colonial Office, in CO129/399, 400, 405 & 406.

with the *S.S. Delta,* and which had carried her fellow passengers on their onward journey. If she had decided to disembark in Singapore, for example, the shipping line would certainly have informed Hong Kong. Had she used the change of ship at Colombo to change direction altogether? When discussing her removal to the UK, the suggestion was made that she return to Shanghai. But a note by one of the Under Secretaries in the Colonial Office writes that if this had happened "she would inevitably have become a White Slave [prostitute] and would have had probably to be deported [back to the UK]". But this man surely underestimates Miriam Monteith. A woman so adept at 'living on her wits' would have done better than that.

However, she does appear in London, in 1916, in rather sorry circumstances, but then five years later in the United States, planning international travel once more. China expert Robert Bickers has researched her story and his website blog post includes the backgrounds of some of her connections and details about her time in China and Japan.[287] Since he wrote this further information has emerged, including the photograph which this author believes to be of Miriam Monteith.[288]

Passport application 1921, ancestry.co.uk.

In and out of trouble: the spirited women of the seventies

For some years, American Augusta Curtis had been caring for a large dog which a gentleman friend had entrusted to her while he was out of the colony.[289] Their understanding included that she would return the dog to him when he came back, or, if she left Hong Kong before that, would give it to a friend of his. The dog became a great pet, living in the house and being well fed and exercised by Curtis and her servants. During the summer of 1878, she decided to go to Shanghai for a time, and so sent

287 Robert Bickers, *Living on her wits,* 2015, https://robertbickers.net/2015/07/28/miriam-monteith-in-shanghai/

288 More of her story can be read at www.socialhistoryhk.com

289 The story appears in *The China Mail,* 20th August 1878 and in *Hongkong Daily Press* the following day.

the dog to her friend's agent, William Reiners, a partner in Melchers & Co, a prominent trading firm. She was told that he had agreed to look after it until the original owner returned. But Curtis did not leave as soon as she had intended, and soon her servants brought word to her that the dog was not being cared for as she had, that it was to be sent away or even put down. Reiners, not being able to keep it in his house, had made arrangements for the dog to be dispatched, perhaps back to its original owner. When the irate woman demanded it back, he refused, and told her of his plan. Thus thwarted, Curtis decided to take out a writ against him, but was advised that she needed to make some financial claim to proceed. The case, for the return of the dog and $100 damages, came to the Court of Summary Jurisdiction on Tuesday, 20th August. Reiners' solicitor, Mr Wotton, told the Puisne Judge James Russell, that the dog had not been maltreated – it was rather that some people had very indulgent ideas about the way an animal should be looked after, feeding it on mutton chops, perhaps. It was no longer in the colony, and he submitted that the plaintiff had made out no case. Augusta Curtis said that she had never wanted the money: it was only the dog she hoped to recover. The judge explained to her that by sending the dog to Reiners without condition, she had relinquished all claim on the animal, and her case was thus non-suited.

At about 10.30 a.m. both parties left the court building, Curtis probably sooner than Reiners. Feeling aggrieved and still furious with the man, she hurried down to Queen's Road and purchased a horsewhip. Her next stop was at Kruse and Co., a cigar and tobacco store in the same road, where she appears to have been a frequent customer, since Mr Schonberger there knew her by name. She confided her troubles to this man and told him she would whip Reiners – pulling the horsewhip out from beneath her jacket to confirm this. He spoke soothingly to her, sitting her down and giving her some iced water to calm her. Although she seemed a little quieter, he could not dissuade her from her intention, although she was using a lot of American slang which the German did not fully understand. Leaving the shop, she got back into her (sedan) chair and instructed the bearers to take her up Queen's Road.

Meanwhile, Reiners had gone to the Hong Kong Club and then home for a few minutes. At 11.15 a.m. he was out again, walking down to the main thoroughfare with Mr Georg of Siemssen and Co. They were approaching the Clock Tower at Pedder Street when the latter alerted him to Augusta Curtis, who seemed to be following them. The men stopped to allow her chair to come alongside them, whereupon she dismounted and set about Reiners with the whip. Startled, he managed to deflect the blows with his stick. Her language was intemperate, with threats to murder him. A shop proprietor nearby rushed out and took the whip from her, while Reiners summoned a Sikh constable close by. He took Curtis into custody and told her bearers to accompany him to the police station. The party all made their way up Pedder Street, Curtis still using foul language, although much of this was fortunately muffled by the chair blinds, which were down. In the charge room, she lamented that she had not struck the man. "I'll do it even if it costs me $5,000 or I have to go to prison for a long time!" was her promise. Reiners told the inspector he believed his life to be in danger from her, so the officer advised him to take out a summons against her, which could be brought to the magistrate that very afternoon.

Both parties had engaged solicitors: Reiners having made contact again with Mr Wotton, while Curtis had instructed Mr Dennys. At the hearing there was some debate about the earlier case, and evidence given by Mr Schonberger of the cigar store and Mr Georg, although the police had not found anyone to testify to the purchase of the whip that morning. The man's solicitor made much of how alarmed and threatened his client had felt, that this was therefore not just a case of simple assault, but had murderous intent – or, at any rate, the threat of such. Mr Georg, whose evidence was more impartial than that of his friend, had less talk of murder, although he had found the whole incident alarming.

Mr Dennys' defence rested on the character and mode of life of Augusta Curtis. The newspaper reports had given her as "a well dressed woman", and then carried the telling line from Mr Wotton, "If women of this description are to be tolerated, it is imperative that they behave themselves." Her solicitor described her as having a certain notoriety and being a woman of such a class as men who associated themselves with were likely to get punished. She had been some years in the colony but was planning to leave for Shanghai at the end of that week. Unlike some of the other western women whose stories are recounted in this chapter, Augusta Curtis would appear to have been an independent – career? – prostitute, who kept herself in a fair standard of living. Mr Dennys sought to impress on the magistrate that such a person, living a very different life to that of most western women in the colony, and possessed of a fiery temperament, could not be judged by the same standards as others. Her reaction to being frustrated in her attempt to recover her pet had to be seen as a natural response for such a woman.

Mr May was not inclined to afford her any leniency. He could not agree with Mr Dennys that this was a case of simple assault, arising from the heat of the moment, nor that her gender or station in life in any way lessened her culpability:

> The defendant has made a very open defiance of law and order in the Colony by using violence of a very grave character to a gentleman who, so far as I can see, had done no injury to her… The defendant's threat to murder Mr Reiners is, I think, just one of those very stupid expressions women use without any meaning attaching to them… but that she had intention to do violence to Mr Reiners is quite apparent from what she did… I sentence her to three days' imprisonment and to pay a fine of $40, and in default to one months' further imprisonment. At the expiration of her sentence she will find security in two householders of $200 each to keep the peace for the next six months.

Nothing more has come to light about this woman. From what we learn of her in the two newspaper reports, it seems probable that she was able to pay the fine rather than to endure the extreme discomfort of the Women's Prison for a whole summer month. And perhaps it was not too difficult for her to find the necessary guarantors amongst her clients and acquaintances. In any case, she would be sailing to Shanghai on the Saturday, the day after her release from gaol.

Disreputable but not defeated

To conclude, let us return to where this chapter started, with more of Hong Kong's western, but home-grown, 'unquiet women', this pair scraping a living on the edges of society, but apparently finding some enjoyment and happiness amidst the squalor and penury.

Screams and sobs, definitely female, came from the house.[290] Surely those weren't the cries of a Chinese woman? A heavy thump followed, as if someone had fallen. As Inspector Grimes, in charge of this western part of the town, decided to investigate and called over a constable to accompany him, the voice shrieked out, "Oh dear! Don't kill me!" In that moment it came to him: this was No. 10 Battery Road, where that infernal nuisance, Mrs Albert, lived. Every day, it seemed, she was pestering his desk sergeant with complaints about neighbours or tradesmen, and often there was more than a suspicion of drink about her. But he'd still better make sure she wasn't being murdered. Entering the house, he found the confusion he'd expect from a woman of her sort, but with the obvious signs of a scuffle and more. She was already on her feet again and fighting with her assailant. Dusk had fallen that Wednesday evening in May, 1875, so with the room lit only by a kerosene lamp, it took Insp. Grimes a moment to realise that the man was her paramour, William Bristow. The inspector and his constable interposed themselves between the warring parties and then tried to get some sense of the problem, but Mary Albert was still shrieking and obviously not sober.

Bristow had hit her, and not with just a slap, either, that much was evident. Although he was now calm again, the incident could not be ignored. Insp. Grimes told them that they would hear from the court about this, that they would both have to attend tomorrow. His sympathies were very much with the man, not only because of his knowledge of Albert's character. Bristow had appeared in Court sometimes, but there were few of the tavern barmen in that part of town who had not. He had worked in the Diver's Arms for some time now and had helped the inspector with an inebriated client on occasions. He wasn't, in the inspector's opinion, a violent man. Probably the man had received plenty of provocation: Bristow was known for being kind to this woman, so this attack seemed

290 *Hongkong Daily Press*, 14th May 1875.

out of character. The summons was duly issued but the next day and, not entirely to the officer's surprise, only Bristow appeared. The barkeeper was probably able to give some idea of the places the police might find the woman, so a constable was dispatched with a warrant for her arrest. Albert was required to attend court on Monday.

The appearance before Mr Russell on 13th May was brief, the officer explaining the situation as he saw it and Bristow realised that he did not really need to say anything more in his own defence. He was required to find a personal security of $25 to keep the peace for three months, but was not fined. Albert had stormed out of the house on the 12th: presumably she had left him and intended to live elsewhere. But she would not let him go without getting the 'last word'. The barman had returned to his post at the Diver's Arms after the hearing, but in his absence Albert went to his home in Battery Road and removed various articles of his property. Returning later, he realised what had happened and went in search of her. By this time she had consumed a few drinks and seemed to want to recommence their fight. Now it was Bristow who received the blows and punches and, with much offensive language, Albert told him she would not give him his belongings back. At this, Bristow called out for a constable, West Point Police Station being just at the end of the road, and P.C. 38 came running. He arrested Albert and took her into custody, but not without receiving a torrent of abuse and obscenities.

Mary Albert probably had to endure two nights in the Women's Prison before she appeared once more at the Magistrate's Court.[291] This time she faced the older and more severe Mr Charles May, who took a very dim view of western women 'letting the side down' and disgracing themselves in public. Not only was she guilty of assault but had given the police much trouble, doubtless in front of many interested local bystanders. Her plea, that the constable had some spite against her, cut no ice and he fined her $5, in default of which she would spend fourteen days in gaol with hard labour. Unless her erstwhile provider was again kind to her, Albert had no option but to be led away, back into the charge of long-time Prison Matron, Mrs Collins.

---

291 *Hongkong Daily Press,* 18th May 1875.

In the 1870s the number of non-Chinese women in the colony was still very small, and any named appearance, even in connection with something as innocuous as attending a civic event or contributing to church work is rare. But the same month as Albert was sullying the reputation of British womanhood, the first of several references to another western woman, who became quite an habitué of the courts appears. Mrs Mary or Molly Voge, alias Miss Molly Cecil or Mrs Murray, lived in Bridges Street above Hollywood Road and close to the Central Police Station. She, too, was in an irregular relationship with a barman, an American, James Mehan. He was not the steady man that Insp. Grime's considered Bristow to be, had worked in at least three taverns in the past eighteen months and was now at the Crown and Anchor.

On the evening of the same day as Mary Albert was arrested for assault, Molly Voge ran out of No. 5 Bridges Street and told a European constable that the man with whom she lived had attacked and beaten her.[292] The marks of injury about her head were obvious and the officer, together with an Indian colleague, accompanied her back to the house. Mehan was asleep now. Voge explained that she had needed to wait until he was worn out with beating her before she could get help. P.C. 94 woke him and tried to question him, but received a volley of abuse, both verbal and physical. With some difficulty, therefore, they arrested him for both assaults.

Since neither Albert nor Voge were married to their assailants, there was no difficulty with them giving evidence against these men. When the case appeared before Mr May on Monday, her story was simple. "I have been living with Mehan for some time now, and all that long while he has used me ill, beating me and hitting me. On Saturday night he beat me dreadfully. He cut my head, and bruised me all over my body. I have had enough, now, Sir, I just want to be rid of him." The erstwhile bartender had a great deal more to say for himself. Yes, he admitted to hitting the woman, but the row was about some letters she'd received from someone living in the Hongkong Hotel. "It's very hard on me, your Worship, after all I've done for this woman, to be treated thus! I've had to pay off all her debts. Last year I managed to get a good position in Japan, and was doing

292 *Hongkong Daily Press*, 18th May 1875.

comfortable, like, making enough money, but she came up to Japan and dragged me back here." He only lived with her because she had implored him – he had the letters from her to prove this. There was no comfort with her, she was always drunk and far too lazy to cook for herself, let alone him, or do anything around the house. Sometimes she was so inebriated that she threw bottles at him the moment he came through the door. He could even show the magistrate the mark of the latest injury to his head. Maybe Mehan felt that his tale of woe was not going down well with Mr May, for then he changed tack and portrayed himself as the honourable man, trying to do the right thing by this woman. He had been thinking of getting away from her, he said, and taking the mail boat the previous weekend, but he did not want to leave her homeless, so he had remained.

Charles May had heard such stories before and was not taken in. Yet neither was he sympathetic towards Voge. Having made up his mind about her, he told Mehan that the punishment he was about to mete out was more to warn him against any similar behaviour than as a penalty for his assault on the woman. To live with such a man as he, for so long and to endure his beatings, she must, Mr May stated, be an idiot or, as Mehan himself had said, a drunkard. Mehan had to find $5 for hitting Voge but $10 for attacking the policemen. He must also provide two sureties of $50 each from amongst his friends and acquaintances to bind him over to be of good behaviour for six months.

The couple's next appearance in Court gives us a little insight into their lives during the summer months.[293] Voge again charged him, this time with both assault and robbery. She was still in his first-floor rooms in Bridges Street and Mehan either lived there or was a frequent visitor. On Tuesday morning, 21st September, the barman had, by her account, stormed into the rooms and immediately started hitting her and threatening to "kick her brains out". "I painted the gallows last time I was in gaol and I swear I'll be the first to hang for you on it", he had snarled. Then, taking up a small writing desk of hers, he had kicked it down the stairs. Voge rushed out of the house and fled for refuge to a friend's, staying away that day and not daring to return. In the evening, she went

293 *Hongkong Daily Press,* 23rd September 1875.

to the Magistrate's office and was given admission to Mr May. There she pleaded with him to give her protection. On this occasion, he was more sympathetic towards her, for he gave her an order to take to the police, such that they would arrest the man.

After taking the paper to the report room of the Central Station, Voge returned home, where she found the rooms in a worse state than she had left them. Her servant told her that Mehan had come back just thirty minutes ago and taken away her wooden box, the one that contained her clothes. The man had also torn down and destroyed an oil painting of which she was very fond. Once more, she went back to the police station and this time P.C. 30, J. Lindsay, agreed to inspect the damage. Another Chinese servant there told him he had seen Mehan break up the box and the picture. The barman would have been a well-known figure to P.C. Lindsay, whose 'patch' this was, and the policeman took off down Queen's Road, in and out of every public house, sure of finding him soon. His first find was Voge's box in one of the beer houses and not long after that he caught up with his man, very much the worse for drink, in the Liverpool Arms. Mehan had no intention of coming quietly and although, with the help of the barkeeper, P.C. Lindsay manhandled him into a (sedan) chair he escaped and the process had to be repeated several times. Eventually he had so broken up the chair that the constable had to procure another and his charge was finally taken to the police cells at Central Station.

But in the Court next day, this time in front of Mr Russell, Mehan, ever the optimist when it came to pulling wool over eyes, explained to the magistrate he had thought the constable was larking with him. Of course, he would have cooperated had he realised earlier that P.C. Lindsay wanted him to come to the station. Mr Russell heard evidence from the complainant who told him of her treatment and her loss. She valued her box of clothes at about $50, no small amount. Then the constable gave his account and that of Voge's servants, but the magistrate would not allow the defendant to go further than his excuse for giving trouble to the police. He adjourned the case and since bail was neither requested nor offered, Mehan went to gaol until the hearing was resumed, six days later. It seems curious that no mention was made of the sureties Mehan had provided in the earlier case, the six months term of which had not yet expired. The clue may come in the man's reference to "when he was last in gaol". If convicted of another offence in the intervening period and on hard labour, he was perhaps given the disagreeable work of painting the gallows. A new scaffold had been made, ready to be erected in the Magistracy compound on Arbuthnot Road when it was next needed.[294] It seems that he had already forfeited those securities.

When he next stood in the dock, Mehan put his case with his customary fulsomeness to Mr Russell.[295] He denied stealing any of Voge's property, but did not account for the box being in one of the public houses. If he had broken up anything in the house, it was only after great provocation from the woman, who had been throwing things at him. He really had such trouble with her, he said, implying that it was he who was the injured party. By now, this magistrate knew the background of this case but despite the defendant's police record, his sympathies appear to be more with him than with Voge. He told the man:

> I have no doubt that there is some truth when you claim that you have been greatly annoyed by the prosecutrix, but you have not shown any determination to shake her off. If you had really wished to get rid of her, you had a remedy to hand. When she so persistently annoyed you, you should have given her into custody. But still you stuck to her, and now, to punish her, you maliciously broke up her property, some of which you know full well cannot be replaced.

Mr Russell was prepared to be lenient with him and gave him just fourteen days' imprisonment, without hard labour, for maliciously damaging property. He did not punish him for any attack or threat to Voge. However, Mehan was yet again required to find two sureties, this time for $25 each for three months. Addressing both, he told them

---

294 *Hongkong Daily Press,* 27th November 1875, 'Execution at the Hongkong Gaol'.

295 *Hongkong Daily Press,* 29th September 1875.

that, should they come before the Court again, they would doubtless be deported.

So now Molly Voge was free of this violent man, at least for a short while. She returned to the house in Bridges Street and picked up her life again, trying somehow to restore what she had lost. But what sort of life was it? Like so many, she appears in Hong Kong only for a brief time and, in her case, achieves a certain notoriety. The little columns that record her appearances in court have headings such as 'Mrs Voge again'. Her aliases, suggest that there had been husbands in the colony earlier on. Bearing in mind James Russell's suggestion of deportation, which would indicate that she was not – at that point – a British national, a life story can conjectured. Since few western women came to Hong Kong independently, perhaps Mrs Murray, the former Miss Molly Cecil, had arrived as a young wife with her soldier husband. He might, like so many soldiers, have succumbed to disease and died early on, or he may have purchased his discharge and freed himself both from the army and his wife. This could explain her re-adoption of her maiden name, distancing herself from the disgrace of having been abandoned. The papers provide no description of her other than as a "married woman": she is probably between 25 to 35 years old. But there was no occupation for a single woman in Hong Kong. All domestic service was undertaken by Chinese (male) servants, known as 'boys', no western family would employ such a woman as a governess and shop work would be limited to the handful of establishments catering for European female requisites. Thus, without independent means, she had to find another man to provide her with a home, unless she was to enter one of the small number of European brothels.

Had she been a prostitute there would have been some reference to this, given that she features in reports on at least six occasions. The administration discretely repatriated British prostitutes, especially those in any way troublesome, to prevent the portrayal of their women-kind as anything other than decorous and virtuous females. Her not leaving Hong Kong until the end of the year, and that by mutual agreement, rather suggests against this, too. There is a reference to the house in Bridges Street as a sly brothel in a later report, but there is nothing to substantiate this, and appears to refer to Voge and a female companion having a series of lovers. This road, running above Hollywood Road and the Man Mo Temple, was on the edge of Taipingshan and well into the Chinese part of the city, but contained some larger properties as well as the usual shop-houses. The slightly Germanic-sounding Voge and the absence of a Mr Voge in any of the other records suggests a German or Swedish seaman, based for a time in Hong Kong, but then not at liberty to take his wife with him when he returned to the sea. Since women, at marriage, generally took the nationality of the husband, this might account for the magistrate's reference. But the conclusion of her story, or at least, the Hong Kong part of it, finds the Colonial Administration taking responsibility for her.

Molly Voge had a friend in living further down Bridges St., one Mrs Lewis. She was rather an exceptional woman at the time, in that she was married to a Chinese, Foong Sing, and still holding down a position with a European family, despite having a child of her own. Her husband was absent and she and Voge were much thrown together. Earlier that summer Lewis/Foong had entertained Private J. Hill from the garrison one evening, but he had become drunk and slept too soundly to get back to his barracks by 5 a.m. the next morning.[296] P.C. Lindsay then found and charged him with desertion. He was taken into custody pending instructions from the military authorities. Although it was an offence to harbour a deserter which normally resulted in a prison term, no charge was made against her. Maybe the penitence the soldier expressed, his assertions that he had not meant to desert and that drink had got the better of him sufficed to exonerate his friend this time.

In the middle of September she had to leave her employment when she became ill, thus losing her means of paying the rent. She moved in with Mrs Voge, perhaps as Mehan went to gaol on remand during the hearing of the assault case. Bridges Street's proximity to the Central Police Station had proved to have its uses, but perhaps there were disadvantages, too. Being part of sharp-eyed P.C. Lindsay's beat meant that the officer knew rather more about her affairs that she would like. The visit of a young soldier to her rooms at 9 p.m. on Friday evening, 1st October,

296 *Hongkong Daily Press,* 13th August 1875.

did not escape his attention.[297] Private Edwin Cooper, also of the 80th Regiment had started drinking in the Hollywood Road taverns, came up to Mrs Voge for more and then stayed longer than he should and was not back in camp when his leave expired at midnight. On the Sunday Voge had to give up Mehan's rooms (in anticipation of his release from gaol) and move a few doors down into a single room. Perhaps Cooper made himself useful carrying the women's belongings, but he was in uniform all this time. That afternoon Constable Lindsay read a report from the military of a deserter and recalled some whispers he had picked up earlier. He went straight round to the women's room in No. 19, Bridges St and asked them if Cooper was there.

They firmly denied that the man was there, but P.C. Lindsay pressed them. "Wasn't he with you in No. 5, didn't I see him go in there?" Still, they would have none of it. But during the brief conversations the constable had caught sight of movement across to the cookhouse. He went downstairs and out across to the kitchen where he found Cooper standing with his back to the wall. "Why haven't you gone back to your barracks, man? You know they've put a call out for you?" Cooper seemed quite taken off his guard and at a loss what to reply. Eventually the soldier said that he had intended to, but would the constable just let him stay till nightfall? By this time the two women had joined them and heard the request. "Do let him stay, Mr Lindsay, you know what it'll be like if everyone can see him being marched off. I'm sure he'll go with you later." But the officer had his duty to do and Cooper, knowing when he was beaten, went back upstairs to collect his coat and cap, which he had hidden from view. Before he left, the constable warned the women. "I'm sorry, ladies, but you know I must report this. There'll be a summons for you tomorrow, for sure. It's a very serious offence, you know, if you let a deserter stay in your house."

The summons duly arrived, and both women had to present themselves at the Magistracy on Tuesday morning. The case opened with the policeman's description of finding Cooper and the conversations they had in the house. The constable also reminded the magistrate he had arrested a deserter in Mrs Foong Sing's house on 10th August. Private

---

297 *Hongkong Daily Press,* 5th & 6th October 1875.

Cooper spoke next, explaining that he had stayed on at Molly Voge's house from 9p.m. on the Friday right through until 1p.m. on Sunday, when the women had moved rooms. Yes, he had been in uniform when he went down the road with them. Trying to do his best for the women, he turned and said to them, "You did beg of me to leave on Saturday morning, and several times". Magistrate May asked him, therefore, why he did not do as his hostesses asked. "Your Honour, I thought that once being late, I might stay and enjoy myself as much as I could as there would be the same punishment inflicted for two days as for one."

Now it was the defendants' turn in the dock. Voge, answering to Miss Molly Cecil on this occasion, knew enough of Mr May not to attempt any explanation other than to tell him she had advised the man to leave, but he wouldn't listen and had fallen asleep. Lewis/Foong protested that she had nothing to do with it and nothing to say. She knew the man was there, but she was only sharing Mrs Voge's home because she had none of her own, "If you can call it a home." Obviously it was a step down in the world for her. "He was no visitor of mine, I assure you, your Honour. He came to the new place with us, but we hadn't invited him. I had no wish to invite him there." Questioned whether she had denied Cooper's presence to the constable, she responded, "Well, I do admit that I told Mr Lindsay he wasn't there, but only with a feeling not to get the man harmed."

Fortunately for the women, Mr May was feeling magnanimous that day. Despite P.C. Lindsay's reminder of Mrs Foong Sing's recent involvement in a similar case, he told the women that although their offence was a serious one and the law had to be carried out in connection with deserters, he would be lenient on this occasion. But they might not expect similar consideration if they were up again on the same charge. He would fine them just $25 each.[298] Could they find that, he asked? If not, could they sell some of their goods and chattels? Oh dear, if not they would have to go to gaol for ten days each. Both women protested that they had nothing to sell, nothing of any value at all. Then Mrs Foong Sing said, "But I have a child, if that is any good?" The turn of phrase

---

298 A huge amount for either woman to find, probably five times their monthly rent and more than half the police constable's monthly pay.

was perhaps unexpected from a western woman, although, as has been seen, Chinese women might put up a child as surety on a loan. Was she really suggesting this to Mr May? Perhaps she was trying to claim some exemption from gaol? But realising that the magistrate was not moved she asked if she could bring her child into the gaol with her. The two women and the child went to prison for the next ten days.

The following day Mehan was released from his gaol term and presumably returned to Bridges Street, doubtless soon hearing about his former mistress. It would seem that this was the final split for the pair and James Mehan disappears from the records in Hong Kong. Lewis/Foong received free medical care for her illness whilst 'inside' and might have found work afterwards, if she could get a character reference from her former employers, although she remained in the Bridges Street area. After her release on 15th November, Private Cooper renewed his friendship with Voge and helped her furnish her new room and visited her on occasions. But, once more, the woman still got her name onto the court list, even before the month was out.[299] On this occasion, she was the named party in a case in the Summary Jurisdiction Court, which ruled on disputed debts and financial cases. The judge found against her to the sum of $15.46, although the case was not reported by the papers. She had not attended the hearing so Thomas McBean, the bailiff and summons server, had to come round to her room on Friday 26th November to serve a warrant to get the money, or goods in lieu. The door was opened to him by Cooper, who called Voge out from the back of the room. Mr McBean had scarcely managed to explain what he wanted before she started screaming profanities at him and trying to hit him. She was obviously drunk, and ran into the cookhouse, emerging with some kitchen utensil with which to attack Mr McBean. Fending off the blows, he said that the furniture might suffice, but Cooper quickly told him of his ownership of that and declared that he would take it away, if need be. Perhaps fearing that the soldier might be as violent as his lover, the bailiff assured him he wouldn't dare touch it in that case, but would return to see Mrs Voge the next day. On Saturday he fared no better with the payment, but at least

---

299 *Hongkong Daily Press,* 1st December 1875.

the woman was not drunk or abusive. She identified her own possessions and Mr McBean put a man in charge over these few things.

The bailiff had reported to the court and to the police of the treatment he had received in Bridges Street, and knew that she would soon receive a summons. But according to her version, the arrival, on Tuesday morning, 30th November, of the order requiring her to answer a charge of assault and making use of offensive language was the first she knew of Mr McBean's initial visit. Even her recollection of his Saturday visit was hazy, she claimed. She wrote an apology to Mr McBean that Tuesday morning, but knew that she still had to appear before Mr May in the afternoon. There she explained that her doctor had ordered her to take brandy and opium (for what complaint was not recorded) but the mixture had made her very stupid. She didn't even know of the summons for debt until that morning. Mr May was not minded to give her any benefit of the doubt and told her that the truth was, she was always drunk. It was no good sending in an apology to Mr McBean. He was not an ordinary member of the public, the bailiff could not rescind the charge, since he was in the employ of the courts. Attacking an Officer of the Court was a serious matter. Voge would go to gaol once more, this time for fourteen days with hard labour.

So for two weeks, Molly Voge joined the other female prisoners 'doing hard'. This likely involved either oakum picking or washing blankets and prison uniforms brought into the women's area, since they were not permitted to enter the main prison laundry, where male prisoners worked. But in that time there were discussions going on at high levels about her and that she had visits from the Acting Superintendent of the prison, Mr G. L. Tomlin, and the clerk to the Colonial Secretary, Mr H.E. Wodehouse. Voge was now destitute and becoming a by-word for low-life scandal, and thus far from the picture of respectable gentility expected of British women in the colony. Perhaps she had friends or relatives in Australia? At any rate, the Colonial Secretary decided that the administration would provide her with a passage to Sydney on the next sailing following her release. She seems to have realised that Hong Kong had little left for her and welcomed the chance this solution gave.

Knowing that an extra few days in gaol would relieve her of the problem of finding her own food and lodging, she obtained permission to stay there until it was time for her to leave the colony. But even now, Mrs Molly Voge could continue to make good material for the papers. On the day that her sentence expired, the Warden, Mr A. Grey, sanctioned her return to Bridges Street to collect her belongings.[300] She was to be accompanied by a turnkey, Robert Forbes. The pair left the gaol at 9 a.m. but found that Private Cooper, who had the key to the room, was not there and would not be coming until later in the day. However, soon Voge was joined by friends: a man named Richardson and then Lewis/ Foong. The group became a party, perhaps an early farewell celebration, and the brandy flowed. Turnkey Forbes had been enjoying himself, even if he did not have too much of the brandy: it was a welcome change from the drudgery of supervising prisoners in the gaol. Some time into the merriment, Cooper turned up along with a fellow soldier and more bottles. By now Voge had succumbed to the intoxicant effects of the cheap and often highly potent liquor. When conscience struck the turnkey and he tried to get her to return to the gaol, she resisted and appealed to her soldier-friend. He stepped between them and promptly gave the gaoler a great punch in the face, blackening his eye.

Eventually, and probably with the intervention of the police, Voge and Turnkey Forbes returned some 600 yards to the gaol. Cooper was brought before Magistrate Russell the next day, with Forbes and Voges as witnesses. At least on this occasion, the hapless woman was not being charged with any offence. Having listened to the tale, Mr Russell passed sentence on Cooper for the assault of Turnkey Forbes and fined him $5. He also informed the gaoler that he would let the Governor, no less, know of his conduct. This had amounted to complete neglect of duty. Forbes, who had only taken up his appointment in April of that year, does not appear on the staff lists of the gaol for 1876. Doubtless he was summarily dismissed.

Meanwhile, Voge spent Christmas in the small Women's Prison. She would have been allowed visitors, who could have brought in gifts of food and clothes (but not alcohol) for her. It was as Miss Cecil that she

---

300 *Hongkong Daily Press,* 16th December 1875.

last appears in the newspapers of Hong Kong, recorded as sailing out of the colony on New Year's Eve, 1875, in a second-class cabin aboard the *S.S. Normanby,* to start a new life in Sydney.[301]

301 *Hongkong Daily Press,* 3rd January 1876.

BIBLIOGRAPHY

Primary sources

Great Britain, Colonial Office, Original Correspondence: Hong Kong, 1841-1951, Series (CO)129.

Great Britain, Colonial Office, Executive and Legislative Council Minutes: Hong Kong, (from 1844), Series (CO)131.

Great Britain, Colonial Office, *Hongkong Blue Books*, 1844-1940, Series (CO) 133.

Hong Kong Civil Service List and General Orders, Hong Kong, Colonial Secretary's Office, from 1904.

Hongkong Government Gazette, Series (CO) 132.

Newspapers: *The China Mail* (from 1845).
Hongkong Daily Press (1864-1941).
The Hongkong Weekly Press (1895-1909).
The Hongkong Telegraph (from 1881).
South China Morning Post (from 1903).
The Friend of China (1842-1848).

The Chronicle and Directory for China, Corea, Japan and the Philippines, etc., Hong Kong, Hong Kong Daily Press Office, from 1866.

Web-based sources

Hong Kong War Diary, built, developed and maintained by Tony Banham. http://www.hongkongwardiary.com

Gwulo: Old Hong Kong, built, developed and maintained by David Bellis. http://gwulo.com

China Families, directed by Robert Bickers, site developed and maintained by University of Bristol. https://www.chinafamilies.net

Bickers, Robert, *Living on her wits*. https://robertbickers.net

Bushak, Lecia, *A brief history of the Menstrual Period: how women dealt with their cycles throughout the ages.* 2016 https://www.medicaldaily.com/menstrual-period-time-month-history-387252

The Industrial History of Hong Kong Group, maintained and developed by Hugh Farmer. https://industrialhistoryhk.org

Purcell Miller Tritton LLP, *The Old Central Police Station and Victoria Prison, Hong Kong.* https://www.epd.gov.hk/eia/register/report/eiareport/eia_1912010/HTML/EIA%20Report/Annexes/Annex%20A1.pdf

Index to CO129, Great Britain, Colonial Office, Original Correspondence, compiled and developed by Elizabeth Sinn and Louis Ha. http://sunzi.lib.hku.hk/co129/

Rev. Dr Carl Smith cards available through Hong Kong Public Records Office website. https://search.grs.gov.hk/en/index.xhtml

Secondary sources – books and articles

Bandon, Mandy, *Administering the Empire, 1901-1968. A Guide to the Records of the Colonial Office in The National Archives of the UK.* London, Institute of Historical Research, 2015.

Bickley, Gillian (ed.), *A Magistrate's Court in Nineteenth Century Hong Kong, Court in Time.* Hong Kong, Proverse Hong Kong, 2009.

Early Beginnings of British Community (1841-1898) in Chu, Cindy Yik-yi (ed.) *Foreign Communities in Hong Kong 1840s-1950s.* New York, Palgrave Macmillan, 2005.

Cameron, Nigel, *An Illustrated History of Hong Kong.* Hong Kong, Oxford University Press, 1991.

Carroll, John M., *A Concise History of Hong Kong.* Hong Kong, Hong Kong University Press, 2007.

Carroll, John M., *Edge of Empires. Chinese Elites and British Colonials in Hong Kong.* Hong Kong, Hong Kong University Press, 2007.

Chan-Yeung, Moira M. W. *A Medical History of Hong Kong 1842-1941.* Hong Kong, Chinese University Press, 2018.

Clark, Douglas, *Gunboat Justice. British and American Law Courts in China and Japan, 1842-1943.* Vol. 1*White Man, White Law, White Gun 1842-1900.* Hong Kong, Earnshaw Books, 2015.

Crisswell, Colin & Watson, Mike, *The Royal Hong Kong Police (1841-1945).* Hong Kong, Macmillan Hong Kong, 1982.

Dobash, Russell P, Dobash, Emerson, R, & Gutteridge, Sue, *The Imprisonment of Women.* Oxford, Oxford University Press, 1986.

Eitel, E. J., *Europe in China: The History of Hong Kong from the Beginning to the Year 1882.* Hong Kong, Kelly and Walsh 1895 reprinted Hong Kong, Oxford University Press, 1983.

Faure, David, *The Common People in Hong Kong History: their livelihood and aspirations until the 1930s* in Pui-tak Lee, ed., *Colonial Hong Kong and Modern China: Interaction and Reintegration.* Hong Kong, Hong Kong University Press, 2005.

Greenwood, Walter *John Joseph Francis, Citizen of Hong Kong, A Biographical Note* in *Journal of the Royal Asiatic Society Hong Kong Branch* Vol. 26 1986 pp 17-45.

Ha Keloon Louis *The Foundation of the Catholic Mission in Hong Kong 1841-1894.* Hong Kong, Joint Publishing (H.K.) Co. Ltd. 2018.

Hamilton, Sheilah E., *Watching over Hong Kong. Private Policing 1841-1941.* Hong Kong, Hong Kong University Press, 2008

Harrop, Phyllis. *Hong Kong Incident.* Eyre and Spottiswood, London 1943.

Hoe, Susanna, *The Private Life of Old Hong Kong. Western Women in the British Colony 1841-1941.* Hong Kong, Oxford University Press, 1991.

Holdsworth, May & Munn, Christopher, *Dictionary of Hong Kong Biography.* Hong Kong, Hong Kong University Press, 2012.

Holdsworth, May & Munn, Christopher, *Crime Justice and Punishment in Colonial Hong Kong. Central Police Station, Central Magistracy and Victoria Gaol.* Hong Kong, Hong Kong University Press, 2020.

Howell, Philip, *Race, Space and the Regulation of Prostitution in Colonial Hong Kong,* in John M. Carroll and Chi-Kwan Mark (eds.), *Critical Readings on the Modern History of Hong Kong, vol. 1.* Leiden, Brill, 2015.

Jaschok, Maria, *Concubines and Bondservants: a social history.* Hong Kong, Hong Kong University Press, 1988.

Jaschok, Maria & Miers, Suzanne, eds. *Women and Chinese Patriarchy. Submission, Servitude and Escape.* Hong Kong, Hong Kong University Press, 1994.

Lethbridge, Henry J. *Hong Kong, Stability and Change: a collection of essays.* Hong Kong, Hong Kong University Press, 1978.

Levine, Philippa, *Prostitution, Race and Politics: Policing Venereal Disease in the British Empire,* New York, London, Routledge Keegan Paul, 2003.

Miners, Norman J. *Hong Kong under Imperial Rule, 1912-1941.* Hong Kong, Oxford University Press, 1987

Morris, Norval & Rothman, David J., eds. *The Oxford History of the Prison. The Practice of Punishment in Western Society.* Oxford, Oxford University Press, 1995.

Munn, Christopher, *Anglo-China. Chinese People and British Rule in Hong Kong 1841-1880,* Richmond, Surrey, England, Curzon Press 2001.

Munn, Christopher, *The Criminal Trial under Early Colonial Rule* in Tak-Wing Ngo, ed., *Hong Kong's history: state and society under colonial rule.* London, New York, Routledge, 1999.

Norton-Kyshe, James William, *The History of the Laws and Courts of Hong Kong,* (2 vols.). London 1898, reprinted Hong Kong, Vetch and Lee, 1971.

Pearson, Veronica & Leung, Benjamin K. P., *Women in Hong Kong.* Hong Kong, Oxford University Press, 1995.

Ryan S.J., Thomas F., *The Story of a Hundred Years: The Pontifical Institute of Foreign Missions (P.I.M.E.) in Hong Kong 1858-1958.* Hong Kong, Catholic Truth Society, 1959.

Sayer, Geoffrey Robley, *Hong Kong 1862-1919 Years of Discretion.* Hong Kong, Hong Kong University Press, 1975.

Sinn, Elizabeth, *Power and Charity. A Chinese Merchant Elite in Colonial Hong Kong.* Hong Kong, Hong Kong University Press, 2003.

Smith, Carl, *A Sense of History: Studies in the Social and Urban History of Hong Kong.* Hong Kong, Hong Kong Educational Publishing Co., 1995.

Starling, Arthur E. ed., *Plague, SARS and the story of Medicine in Hong Kong,* Hong Kong, Hong Kong University Press, 2006.

Wang Gang, *An illustrated story of Wyndham Street 1840s to 1960s.* Hong Kong, 2008.

Welsh, Frank, *A History of Hong Kong.* London, Harper Collins, 1997 (revised edition).

Wesley-Smith, Peter, *Unequal Treaty 1898-1997: China, Great Britain and Hong Kong's New Territories.* Hong Kong, Hong Kong University Press, 1980.

Zedner, Lucia, *Wayward Sisters. The Prison for Women* in *The Oxford History of the Prison* (above).

Index

Cases concerning	
arms & ammunition, possession of	114-118, 303-308
assault	57-59, 85-87, 301-302, 318-323
assault and threatening behaviour	313-316
bottle throwing, 1915	300
brawling	99-100, 299-300
burning a child	59-60
child stealing	63-72
debt	53-54
decoying a girl	64-72
discharging a firearm	302-303
disorderly conduct/ breach of the peace	62-65, 72, 303-308
dogs	73, 313-316
drunk and disorderly	300
ear-ring snatching	244-245
exposing a woman in a public place	55
forgery of notes & coin	102-105, 201
fraud (boat licence)	50-51
gambling den keepers	177
harbouring a deserter	325-327
hawking	243-244
heroin, possession, production & smuggling	129-135
indecent assault	61-62
involuntary manslaughter	90-92
keeping a bawdy house	52-53, 300
kidnapping/unlawful detention	63-72, 79-81, 137, 177, 201-202
motoring offences	109-112
mui tsai, ill-treatment of	82-87
mui tsai, keeping an unregistered	87-88

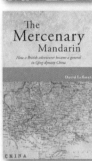

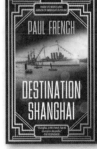
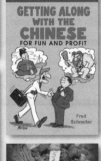